MODERN AMERICAN LITERATURE

Edited by

RAJESHWAR MITTAPALLI
CLAUDIO GORLIER

ATLANTIC
PUBLISHERS & DISTRIBUTORS (P) LTD

Published by

ATLANTIC

PUBLISHERS & DISTRIBUTORS (P) LTD

B-2, Vishal Enclave, Opp. Rajouri Garden,
New Delhi-110027
Phones : 25413460, 25429987, 25466842

Sales Office
7/22, Ansari Road, Darya Ganj,
New Delhi-110002
Phones : 23273880, 23275880, 23280451
Fax : 91-11-23285873
web : www.atlanticbooks.com
e-mail : info@atlanticbooks.com

ISBN 81-7156-978-1

Printed in India
at Nice Printing Press, Delhi

PREFACE

This collection of essays aims at contributing to investigate, discuss and to redefine some fundamental issues and works which substantiate the topicality of the literature of the United States, from the eighteenth century to the present time. In this respect, expressions such as "Crossing Borders" and key words such as "Humanism" emerge as significant signposts. Conversely, confronting Thoreau's *Walden* and Whitman's poetry amounts to exploring two indispensable and crucial, founding stages. Any study of *Walden* and of Thoreau propitiates a variety of approaches. For one thing, *Walden* undoubtedly expresses a credo, a profession of faith; furthermore, it represents a turning point in intellectual autobiography, and creates an original, unique kind of genre, unencumbered as it is with the heritage of the past: an American prose epic.

Not by chance Matthew Arnold, who in a previous essay had resolutely discounted the very existence of an American Literature, in his view simply a foreign branch of English Literature, vis-a-vis Whitman's *Leaves of Grass* came to the conclusion that Whitman represented an unmistakably American voice. In that Whitman voices a genuinely American experience simultaneously conferring a universal significance on it, and to do so he actually re-invents the language of any poetry in English. To the extent that he combines the individual frame of mind and experience, the urban and the natural landscape, the phenomenon and the numinous, he can be legitimately considered a poet of all ages and of all nations.

Here, again, the critical exercise can be fruitfully put to work. Both Thoreau and Whitman almost prophetically open the way to the modern; specularly, Hemingway, a modernist writer par excellence, consciously relates to the American literature of the eighteenth century, on the literary and on the speculative level (he could be considered one of the genuine heirs to transcendentalism). *The Old Man and the Sea* in many respects renews the crucial American paradigm of the allegorical adventure, where realism and symbolism set up a necessary dialectics, as Eric Auerbach has impeccably demonstrated in *Mimesis*. Consequently, the literary dimension as such is being transcended (again, Hemingway's debt to the Emersonian tradition), and diverse perspectives call for a detailed analysis.

It has been appropriately stressed by some scholars that Faulkner's *The Sound and the Fury* and Thomas Wolfe's *Look Homeward, Angel* came out in the same year, 1929, which also marked the beginning of the Depression. Wolfe's novel, an actual, often unchecked torrent, still has to be recognized in all its decisive relevance to the American literature of the twentieth century. One could be tempted to say that Wolfe is Whitmanian; in point of fact, he sums up in his work, and particularly in this novel, the individual and collective tragedy of the South. Paradoxically, the struggle of its hero to go out of the South carries in itself some of the crucial, anguished paradigms of Southern culture: in the backstage we face Gettysburg; the present expresses the effort to build up or to reconstruct a myth which (this is peculiar to the defeated, post Civil War South) can only be fragmented, individual, desperately introverted.

Albee is usually the object of careful analysis for his early plays. But *A Delicate Balance* marks a very important phase in his work, and here again we come to grips with a typically American paradigm, the family. In this context, the typical dilemma of Albee stages the effort of a family to take refuge in itself in order to exorcise the mystery and the horror of the world, embodied by "the others." The ambiguity surfaces in *Tiny Alice*, where, as it has been observed, the "secular martyrdom" of Brother Julian, his spiritual torment, is tragically enhanced by sexuality, with a tormenting homosexual strain.

Toni Morrison effectively represents the African-American literature in the era of post-militancy, and obviously of the postmodern. The alienated self of the blacks mirrors in its own way the alienated self of the whites, and it can be even more excruciating, though not self-conscious.

These are some of the random thoughts we wish to share with the readers and invite them to have an intellectually stimulating experience which a reading of this book promises.

—EDITORS

CONTENTS

INTRODUCTION

Modern American literature yields to easy categorization under certain heads: mainstream (canonical?) American, African American, Jewish, feminist and Asian American (the last of which is still in the nascent stage). Add to this the popular fiction which is the only genre of American literature read by the vast majority of the uninitiated readers at home and abroad.

There are in this anthology articles which focus on the important writers belonging to several genres of modern American literature. Starting with an essay on a new paradigm for modern American literature, it goes on to probe the wealth that American literature is with studies on Thoreau and Whitman who find a place here not because they are 'modern' in any sense of the term but because of their immense value for modern American literature and for their shaping the American thought and literature. These two great men ushered in a new stage of human development in America. Some of the ideas dearest to the Americans were first propounded by them in their own different ways: oneness of humanity, equality of women, democracy, sensitivity to nature, cultivation of the mind, spirit of discovery, hatred for ignorance and non-critical thinking, love for truth and frankness of statement. They are hence regarded as the undisputed representatives of the American canon. The American nation, including the literary men are forever indebted to them. "*Walden*: A Way of Life" and "Walt Whitman: A Poet of All Ages," both essays by Mallikarjun Patil, bring out the contribution of these great masters of American letters.

The rest of the articles deal with individual works of influential American novelists, playwrights and others. First comes Ernest Hemingway whose ability to create mood and evoke sensation are universal and whose "mordant irony," "unremitting bleakness" and whose lifelong engagement with death characterize his fiction.

Hemingway has been much written about, but here for a change his Nobel Prize winning novelette *The Old Man and the Sea* has been proved to have entered the realm of the folklore, is compared to another great book to establish their intertextuality and finally judged as a fictional work capable of inspiring the twenty first century writers as well.

> ...the reason why the artist works and lives...is to snare the spirits of mankind in nets of magic, to make his life prevail through his creation, to wreak the vision of his life, the rude and painful substance of his own experience, into the congruence of blazing and enchanting images that are themselves the core of life, the essential pattern whence all other things proceed, the kernel of eternity.

This is how Thomas Wolfe would like to describe his craft. It was further elucidated by Margaret Mills Harper in her book *The Aristocracy of Art in Joyce and Wolfe*. Even earlier he was studied from race and nationality perspectives, from the psychoanalytic critical angle (Richard Steele) and viewed as Ulysses and Narcissus put together (William U. Snyder). Quite apart from all these studies, Prem Prakash in the present anthology draws attention to the "incommunicable mythography" in his *Look Homeward, Angel* which is close in spirit to his stated aim as an artist.

Toni Morrison's purpose of writing is to demonstrate "how to survive *whole* in a world where we are all of us, in some measure, *victims of something*." Of her first novel *The Bluest Eye* she says that it "is about one's dependence on the world for identification, self-value, feeling of worth." The novel dramatizes the evil effects of dependence. The protagonist Pecola Breedlove is constantly frustrated in her effort to forge an identity of her own and is finally driven to madness. Morrison's *Sula* examines a four-decade long deep relationship between two women who traverse the journey of life differently – Nel Wright staying home, raising a family and thus representing all that the black community stands for and the heroine Sula defying it all by moving away from the community's code. Their confrontation however only leads to a final reconciliation. The article "The

Alienated self: Searching for Space in Morrison's *The Bluest Eyes* and *Sula*" takes this argument further.

Harold Robbins, for that matter all other popular novelists, have been completely ignored by the literary establishment. But no longer so. Here is an article on his *Where Love has Gone* which studies the theme of marriage with deep understanding and brings out its many literary merits.

Of all the American playwrights, Eugene O'Neill and Edward Albee are certainly the finest and the most representative—the former raised the American theatre from its humble origins to the exalted heights of an art and is hence often bracketed with Shakespeare and Shaw and the latter took the American drama to the pinnacle of achievement. O'Neill's tragic genius gave the American theatre its character and his innovative themes and techniques led to the birth of the avant-garde movement in America. His genius is nowhere better at work than in *Desire Under the Elms* which is a play based on the classical Greek themes of infanticide, incest and retribution. This play marked a great departure from the well-established traditions of the Broadway theatre in terms of theme and treatment. O'Neill's tragic vision is studied perceptively in at least two of the articles in this anthology.

Edward Albee's contribution to the theatre of the absurd is undisputed. For Albee this new trend is "an absorption-in-art of certain existentialist and post-existentialist philosophical concepts having to do, in the main, with man's attempts to make sense for himself out of his senseless position in a world which makes no sense." We have two well-written articles here which focus on his masterwork *A Delicate Balance* and his great allegory *Tiny Alice* and assess his dramatic genius.

Albee had an "American dream" which has perhaps gone sour. Similarly, we the editors have a dream of presenting a fine anthology of articles on American literature but are not sure whether we have been successful. Maybe we have just built castles in the air but, "If you have built castles in the air, your work need not be lost, that is where they would be. Now put the foundations under them" avers Thoreau. Have we also put the foundations?

1

Humanism: A Quest for New Paradigm in Modern American Literature

ARJUN KUMAR

Humanism, a profound philosophy has dominated the literary horizon of Modern American Literature. Humanism, in its strict sense, is the Renaissance literary cult of the so-called New Learning, a revival of Greek and Roman studies. "It was 'new' mainly in that it approached the classics for their own sake, rather than for their use to Christianity, and in that it believed that such studies, rather than religion, were the highest expression of human values and a means to developing the free responsible individual."[1] The term derives from the 15th century *Italian humanista* or teacher of the *Studia humanitatis,* or humanities. Humanism, in its broad sense, is a concept as old as classical Greece and as modern as the twentieth century. Subject to a wide diversity of expression it is basically a philosophical outlook centered on the autonomy of the human being as a dignified, rational being, possessing the source of truth and right. Humanism's final court of appeal is human reason rather than any external authority and its goal is the greatest good in this finite existence. Humanism may or may to be linked with religion, science or any specific political system. Its spirit is secular, liberal, and tolerant; its method, education, free inquiry and enlightenment.

The basic ideals of Renaissance humanism, summed up in the dictum of the Greek philosopher Protagoras "Man is the measure of all things,"[2] are a part of the rich legacy of Greco-Roman antiquity. That heritage was transmitted to the Western world partly through Byzantium and by Arabs in Spain but chiefly by the medieval church. Literary Humanism took firm root in the early Middle Ages and was given new vigour in the twelfth century. It has remained as vital ingredient of Western thought. In the eighteenth century Enlightenment, Humanist Rationalism, Individualism and Secularism were given a new dimension by their association with political and scientific outlook. Not until the late 19th and 20th centuries, however, in response to the dominant role of science and in reaction against the growth of naturalism did humanism reappear as an articulate movement. It assumed a bewildering variety of forms. Scientific humanism aims to supplant religion and make scientific knowledge the instrument of freeing man and enhancing his life. To this end science and technology must be humanized and socialized, and man must be educated to respond positively to rapid change.

The humanism of Irving Babbit and Paul Elmer More in the 1930's was a reaffirmation of the humanism principle of man's innate ethical sense the "high will" pointing to a spiritual order beyond man. Babbit remained uncommitted about religion. More ultimately finding in it a necessary dynamic and discipline, became an exponent of religious humanism, followed by Jacques Maritian, another religious humanist. Other 20th century expressions of so-called Christian humanism reject the traditional concept of God, Church, prayer and worship as anachronistic. Ultimate reality, it is said, is to be found within human beings and expresses itself in a Christ like dedication to their total well-being. The term 'humanism' is also claimed by pragmatists, existentialists and Marxists.

Humanism in all its expressions, considering education as man's single and most important enterprise means education in the humanities no less than in science and technology. And thus the living tradition of human knowledge and wisdom alone can give direction to scientific development and prepare people for a change.

Humanism in Post War

Humanism, in its strict sense, is a study in the Renaissance of ideas of the ancient Greeks and Romans not concerned with religious principles. As the highest expression of human values meant to develop free and responsible individual, it emerged as a philosophy of mankind. The term 'humanism' derived from the *Italian humanista* or *Studia humanitatis i.e.,* the study of humanities, came into use in the early sixteenth century to refer to the most enduring values of European Renaissance humanism. The humanist movement started in Italy by Picodella Mirandola who championed the humanistic ideal in his oration and upheld the dignity of man. According to Cheyney, American historian, "humanism means many things: It may be the reasonable balance of life that the early humanists observed in the Greeks; it may be merely the study of humanities or polite letters; it may be responsive to all human passions of a Shakespeare or Goethe; or it may be a philosophy of which man is the centre and sanction."[3] Corliss Lamont has defined the twentieth century humanism as "a joyous service for the greater good of all humanity in this natural world and according to the methods of reason and democracy."[4]

But "Humanism" in general is not merely a philosophy. It is for the average men and women a way of thinking and doing for a happy and useful life, concerned with the dignity and worth of individual, and his capacity for truth and virtue. It believes in the goodness of man subscribing to the welfare of the whole community. It is not a new dogma, but has developed as a system of beliefs and human standards subjected to testing in the light of newly discovered facts and more rigorous reasoning.

Renaissance Humanism

Renaissance, the revival of learning and art in the fourteenth and fifteenth centuries in Italy and France and in sixteenth century in England, is characterized as a glorious period of individualism when creative energy flourished and religious tyranny faded loosing much good of medievalism and creating nothing very significant. Etienne Gilson has observed that "the Renaissance...was not the Middle Ages plus man, but the Middle Ages minus God, and the tragedy was that in loosing God the Renaissance was loosing man himself."[5] The Renaissance humanists enthusiastically promoting ancient pagan writing and ideals of liberty and sometimes stressed secular activity but had neglected spiritual subservience to Christ or to the Church, as John Lyly, Elizabethan novelist and playwright put it: "Is Aristotle more dear with his books than Christ with his blood?"[6] But humanism in the Renaissance period was usually fused with Christianity, a "Christian humanism" as with Eramus and Milton. When Eramus said, "Holy Socrates, pray for us."[7] He sought to unite the reasonableness of the ancients with the Revelation of Christianity. Milton too avoided the excesses of godless humanism. His treatise "Of Education" did not simply define complete education as "that which fits a man to perform justly, skilfully and magnanimously all the offices, both private and public, of peace and war," but also said that the aim of learning was to "to refrain the ruins of our first parents by regaining to know God aright, and out of that knowledge to love him, to imitate him, to be like him, as we may be nearest by possessing our souls of true virtue, which being united to the heavenly grace of faith, makes up highest perfection."[8]

Renaissance humanism concerned with the dignity and position of man in the universe, and becoming part of the study of classical imaginative and philosophical literature, as against natural science, emphasized moral and practical rather than purely aesthetic values. It insisted on the primacy of reason as opposed to the instinctual appetites and the animal passions, in ordering human life. Many humanists also stressed the full need for development of man's diverse powers—physical and mental, artistic and moral as opposed to merely technical or specialized training. And the contemporary humanist has often based the truths on human experiences and human nature rather than on the truths and sanctions of supernatural creed. With few exceptions, however, the Renaissance humanists were pious Christians, but had also inherited the concepts and ideas from pagan antiquity that went into the making of Christian creed. The emphasis on the values that could be achieved in this world, and scant regard for Christian belief in innate corruption of man and ideals of extreme asceticism and withdrawal from this world obsessed with the world hereafter, gave rise to Christian humanism of Sir Philip Sidney, Spenser and John Milton. Further, the material, scientific and technological advancement after the Renaissance stressed the need to study humanities resisting the influence of natural philosophy and practical arts. Dr. Johnson, the eighteenth century humanist, observed: "We are perpetually moralists, but we are geometricans only by chance...Socrates was rather of opinion that what we had to learn was, how to do good and avoid evil."[9]

Mathew Arnold, the great exponent of humanism in the Victorian period, strongly defended the significance of human studies in general education. Many of Arnold's prominent studies are adaptations of the tenets of the older humanism—his view, for instance that culture is a perfection "Of our humanity proper, as distinguished from our animality"[10] and that it consists of "a harmonious expansion of all the powers which make the beauty and worth of human nature,"[11] his emphasis on knowing "the best that is known and thought in the world and his assumption that much of what is best is in the classical writers and the conception of poetry as essentially a criticism of life."

Robert Frost's poem, 'The Tuft of Flowers' that speaks of the spirit of human participation, reflects some sort of Renaissance humanism:

> "Men work together, I told him from the heart Whether they work together or apart."[12]

And Robert Penn Warren, like Renaissance humanist, too speaks of the reality of evil in human nature; and presents in his narratives the 'Original Sin' through some of his most memorable characters and episodes, for example, in the two hatchet—wielders, Lilburn Lewis and Big Billie Potts. He has dramatized self-discovery and makes his character realise his deeper self enclosed like a beast in a cage.

In *Ethical humanism* human interest is preponderant. It has emerged as a movement for survival and social justice of minorities. Frost is a humanist par excellence and has centered his world view on man himself. His is the ethical humanism. Like Wordsworth he is affected by 'the still sad music of humanity.' His poem *Mending Wall* expresses his philosophy of brotherhood and tolerance, the twin virtues of honest living, against the neighbour's dogmatic assertion that "good fences make good neighbours."[13] The poem is a symbolic interpretation of the modern situation where national boundaries are fast disintegrating facilitating international understanding, though at the same time in certain quarters, militant, nationalism is also showing up its head, and thus damaging the spirit of internationalism. We do not like to be taught that we must to be islands unto ourselves, though we prefer understanding and universal brotherhood to tension and misery. This seeming paradox is at the root of human existence, which is the theme of 'Mending Wall.'

Warren's osmosis postulates as an ethic of community that includes and transcends self and family and also tribe. It transcends the separations worked by time or sin or ignorance. And in the end, the Warren protagonist must accept osmosis even as Jack Burden finally accepts the 'Great Cobwebs' concept of Cass Mastern in *All the King's Men:* "he learned that the world is all of one piece...that the world is like an enormous spider web and if you touch it, however lightly, at any point, the vibration ripples to the remotest perimeter."[14]

Philosophical humanism is sometimes used for pragmatism, as opined by Charles S. Pierce and William James. William James has contended that since pragmatism is concerned with man and his action and since all philosophical endeavours are connected with man and mankind, that the term philosophical humanism could be termed as pragmatism, even though some of its ideas are opposed to humanism. In *Mowing* Robert identified himself as a labourer with his scythe. "As the man and his tool perform their function, their earnest love experiences the simple and profound lesson, the fact is the sweetest dream that labor knows."[15]

Sociological humanism tries to define close human relations between families, common members of small community, etc., and their relation to larger impersonal groups. The ideals of sociological humanism are achieved. When loyalty, pity, mutual service and love outline the relationship between members of small group. In this respect sociological humanism becomes almost identical with what is more generally called humanitarianism.

Regarding man's relations with his fellow beings Frost said that these relations should be imbued with the spirit of service and dedication. Since human life is not perfect on this planet, human relations should be guided by the principles of 'love and need.' Most of Eliot's poems set in some metropolis, the hub of modern individual life. His poems, "the Love Song of Alfred J. Prufrock" and "The Rhapsody on a Windy Night" speak of sordid city streets, and "the muttering retreats" of lonely man. *The Wasteland,* besides other urban features, presents unreal city with dissipated London crowds. *Gerontion* resides in a decayed city tenement and the scene of 'Sweency Among the Nightingales' is a city of underworld.

Socialist humanism is consistently materialistic and historical. It is based on the working class of society resisting the influence of upper classes and pining hopes for the progress of humanity, the development of consciousness, organisation and power of that social force and on the success of working class struggles. Socialist humanism believes firmly in the power of intelligence and clean cultivation of consciousness and believes no less strongly than any other creed in human decency, dignity and fellowship. But just as it is rational without being rationalistic so it is moral without falling into empty moralizing. A genuine and progressive morality cannot be separated from the actual conditions, contending forces and basic issues of class society. The ultimate aim of the new socialist order is to bring about conditions that will make both individual and the entire class become conscious of the new milieu.

Liberal humanism is essentially liberal, expressing the ethical attitude of middle class individuals violating religious practice and evincing interest to some degree in social reform and political progressivism. Like Marxism it is humanistic in approach, and deals with the middle class workers common interests and also defending science and modern education. But liberal humanism strictly speaking is a philosophy of the working class, either in origin or in intent. In fact, it explicitly repudiates any founded upon the facts of economic life but upon allegedly universal ethical standards which are binding upon all people because of their common human nature. This view point confirms to the abstract individualism, that is, an axiom of the ideology of bourgeois democracy.

On its social and political side, humanism not only preaches peace and settlement of disputes between sections through negotiations but also reconciliation of classes as the general interests and aims of all members of human race or inhabitants of a given country transcend their particular social divisions. The liberal humanists contend that it is sectarian, decisive, and self-defeating to expect one special class to emancipate human kind from this predicament. They insist that the task of eradicating social evils be entrusted to all men of goodwill. But they are not totally consistent in their argument, as the humanist expect only a section of humanity to lead the rest to a better life. But they select even these pioneers, not on the basis of their economic function or material interests but because of their superior quality of intelligence, goodwill, loving nature and kindness.

Religious humanism is a movement developed from unitarianism and is best defined in the *Humanist Manifesto* 1933 : "Religion consists of those actions, purposes and experiences which are humanly significant. Nothing human is alien to the religious."[16]

There is no metaphysical motivation for ethical behaviour. Anyway of life as Christian humanists think, is based on human values; even future is not held out as a reward or a punishment for ethical behaviour.

T.S. Eliot pleads for a revival and restoration of religious faith relating contemporary living to the universal experiences of man. His poetry is not a mere rendering of contemporary disillusionment. "It has a relevance not merely to the modern peculiar, human situation, but also to the universal human predicament."[17]

Eliot's view of life is first existential, and secondly, religious. To him, the word 'religion' signifies a particular kind of attitude towards life which is opposed to the secular. He uses the word to denote an attitude of passionate concern for man's spiritual destiny. The religious man need not be a Christian, he may even be an atheist. He becomes religious even if he gives earnest and sincere thought to religious matters. It is this concern with matters spiritual, as contrasted with the worldly and the secular, and not the adherence to any dogma, that makes a man truly religious. Secondly, religion for Eliot implies a faith in "the primacy of the supernatural over the natural life." In this lies the essence of his religious attitude. This religious strain appears even in his earliest poems. He takes themes of a secular nature and satirizes man's materialism and his lack of concern for spiritual problems. In the volume entitled "Prufrock and other observations" (1917) the mode is that of a satirist. The evils of pre-occupation with the material and the worldly, and the exclusion of the spiritual, are exposed and ridiculed, the satire and scorn of Eliot in his early poems indicate his contempt for the second volume entitled 'Poems 1920' contains decidedly Christian poems, "The Hippopotamus" and "Mr. Eliot's Sunday Morning Service" present satirical pictures of the degeneration of the Church and Christian theology:

"God works in a mysterious way
The Church can sleep and feed at once."[18]

and

"Under the penitential gates
Sustained by staring Seraphim
Where the Souls of the devout
Burn invisible and dive."[19]

Traditionally humanists have affirmed the anthropocentric nature of truth, values and religion. Their major focus has been on life in this world, the only life and the only world of which they can be certain. So they must create a place fit for people. In contrast, the traditional Christians are ambivalent toward this world, for having been admonished to have just been in it but not of this world. They are not certain whether suffering is a part of the divine plan whether heaven or humans should attempt to alleviate it, whether in the scheme of things the promise of a future in a spiritual realm is not more significant than life in the natural world. On these issues, the humanist does not experience such ambiguity and reluctance. A world with less suffering is better than the one with more. Suffering is evil and it should be reduced or eliminated if possible. The means to accomplish all this are human intelligence and skill. Unless they are effective suffering will continue.

Humanist take this life seriously for they have great doubts about future. They believe that evil and suffering must be fought by humans in the absence of anything else to fight. Traditional Christians have an ambiguous view of this life. And hence, they tend to neglect it by preparing for the next. The liberation theologians appear to take a position between these two poles. They tend to take the present seriously without denying a future. They also believe that the dice of the universe are loaded in favour of support for the promotion of morality.

Masonolds has observed that "Liberation either will or will not be brought by human effort, for the evidence suggests the universe is indifferent to the existence of oppression. The application of human intelligence and skill will determine whether the human enterprise will be saved or lost. Humans are their own messiahs; it is indeed time that they grew up and accepted this simple fact."[20]

Warren's metaphysical dimension of osmosis manifests itself in the "Ballad of Billie Potts," reflecting the sacramental conception of the universe. In his earlier 'Kentucky Mountain Farm' Sequence Warren has identified the larger being as "the spirit that moves and never sleeps, in the tall, profound shadow of absolute deeps.' 'Perfect adjustment' being 'at one with God' and 'knowing at last,' 'who you are'—such are the final rewards of Warren's Osmosis, though its final price is the death of the conscious ego. "And the death of the self is the beginning of selfhood."[21]

Literary humanism an intellectual movement starting in 1910 in America popularly known as 'New Humanism' was pronounced and propagated by Irving Babbit and Paul Elmer More. Stuart Sherman, Norman Forester and the rest of their group later became known as 'the New Humanists.' They contended that man's free will is guided by intuition and he might strive for his own progress, and his community unhampered either by theological or scientific determinism. Thus, he has to fight against the so-called modern mechanistic materialism. It is logical to say that these ideas of classical art and the philosophy of antiquity as human expressions of their convictions also constitute the cultural value system. Further the New Humanists had also objected to the romanticism and materialistic naturalism of the enlightenment, since both made men become irresponsible.

'The New Humanism' sprang from the discontent of modern age. The New Humanists tried to remedy the social malady of the society through adequate perception and conception of the nature of man and man's relation to the universe. The 'New Humanism' created a kind of intellectual conservatism in the twentieth century in America. The 'New Humanists' were not popular in their own time. But their effort to restore the Western classical tradition in America provided noteworthy voice of dissent to reconstruct modern life.

Humanism, as Babbitt and Paul Elmer More conceived it, was opposed to romanticism and naturalism. These two tendencies were viewed as potential threats to a sense of the social order. Romanticism placed the individual above society, without responsibility while naturalism has debased the individual to the position of animals. Humanism offered instead a broad spectrum of traditional values. As a former student of Babbit has recorded, "...it drew from sources as widely separated as the Aristotelian ethic and the oriental religions, finding authority and sustenance wherever doctrines of moderation, the dignity of the human will, the sense of permanent values, a perception of dualistic order or existence were upheld, and maintaining steady opposition to intemperance materialistic determinism, relativism or nihilism mystical monism or any other ism that failed to see that man and things are forever twain."[22]

Foerster opined that "in its broadest signification, it denotes a belief that the proper study of mankind is man, and that this study should enable mankind to perceive and realise its humanity. Since man may be conceived as being on three planes, the natural, the human and the religious, the content of the middle term will frequently tend to be invaded by that of the extremes—the word humanism should be confirmed to a working philosophy seeking to make a resolute distinction between man and nature and between man and the divine."[23]

T.S. Eliot in "The Humanism of Irving Babbitt" (1928) and "Second Thoughts about Humanism" (1929) attempts to refute the views of Babbitt and Foerster on this vital doctrine 'humanism' pronouncing his own formulations about its nature and function.

The first essay, "The Humanism of Irving Babbitt" (1928) states that at the centre of Babbitts philosophy is the doctrine of humanism and that Babbitt has put religion in conflict with humanitarianism and naturalism. However, Eliot has contrary views about and contrasts humanism with religion. Eliot admits that all humanists have been individualists and intellectuals applying their critical reason to the problems of human life. He points out that Babbitt frequently mentions of the importance of the doctrine of 'self control' and 'higher will' which render life into an act of faith. Babbitt also questions the existence of 'civilization' which can hardly endure without religion, and without Church *i.e.*, with Catholic Church. At the end of the essay, Eliot suggests that all the hopes of humanity cannot be placed on one institution *i.e.* the Catholic Church, and that Humanism is neither an alternative to religion nor is ancillary to it.

In the second essay, "Second Thoughts About Humanism" (1929), Eliot concedes that in the past 'humanism' has been allied with religion, but asserts that in the future it can afford to ignore positive religion. Eliot apparently thinks that Foerster is right in recognising the fact that humanism cannot accept 'a formal theology' or 'a romantic idealism' in defiance of reason and that unlike religion it assigns an important place to the instruments of both 'science and art' but like religion, it holds 'the ethical will as a power above the ordinary self.' Foerster's humanism like religion, enjoins 'the virtue of humility' and Eliot comes down heavily upon him for this. Eliot remarks that Mr. Foerster's humanism, in fact, is too ethical to be true, and defines 'Humanism'...thus "Humanism depends very heavily...upon, the tergiversations of the word 'human' and in general, upon implying clear and distinct philosophic ideas which are not there."[24] His main objection to the theory of Foerster springs from the humanist's use of the "supernatural" he objected to. Eliot observes, "My objection is not to Humanism; but to Mr. Foerster for not being humanistic enough; and for playing the games of philosophy and theology without knowing the rules."[25]

To Eliot, 'Humanism' does not provide dogmas or philosophical theories and is concerned less with 'reason' than with common sense, and operates against fanaticism. He has also observed that it does not refute anything, but only persuades according to its unformulable axioms of culture and good sense, and that humanism is critical rather than constructive in socio-political terms of the existence of man. Though 'humanism' is concerned with the nature of civilization, philosophy or religion it is no substitute for either and it has become popular with the so-called intellectual aristocrats following a common culture. T.S. Eliot agrees with T.E. Hulme who believes in the perfection of man and nature and in his arguing that both Babbitt and Foerster are nearer to the romantic view of Rousseau than the religious views.

While Babbitt maintained that "humanism" was an idealistic belief in the goodness of human nature towards creating a sound society by means of rational discipline, Eliot is of the view that there would be no pure humanism without religious discipline. Eliot is a highly sensitive person whose primary concern as a poet to shun "the mores" of modern man and awaken him to that of certain human values to merge out of the engulfing morass of self-centredness and deep cultural, even moral and spiritual crises in which he is rolling today. He knew well that the old world order was changing past, and that the old European Renaissance had become a spent up force. The mushroom growth of industries had ushered in an era of commercialism, colonialism and imperialism, eating into the vitals of simple human values like—love, justice, humility, tolerance, equilibrium, sanity, truth and beauty. Eliot was convinced that the present-day universal chaos could not be got rid of only when we would evolve a fresh code of conduct for ourselves, based on tolerance, mutual trust and understanding.

Existential humanism in our sense of the word, "is a doctrine that does render human life possible; a doctrine also which affirms that every truth and every action imply both an environment and a human subjectivity."[26]

Existentialism preaches that the glory of the free individual lies in rebelling against the tragic human condition even though defeat is inevitable. A major voice in existentialism that has deeply affected the recent critical theory is that of Martin Heidegger whose monumental but seemingly contrary writings on 'Dasein' (existence), time, death and poetic language profoundly influenced structuralistic and deconstructive criticism in France and later in the United States. "Dasein exists as an entity for which," says Heidegger, "in its Being, that Being is itself an issue."[27]

Humanism places humanity, rather than God or nature, in the centre of consideration and makes the lot and destiny of our species on earth its prime concern. The materialist Ludwig Feverbach expressed the priorities saying, "My doctrine or view can, therefore, be summed up in two words 'nature' and 'man.' The being which, in my thinking man presupposes, the being which is the 'cause' or 'ground' of man to which he owes his origin and existence is 'not God'—a mystical, indeterminate, ambiguous word—but 'nature,' a clear, sensuous, unambiguous word and thing. And the being in whom nature had become personal, conscious and rational is man. To my mind, unconscious nature is the eternal, uncreated being—first, that is, in time but not in rank, physically, but not morally; man with his consciousness second, in time but in rank the first."[28]

The twentieth century existentialists have made the senselessness of human life the cornerstone of their creed. They proceed from the premise that there is no objective basis for discerning any meaningful direction to human development. They distrust both natural and social science and disparage their findings as guide to life. G.E. Moore, the parochial Cambridge Philosopher asserted in *Principia Ethica* that the most valuable experiences of human being are the pleasures of friendship and the enjoyment of beautiful objects. A conception of the highest good that does not equip humanity and thereby to rationalize human relations so that all people can be friends and create as well as enjoy things of beauty.

American humanism as envisaged by Howard Mumford Jones conveys that people in America became more self-conscious and aware of human dignity rights, liberty and fraternity, pursuing real happiness. In the words of Howard Mumford Jones the new republic of the United States became "the best single gateway...to the manifold hopes than stirring the minds of men and reason and justice could substituted for authority and superstition in guiding human affairs."[29]

There is a great deal in the American tradition, that is, fundamentally humanistic in character. America's belief in democracy and progress, its buoyant-optimism and idealism, its relevance on science and invention, all fit into the Humanistic pattern. Current Humanism reaffirms the spirit of cosmopolitanism of international friendship and essential brotherhood of man. The cosmopolitan outlook of this profoundly democratic and militant humanism was best exemplified in the life and work of Tom Panine, Franklin's protege, who profoundly proclaimed, "The word is my country and to do good is my religion."

Humanism has finally emerged as a profound philosophy of mankind. Corliss Lamont says "Humanism believes in the beauty of love and the love of beauty. It exults in the pure magnificance or external Nature. All the many sided possibilities for good in human living...the Humanist would weave into a sustained pattern of happiness under the guidance of reason."[30]

NOTES AND REFERENCES

1. Quoted in *The Encyclopaedia Americana,* vol. 14, Grolier Incorporated International Headquarters: Danbury Connecticut, 1983, 553.
2. *The Encyclopaedia Americana* 553.
3. Lamont Corliss, *The Philosophy of Humanism* (London: Vision Press Ltd., 1962) 9.
4. Corliss 9.
5. Sylvan Barnet, Morton Berman and Burto William, eds., *A Dictionary of Literary Dramatic and Cinematic Terms* (Boston: Little Brown and Co., 1971) 92.
6. Barnet 93.
7. Barnet 93.
8. Barnet 93.
9. Abrams, M.H., ed., *The Glossary of Literary Terms* (Madras: Macmillan, 1971) 174.
10. Abrams 174.
11. Abrams 174.
12. Frost, Robert, *Complete Poems* (New York: Holt, 1960) 32.
13. Robert 32.
14. Warren, Robert Penn, *All the King's Men* (New York: Modern Library, 1953) 172.

15. Frost 25.
16. *World University Encyclopaedia,* vol. 8 (Washington, New York : Book Inc., 1968) 2441.
17. *The Waste Land and Other Poems* (New Delhi: Rama Brothers 1994) 36.
18. T.S. Eliot, *Collected Poems, 1909-1962* (Calcutta: Rupa and Co., 1962) 52.
19. Eliot 58.
20. Masonolds, *Humanism and Liberation Theology* from the *Journal Religious Humanism* 21.3 (Summer 1987): 108.
21. Warren, Robert Penn, *Brother of Dragons, A Tale in Verse and Voices* (New York: Random, 1953) 215.
22. Clarence D. Thorpe and Nelson Normant, *Criticism in the Twentieth Century, A Bird's Eye View," The English Journal* (April 1947): 169.
23. Greenbaum Leonard, *The Hound and Horn* (The Hague: Mouton and Co., 1966) 79.
24. T.S. Eliot, *Selected Essays* (London: Faber and Faber, 1951) 485.
25. Eliot 485.
26. Kaufmann, Walter Arnold, *Existentialism* (New York: Penguin Books, 1989) 346.
27. Jay, Gregory S., ed., *Modern American Critics Since 1955* (Michigan: Gale Research Co., 1988) 290.
28. Feverbach, Ludwig, *Lectures on the Essence of Religion* (New York: Harper and Row 1967) 21.
29. Jones Mumford Howard, *American Humanism: Its Meaning for World Survival* (New York: Harper and Brothers, 1957) 105.
30. Corliss 9.

2

Walden: A Way of Life

MALLIKARJUN PATIL

Only a few books in the world are useful for the majority of mankind either to delight or to enlighten them, at the same time guiding them for a better mode of life. Such useful documents are not always written. However a few such greatest classics of art, science, culture and the like exist, they surely guide the mankind towards nobility and greater consciousness. No doubt, *Walden* is one of such *magnum opus* by the famous American writer-thinker Henry David Thoreau. The work *Walden,* like Plato's *Republic* or Mahatma Gandhi's *Hind Swaraj* can guide the confused the citizenry and inflected minds. In fact, *Walden* is a lay Bible to set right things; to correct the misled and to make them aware of the significance of primitive and simple life that is close to the life lived in woods. In fact, the subtitle of the book is "Life in the Woods. *Walden* is the result of Thoreau's experiment of life; it is a recreation of his experiences and it is his manual to the weary mankind. Henry Salt, one of Thoreau's early biographers wrote of *Walden* in 1886: "It is incomparable alike in matter and style and deserves to be a sacred book in the library of every cultured and thoughtful man."[1] Thoreau's great works like *Walden, Civil Disobedience* and his ideas reflected in his journals have influenced many a great man of mankind. Mahatama Gandhi and Leo Tolstoy's reading of Thoreau changed them into humanitarians. W.B. Yeats admired Thoreau, while Anton Tchekhov found the thoughts of *Walden* fresh and original. Likewise W.H. Hudson called it: "the one golden book in any century of books."[2]

Thoreau's *Walden* is a treatise in the line of Matthew Arnold's *Culture and Anarchy*. It also bears a comparison with Sir Thomas Moor's *Utopia*. But one has to think of the substance of *Walden* in a philosophical vein lest he/she has to misinterpret it. Secondly and more importantly, as analysis of *Walden* must be undertaken according to the New Criticism. This means one has to avoid much of Thoreau's autobiography while interpreting it. Though *Walden* is a poem of Thoreau's life, Thoreau's life is full of contradictions. For example, Thoreau bore an eccentric nature. He had no ambitions in life as Emerson says. Nor did he have any heroism in his character as such. He was timid, unsociable, and at times anti-social and crooked. Some of the critics' derogatory phrases about Thoreau such as 'intellectual selfishness,' 'itch of originality,' 'perversity of thought,' 'no humour' illustrate the oddities of Thoreau, the man. Therefore R.L. Stevenson calls him a 'Skulker,' while others called him 'a crooked genius.' According to Henry James Thoreau was a parochial representing a documented projection of his self. Besides, many critics have exposed his 'morbid dislike of humanity.'

In the light of this, the best thing is to assess the text without looking at Thoreau's life elsewhere. So then only for us *Walden* will appear a social document about one's simple life in the woods—primitive but happy, isolated but harmonious and pure, noble and virtuous. In the words of Martin Bickman, *Walden* is a "jeremiad calling for a retreat from the corruption of American society."[3] Definitely *Walden* is a philosophical work of art advocating a life of simplicity, independence, magnanimity and trust. However it is a riddlesome embodiment of propositions for scholars, it is a depiction of life in the woods. Even one can call it a lay Bible.

Walden is an honest critique on American life criticising its materialism. Bickman observes, "*Walden*, then, is most thoroughly American in its heartbreaking awareness of the gap between American ideals and the immediate social and political realities betraying that ideal at every turn."[4] This statement can be illustrated with several propositions Thoreau has made in the text. *Walden*, however is loosely constructed into many chapters each highlighting one or the other aspects of free and simple life. It is the uniquintessence of Thoreau's vision of life recorded over a period of nine years. Thoreau's views of life are categorised on different topics such as 'Economy,' 'Life,' 'Reading,' 'Sounds,' 'Solitude,' 'Visitors,' 'The Bean-Field,' 'The Village,' 'The Ponds,' 'Baker Farm,' 'Higher Laws,' 'Brute Neighbours,' 'House-Warming,' 'Inhabitants,' 'Animals,' 'Spring' etc.

Like all the great philosophers Henry David Thoreau believes that happiness and contentment lie in simplicity, service, sacrifice and trust. According to him, "the cost of the luxuries and many of the so-called comforts of life are not only not indispensable, but positive hindrances to the elevation of mankind. With respect to luxuries and comforts, the wisest have ever lived a more simple and meagre life than the poor" (14). Thoreau thinks comforts of life like food, clothing, shelter and fire are quite essential. But in the name of food or any other of the rest, one ought not to indulge in any kind of crime, atrocity and the like. Like Wordsworth before and Gandhi after, Thoreau tired of the worldly ways, one day wished to live in the woods. The other reasons for his settling in a hut at Walden pond had been to devote much of his time of studies. Of course, a wish to experiment with primitive mode of life had been always his greatest obsession. So he became a self-appointed surveyor of forest paths and an inspector of the snowstorms and rainstorms. He states, "My purpose in going to Walden Pond was not to live cheaply nor to live dearly there, but to transact some private business with the fewest obstacles" (19-20). By constructing his home, earning his own livelihood and cultivating his own simple habits of study and meditation and by establishing his relationship with the woodland and animals and birds, Thoreau criticised the modern Americans' foolish imitation of Europe. This is what Emerson, his mentor did in his essays. Here Thoreau seems always to be practising the basic tenets of the philosophy of transcendentalism. Fine it is that he says, "The head monkey at Paris puts on a traveller's cap and all the monkeys in America do the same" (25). Like Emerson, Gandhi, Tolstoy, Thoreau values moral character more than he values our advanced materialism. In his view, "Bankruptcy and repudiation are the spring-boards from which much of our civilisation vaults and turns its somersets.... This is the reason we are all poor in respect to a thousand savage comforts, though surrounded by luxuries" (33). No doubt, he quotes Chapman in support of his assertion that,

> The false society of men for earthly greatness
> All heavenly comforts rarefy to air.

May be for this reason the noble savages have become extinct; modern civilisation has corrupted the old but pure mode of life; and 'men have become the tools of their tools.' He says, "We now no longer camp as for a night, but have settled down on earth and forgotten heaven," and as far our art, says he, "The best works of art are expression of man's struggle to free himself from this condition, but the effect of our art is merely to make this low state comfortable and that higher state to be forgotten" (37). Being a man of self-reliance, Thoreau constructs his own house. He tells man should not resign the pleasures of construction to the carpenter alone. Nor should he permit others to think on his behalf. Like the 12th century Indian Sharanas of Karnataka, he is of the view that truthfulness is heaven and untruthfulness is hell. Life to him did not look an illusion, but a reality to be felt and lived. He says,

> Heaven is under our feet
> As well as over our head

It is in this light Walden pond is a 'God's Drop,' and an image of the universe. According to Thoreau if we talk of heaven, it is like disgracing the earth. Thus the Walden pond becomes a metaphor for a truthful life.

In Thoreau's view to live happily, one has to live his own life, his own self. In this regard, good character is indispensable. So there is no odour so bad as that which arises from goodness tainted. His word of advice is to avoid the beginning of evil because,

> "The evil that me do lives after them" (67).

Service and sacrifice for others should be practised for the sake of merit. But we need not follow any saints as they are irresponsible citizens. Besides, one should live uncommitted to life's oddities.

Thoreau, as a lover of nature advocates us a way of life amidst the biological surrounding. He records his experience at the pond. Life in the woods, he thinks, is simple and happy as the seasons bring all the necessities. He also hates machines. He asks "if we stay at home and mind our business, who will want railroads? Why should we live with such hurry and waste of life? What is the need of reading newspapers? Travelling across the globe? He writes,

> What's the railroad to me?
> I never go to see
> Where it ends.
> It fills a few hollows,
> And makes banks for the swallows.
> It sets the sand a-blowing.
> And the blackberries a-growing.

But I cross it like a cart-path in the woods. I will not have any eyes put out and my ears spoiled by its smoke and steam and hissing" (122).

Thoreau thinks reading is a means for polishing life. So for this the classics are the noblest recorded thoughts of man. He says to read well is a noble exercise and "books must be read as deliberately and reservedly as they were written." According to him good books are the treasures of antiquity and the wealth of nations, fit for inheritance. One must also read widely and acquaint with all type of knowledge. For this he advocates the establishment of more education systems. He states, "That is the uncommon school we want. Instead of nobleman, let us have noble villages of men. If it is necessary, omit one bridge over the river, go round a little there, and throw one arch at least over the darker gulf of ignorance which surrounds us" (110).

Perhaps Thoreau is one of those few persons who know the importance of solitude better. He says he had his own sun and moon and stars and a little world all to himself. "There can be," he says, "no very black melancholy to him who lives in the midst of Nature and has his senses still." Solitude is good for everyone.

Thoreau never felt lonesome in Nature. He says, "In the midst of a gentle rain while these thoughts prevailed, I was suddenly sensible of such sweet and beneficent society in Nature" (132). Every natural entity befriended him there. So he loved to be alone. But in company of birds, beasts and trees, he was no more alone than the weathercock or the northstar. Of course occasionally many visitors might have disturbed him.

Thoreau lived in nature happily. He followed husbandry. *Walden* gives an account of his mode of cultivation of many corns. In Thoreau's view husbandry is a sacred profession as it is everywhere held and followed. Similar to this is his strong advocating that an independent man should not be disturbed by an institution of governance. Like Gandhi, Thoreau opposes the state's poking its nose into an individual's humble affairs. For evidence, when he had been to a village and did not pay tax, he was imprisoned for a day. Mostly this led him to write on civil disobedience. He writes "I am convinced, that if all men were to live as simply as I then did thieving and robbery would be unknown. These take place only in communities where some have got more than is sufficient while others have not enough. You who govern public affairs, what need have you to employ punishments? Love virtue and the people will be virtuous. The virtues of a superior man are like the wind, the virtues of a common man are like the grass, when the wind passes over it bends" (172).

The next chapter, 'The Ponds' is a vivid description of Walden pond which is surrounded by White Pond, Goose Pond, Fair Heaven Pond, Flint's Pond and others. A lake or pond is the landscape's beautiful feature. It is the earth's eye. Man is born and dead but Nature remains alive. Walden merits our admiration especially for its water, which is pure, blue in colour, and it does not dry.

In the section "Higher Laws," the extent of Thoreau's concern not only for human beings but also for the flora and fauna is faithfully displayed. Like Hardy and G.B. Shaw, he says sporting with birds and animals is unlawful. Nor should we eat meat? He writes: "The practical objection to animal food in my case was its uncleanness; and, besides, when I had caught and cleaned and cooked and eaten my fish, they seemed not to have fed me essentially. It was insignificant and unnecessary, and cost more than it came to. A little bread or a few potatoes would have done as well, with less trouble and filth" (214). So man must stop eating animals as ancient savage tribes left off eating each other when they came into contact with more civilised people. Thoreau advocates us to avoid liquor as it intoxicates. According to him intoxication destroys everything one day as the Grecian civilisation succumbed to it. We should practise chastity too and work hard to acquire necessary wisdom and wealth in life. Besides one has to make his body as noble as a temple.

One striking thing about Thoreau is that he is much with the world of Nature. In fact, he is studied as an ecologist today. To read about his association with as wonderful creatures as that of wasp, mice, ant, phoebe, partridge, loon etc. is amusing. His description 'Morning is the spring of the day' recollects us Kalidas' observation of the seasons. Evidently the author of *Walden* writes, "As every season seems best to us in its turn, so the coming in of spring is like the creation of cosmos out of chaos and the realisation of the Golden Age" (313). Winter animals like squirrel, foxes, jays, chickadees, hounds, hares commune with the poet Thoreau. The pond in the winter looks gorgeous. Self-introspection is necessary for one's progress, says this transcendentalist. He writes "It is not worth the while to go round the world to count the cats in Zanzibar" (322). 'Explore thyself' is the heartfelt expression here. He questions us satirically "While England endeavours to cure the potato-rot, will not any endeavour to cure the brain-rot, which prevails so much more widely and fatally?" (325). He tells everyone must mind his business; say what he has to say, meet his life however mean it is, cultivate poverty, be humble, lead a simple life as superfluous wealth can buy superfluities only. Thoreau's beautiful sayings are thus: 'Money is not required to buy one necessary of the soul'; 'goose is a goose still, dress it as you will,' 'Rather than love, than money, than fame, give me truth.'

Thoreau concludes that, "I learned this, at least, by my experiment, that if one advances confidently in the direction of his dreams, and endeavours to live the life which he has imagined, he will meet with a success unexpected in common hours" (324).

Walden is Thoreau's idealised and romantic account of sojourn in the woods. This shows how he had been in a constant self-contemplation and self-observation. To avoid mankind leading a life of quiet desperation, he makes an experiment of life thus highlighting the human will power for transcendental bliss. He writes, "Man has an unquestionable ability to elevate his life by a conscious endeavour." In the world of Nature, which was his second mother, Thoreau, an active and amateur naturalist, as an inventive genius, and as a man of the world, constantly searched for his selfhood. Lean Edel says "Thoreau made his life a sylvan legend, that of man alone, in communion with nature."[5] Indeed, for this reason, Thoreau is read everywhere.

REFERENCES

The references to Thoreau *Walden* are from H.D. Thoreau's *Walden*.

1. H.D. Thoreau, *The Critic,* 8 (Dec. 1887): 291.
2. W.H. Hudson, *Birds in a Village* (Philadelphia: J.B. Lippincott Co., 1893) 190.
3. Martin Bickman, *Walden Volatile Truths* (New York: Twayne Publishers, 1992) 13.
4. Bickman 5.
5. Lean Edel, "H.D. Thoreau," *American Writers,* vol IV, ed. Leonard Unger (New York: Charles Scribner's Sons, 1974) 168.

3

Walt Whitman: A Poet of All Ages

MALLIKARJUN PATIL

The world has seen only a few poets who live for all ages, who speak of all ages; and who lead all by their kind words. What is true of rarity with Jesus, Buddha, Gandhi, is also true of Shakespeare, Wordsworth and Whitman. May be the list of greatmen may be long, but the list of great poets like Whitman is very short.

Walt Whitman is one of the modern world's greatest poets. His *Leaves of Grass* pioneered a vision of humanity based on egalitarian democratic ideals and it unveiled an ambitious poetic voice designed by Whitman to serve as the embodiment of not only America but also the whole world. The influence of *Leaves of Grass* is as pronounced and everlasting as that of Emerson's declaration of American independence in literature with his essay "American Scholar," Wordsworth's announcement to the world on the benevolence of nature and Gandhi's invention of satyagraha for the universal welfare.

Like Wordsworth, Whitman heralded a new kind of poetry; like Thoreau he reached a new mode of life; and like Gandhi he set a new pattern of life.

Despite the initial negative critical judgements, Whitman's *Leaves of Grass* has come to the English speaking world, as a remarkable accomplishment. In this magnum opus, Whitman declares "Of all mankind the great poet is the equable man. His brain is the ultimate brain...he is judgement...he sees the farthest he has the most faith. The greatest poet hardly knows prettiness or triviality. Poet is a seer...he is individual...he is complete in himself. Nothing can jar him...suffering and darkness cannot—death and fear cannot...." This evokes Wordsworthian saying that 'Poet is a man speaking to men and poetry is the breath and finer spirit of all knowledge.'

Walt Whitman's poetry is the poetry of God, his creation about man and his life on the world about nature and her role in assisting God's creatures. In Clarence Darrow's view, "The work of Whitman stands alone in the literature of the world." Both in form and substance, Whitman's poetry is Whitman only. It is individualistic, special and pristine. It is original, delightful and instructive. It is the uniquintessence of Whitman, the poet of Body and Soul. His poetry is a breeze in the morning. Whitman sounds a primitive bard, and his poetry, a great song on the miracles of the universe and the mysteries of life. For this as Darrow thinks, he alone in all the ages seems to have been specially given to the world. Still fresh is his poetry with the imprint of the Creator's hand. No one else has ever looked on the universe and life as Whitman did. Whitman sings all the things—the high mountains and deep valleys, the broad plains and wide seas, the springtime and winter, the day and night, the birth and death:

And I will show that there is no imperfection in
The present and can be none in the future,
And I will show that whatever happens to any—
Body it may be turned to beautiful results,
And I will show that nothing can happen more
Beautiful than death.

Whitman thinks the imperfection on the earth is due to man's narrow vision but not due to God's faulty creation.

Happy are the people that read his poetry, for it has an enlightening power. Whitman guides us by his views and visions, ideas and thoughts, feelings and pity. For example, he did not like to write only on the brighter aspects of life:

I am not the poet of goodness only. I do not decline
To be the poet of wickedness also.
What blurt is this about virtue and about vice?
Evil propels me and reform of evil propels me,
I stand indifferent.

This Adam's child Mr. Whitman is an embodiment of perfect courage. No one else but he alone defends himself for thoughts he expresses:

If anything is sacred, the human body is sacred,
And the glory and sweet of man is the token of
Manhood attained,
And in man or woman a clean, strong, firmfibred body,
Is more beautiful than the most beautiful face.

Walt Whitman stands more for this worldly life and democracy than for anything else. His is deep, broad and fundamental democracy. To Whitman there can be no thought of class, creed and class. He naturally forms an order of life in tune with nature than in tune with human ingenuity. So he places the work of nature above the works of man.

Whitman does not have any faith in the man-made laws and institutions, which defraud many a man and enslave them denying the common brotherhood. To him everyone and everything is inevitable:

Each of us is inevitable,
Each of us limitless—each of us with his or her
Right upon the earth,
Each of us allowed the eternal purports of the earth,
Each of us here as divinely as any is here.

Whitman's democracy is higher democracy, deep-rooted in universal ethos. Also is seen his humanitarianism in the following:

I speak the password primeval, I give the sign
Of democracies,
By God! I will accept nothing which all cannot
Have their counterpart of on the same terms.

So characteristically he does not call one greater and one smaller. For him, everyone is equal. Mostly Whitman is the first greatest American poet before that of Emerson and Thoreau, who advocate equality between the sexes. He thinks woman must stand equal to man as Negro has to stand on the same plane of the White. Besides, he advocates for woman's economic independence:

I am the poet of the woman the same as the man,
And I say it is as great to be a woman
As to be a man,
And I say there is nothing greater
Than the mother of men.

Whitman by precept and example, echoes the 12th century Karnataka Sharana's sense of help and sacrifice. His keyword is concern for others. He asks us whether man should not be as kind as the Nature. So he says:

I will play a part no longer, why should I exile
myself from my companions?
O you shunned persons, I at least do not shun you,
I come forthwith in your midst, I will be your poet,
I will be more to you than to any of the rest.

Whitman is a lone man's friend—a friend of the poor, sick and weak. To a destitute prostitute, he says:

Be composed—be at ease with me—I am
Walt Whitman, liberal and lusty as Nature.

His ideal is to establish a robust hope for the rotting mankind. The degenerated world can be built upon the democracy Whitman has taught:

I will establish in every city of these states
Inland and seaboard,
In the fields and woods, and above every keel,
Little or large that dents the water,
Without edifices or rules or trustees or any argument,
The institution of the dear love of comrades.

Whitman is the Browning of English poetry—a robust optimist. He also evokes Shawian and Hardyan 'evolutionary meliorism.' He looks forward and turns everything good. His poem 'Song of Myself' with which aptly his *Leaves of Grass* began heralds hopes to the groping mankind:

I celebrate myself, and sing myself,
And what I assume you shall assume,
For every atom belonging to me as good
    Belongs to you,
I loafe and invite my soul,
I lean and loafe at my ease, observing
    A spear of summer grass.
My tongue, every atom of my blood,
    Formed from this soil, this air,
Born of parents born here from parents the
    Same, and their parents the same,
I, now thirty-seven years old
Hoping to cease not till death.

This also means Whitman did not dislike death. Death, he says, is a boon to man given by God. In Darrow's words, the close of a lovely life is really as peaceful and as beautiful as the decline of a perfect day.

In his immortal poem 'Passage to India' with which, as critics say, Whitman's significant poetry is complete, Whitman sings of death as lively as he sings of life in the beginning. His views on Death are splendidly expressed.

Come, lovely and soothing Death,
Undulate round the world,
    Serenely arriving, arriving,
In the day, in the night, to all, to each,
Sooner or later, delicate Death.
....
I float this carol with joy.
    With joy to thee, O Death.

Whitman's poetry, it is aptly observed, is better in its enlightening force, than much of preaching. He is an immortal poet of Body, Soul, Love, Faith and Preaching. He thinks love is the law of man and of life. So is he:

So I be written in the book of love,
I have no care about that book above,
Erase my name, or write it as you please,
So I be written in the book of love.

So nothing is pleasing than hearing Whitman sing on the passion of love as the true philosophy of life. When the world moves to a den of darkness, Whitman is a guiding force for the confused man. For such men who inhabit this earth, Whitman is sweetness and light—the greatest, truest, noblest prophet of all ages.

4

Crossing Borders: Ernest Hemingway's *The Old Man and the Sea* in Literary Anthropological Folkoristic Perspective

JANET WILSON

In America, 'each individual must find his own way of dealing with chaos.' Yet at the end of the nineteenth century, a coherent mythology and recognizable attitudes had emerged so that twentieth century writers have been able to analyse, interpret and modify.[1]

In American literature, the relationship between literature and folklore is subtle and complex. What was initially borrowed from European tradition gradually grew into a literary tradition and folk tradition that had a distinctive cultural identity as it acquired a history and heroes and raised up a diversified body of rich indigenous legend and lore. Folklore, in American literature, was used in two ways: passively, as a transcript or actively and functionally. Writers concerned with creating conscious works of art, like Hemingway does, use folklore functionally and not merely as providing transcripts from life. Folklore in literature, consequently, has various functions: to advance a plot, to characterize, to provide structure and to defend, explain and raise questions about the nature of society; in other words, a Kay asserts to analyse, interpret and modify life.'[2]

The scope of this case study of Hemingway's novel *The Old Man and the Sea* comprises a combination of literary, folkloristic and anthropological approaches with the resultant patterning, *i.e.*, literature nourishes folklore and folklore nourishes literature. The term 'folklore' itself may be broadly defined as

> the songs, proverbs and riddles, beliefs and susperstitions, the traditional ways of doing and saying things, that are passed along by imitation among, a relatively stable, homogeneous people and created anew with each repetition.[3]

There are, of course, mythic pattern, ritual, archetypal figures and American stereotypes like the Yankee peddler and Uncle Tom, the frontiersman which also describe in a general way how folklore appears in American literature. Hemingway uses folklore to provide a setting for his novel, to bring alive the culture of Cuban fisherfolk, their life and customs, and moves further on from the individual to the universal, from his interpretation of a single culture to that of all cultures with the same vision of Socrates who declared 'My country is the world' and 'My countrymen are all mankind.'

The American artist's concern to depict the two primary experiences of that autochthōnous questing man who is the characteristic American, and the feeling that man is forever a stranger and alone is distinctly evident in most twentieth century writers. Although Ernest Hemingway is commonly credited to being the 'archpriest of naturalists' there is more to his art than mere naturalistic presentations of things as they are or were. In deceptively simple style, he uses the non-human universe to gain further understanding of the complex, unplumbed depths of the human psyche, and the endless surprises encountered in life's journey of what man can achieve and endure.

In days of yore, the great deeds of man on land and sea were recorded in song and ballad. The old, weather-beaten sailor relates the strenuous hardships of a life out at sea to an undeterred youngman impatient to start his own saga. Centuries later, Hemingway repeats the same cycle in *The Old Man and the Sea* with Santiago as the mentor narrating his struggle with the marlin to his admiring 'apprentice,' the body Manolin. The story takes us directly to the fishing community on the long Cuban island, to folk fishing in the Gulf Stream. The uninterrupted narrative of the novel and its style 'not spoiled or weakened by literature,[4] but deepened by a natural Wahrheit (Truth) and a natural Dichtung (Poetry) levels with a parable or folktale rather than mere fiction. Hemingway's novel may, therefore, be identified with folklore in American Literature, used not as a transcript, but actively and functionally to advance the plot and like Hawthorne, as a means to exploring social and spiritual questions. It is in this sense that folklore is made to function in *The Old Man and the Sea** and retains its charm and vitality.

The Old Man offers a study of both folklife and folk hero. As Don Yoder avers,

> The chief value of folklife studies is that their data shows us the range of human thought.... In showing us what life was before urbanisation and industrialisation, we are shown the long roots of the life that we share.[5]

The seaman's life is a hard one. As he faces constant danger the sailor is insensible to much of the trivia of life. He is possessed with one strong emotion: that the sea is his provider. He also has his own customs and superstitions beliefs compounded by a large amount of sentimentality.

The use of ritual, superstition and formulistic number are other folkloristic features woven around Santiago's character as a typical fisherman. The native innocence and wisdom that pervades the lives of simple fisherfolk is faithfully captured in Santiago's method of solving the perenial problem of poverty. Santiago cannot provide himself one substantial meal on most days, but he has learnt to live with this situation with cheerful, child-like, ritualistic make-belief:

> 'What do you have to eat?' the boy asked.
> 'A pot of yellow rice with fish—Do you want some?'
> 'No. I will eat at home. Do you want me to make the fire?'
> 'No. I will make it later on. Or I may eat the rice cold.'
> 'May I take the cast net?'
> 'Of course.'

There was no cast net and the boy remembered when they

---

* All references to this book will be cited parenthetically within the text as (OM, ...).

had sold it. But they went through this fiction every day. There was no pot of yellow rice and fish and the boy knew this too (OM, 12).

They go through the same ritual for newspapers. Santiago and Manolin fall upon this simple scheme to retain dignity even in poverty.

Santiago has his own brand of religious beliefs and superstitions. He has no sophisticated philosophy to sustain or guide him. It is his own ethical/religious beliefs and 'fear of the gods' that plague him in his crucial moments of conflict with the marlin. After Santiago gets his first vision of the great marlin, he becomes assiduously bent on making his prize catch.

> 'I am not religious,' he said. 'But I will say ten Our Fathers and ten Hail Marys that I should catch this fish, and I promise to make a pilgrimage to the Virgin de Cobre if I catch him. That is a promise' (OM, 63).

He is still enamoured of the fish and optimistic when he adds "Blessed Virgin, pray for the death of this fish. Wonderful though he is." Later, however, when sharks begin to attack and multilate the fish, Santiago is beset by primitive fears of having somehow displeased the gods. "I should n't have gone out so far, fish' he said (OM, 110). Again, "I should have some luck." "No," he said. "You violated your luck when you went too far outside" (OM, 117). He speculates on whether killing the fish was a sin, having killed him for pride, but he quickly recovers his poise and avers "I killed him in self-defence and I killed him well" (OM, 106). Nevertheless, there is a sense of defeat when he mutters under his breath, "It was too good to last."

The old man, Santiago, had gone eighty-four days without taking a single fish. After forty days, the boy Manolin's parents put him in another man's boat saying that "the old man was now definitely and finally salao, which is the worst form of unluck" (OM, 5). Superstitions abound among these unlettered folk. For the protagonist, Santiago, eighty-five is 'a lucky number': he often wonders which is better, luck or precision and even considers buying luck if possible as a commodity in a shop, although he is too practical a fisherman to depend on luck alone.

Yet, there are moments when superstition gets the better of him. When he senses that the marlin had taken the bait and can feel the weight of the fish, he calculates that it will turn and swallow the bait. However, 'He did not say that because he knew that if you said a good thing it might not happen' (OM, 40). Again, like Coleridge's *The Rime of The Ancient Mariner*, where the sailors fear ill-luck because the friendly albatross had been killed, Santiago also experiences superstitious dread saying "I am a tired old man. But I have killed this fish which is my brother and now I must do slave work" (OM, 94).

'Three' becomes a formulistic number in the novel. "If the boy were here," thinks the old man thrice in quick succession (OM, 82), and later on says with ritualistic fervour, "I wish the boy were here," which is not so much an expression of his desire to have the boy for company as an affirmation of his strength and self-confidence by invoking incantation-wise the presence of the boy who intrinsically represents the physical strength he sadly lacks.

The 'primitive' folk are said to show a surprisingly distinterested and an intellectual way of thinking, which though not exactly scientific yet displays a precise knowledge of their environment and their resources. As Levi-Strauss observes:

> ...these people whom we usually consider as completely subservient to the need of not starving, of continually able just to subsist in very harsh material conditions, are perfectly capable of disinterested thinking; that is they are moved by a need or a desire to understand the world around them, its nature and their society.[6]

Santiago, like any sailor, has the ability to judge weather conditions and predicts a storm three days in advance. So can he judge the distance of the different lines down the sea. His sensory perceptions are alert. He does not need a compass. He marks directions by the sun and the stars. He follows a sea bird that leads to dolphins and watching the movement of the flying fish surmises that his big fish must be somewhere nearby. There are simple home remedies Santiago adopts to keep himself alive and healthy. He eats turtle eggs when they are plenty, and drinks a lot of shark liver oil to preserve his eyesight. He makes his own hand-forged hooks, measures the marlin against the skiff saying it is "two feet longer than the skiff," simply washes his bleeding hand in sea water to let it heal quickly, and knows he can make salt on the bow of the boat, if needed.

The anthropological folklorist's interest in cultural history has its starting point in the novel in the author's presentation of the shift in the societal environment of the fishing community. It would be very much in place, at this juncture, to quote E.B. Tylor's classic definition of culture:

> Culture or civilization, taken in its wide ethnographic sense, is that complex whole which includes knowledge, belief, art morals, laws, customs, and any other capabilities and habits acquired by man as a member of society.[7]

Santiago depicts the lore of the humanist replete with the deposit left by the succession of vanished generations, of its craft, philosophy, ethical searching and superstitions. He becomes the centre of values beside the automation and uniformity imposed on a culture by the progress of science and technology. In fact, the old man becomes a veritable relic when pitted against the younger fishermen who venture further out into the sea in their motor boats with transistors to entertain them, and haul in huge sharks and marlins to the factories on the shore. Characteristically, their attitude to the sea is also diametrically contrastive:

> Some of the younger fisherman, those who had used buoys as float for their lines and had motor boats...spoke of her (the sea) as *el mar* which is masculine. They spoke of her as a contestant or a place or even an enemy. But the old man always thought of her as feminine and as something that gave or withheld great favours, and if she did wild or wicked things it was because she could not help them. The moon affects her as it does a woman, he thought (OM, 26, 27).

To Santiago, the sea was *la mar* a woman, sometimes kind and very beautiful, sometimes cruel.

Ultimately, the resistance to change in core institutions, attitudes and values is contextualized in Santiago's passing on his trade tricks to the young initiate/disciple, Manolin, who in all probability

they exhibit—not animosity or insensitivity—but rather a degree of awe, respect and even sympathy for the animal they kill. It is in their respective perceptions of the victim they must kill that the fishermen of the two novels show their mutual kinship.

Because of the authors' use of a common archetype, many of the intertextual echoes here may be traced to the collective heritage of the human race. Both the works seem to reverberate with echoes from myths prevalent among the fishing people all over the world, from Ireland to Canada, Japan to South-east and South Asia. At the same time, in view of Samaresh Basu's modern awareness, and of the average educated Bengali readers' awareness of contemporary English and American writings, it seems quite likely that Basu had read this book by Hemingway which came out in 1952 and received wide publicity because of the subsequent Nobel prize award to the author. The many intertextual links connecting the two books may also be taken as circumstantial evidence of Baus's knowledge of the precursor text. Finally, the similarity of the two novels in the conceptualization and presentation of an age-old folk-theme in the modern context, as well as the proliferating intertextual echoes are remarkable; and it is an aesthetic pleasure to recognize the intertextual links as well as the authors' use of a common folk theme, along with their respective traditions and myths, in the context of the experience of a fisherman of the mid-twentieth century. The intertext, here is not ironic or parodic like many a postmodernist texts of our times. Rather it imaginatively absorbs the previous text, and then recreates it by indigenizing in such a living way as to add even more fascinating dimensions to the folk-theme than given by Hemingway.

Hemingway's Nobel Prize speech contained remarks about the past driving a writer "far out to past where he can go, out to where no one can help him" (quoted by Sheridan Baker 129). As Hemingway depicts a man as being engaged with an animal in a fierce but almost equal battle, he is actually staging a journey "far out to past." Both Hemingway and Basu wrote in the fifties—with a brief interval of five years between them—on one of the most ancient themes of art and culture. At the centre of the novels, and also covering the bulk of the space, are the descriptions of an act which has been primordial, and has thus remained implanted in the racial memory. It is hunting, *i.e.*, fishing in this case, which also formed part of the primitive man's hunting for food. Since hunting had been man's first livinghood it had naturally made deep dent into his consciousness and powerfully coloured his imagination. The earliest cave-paintings were about hunting. Among the gods/goddesses man came to envisage in the ancient ages were hunters and huntresses.[4] This suggests the grip of the idea of hunting on the primitive consciousness. What was originally a compulsive act, seeped deep into the psyche and re-emerged in the form of mythicized imagination.

Again, the way the primitive hunter perceived his target was radically different from the modern killer who has become cut off from the roots. Margaret Atwood brings out this contrast in *Surfacing* and stresses the ugly nature of the killing where the hunter-turned-murderer, demonically equipped with modern technology, gloats over his insensate, unnecessary mass-killings of helpless creatures in water and on land.[5] For the primitive man, on the other hand, hunting was necessary, and it was a challenge, a game between equals, as it were. For him the hunted was not an undignified animal to be murdered, but often an awe-inspiring mysterious spirit, at least equal if not superior to the hunter. As the primitive man pursued his target he was also imaginatively stirred by the victim; it was, as it were, his fellow, his alter-ego. He had to respect the animal; he was compelled to kill for his sustenance or survival. Thus his perception of the victim was not that of just a kill. It had a mysterious life somehow destined to be intertwined with his own; it was a kind-ruthless, generous-tricky, strong-weak friend-enemy who was to be admired and pursued, respected and killed at the same time.

Frazer describes the practice of fish-worship among the Indians of British Columbia who lived largely on the fish in their seas and rivers and performed certain rites on the eve of the fishing season and prayed to the fish to come (Frazer 18). Frazer also speaks of the practice in savage societies by which the hunter and the fisherman have often to observe rules of abstinence and purification "of the same sort as those which are obligatory on the warrior and the manslayer" (216); this obliquely suggests a parity between the fish and man in the perception of this society. Though Frazer tentatively explains this ("we may with some probability assume") as dread of the spirits of the animals killed or to be killed, he also observes: "the savage commonly conceives animals to be endowed with souls and intelligences like his own, and hence he naturally treats them with similar respect" (217). In another context, with reference to the propitiation of wild animals by hunters, Frazer claims: "a tribe which depends for its subsistence, chiefly or in part, upon fishing, is careful to treat the fish with every mark of honour and respect" (527). Thus the Indians of Peru "had whatever fish was most serviceable to them as their gods" (527). The Hurens (of Canada) implored the fish to come and be caught, "for it was all to serve friends who honoured them and did not burn their bones" (Frazer 527) (thus helping the dead souls to pass into other bodies of fish). In British Columbia the Indians used to go out to meet the first fish as they came up the river: "They paid court to them...thus: 'You fish, you fish; you are all chiefs, you are; you are all chiefs'" (Frazer 528). For the primitives "chief" means the supreme authority, the most respected person of the community; thus the address "chief" itself is meant to be a kind of ovation.[6]

The way Santiago and Panchanan, the two old fish-killers in the respective novels of Hemingway and Samaresh Basu, perceive the fish may be related to this racial memory of fishing which may explain the striking correspondence between the perceptions of the two old men who are separated by great gulfs of space and culture. In this last half of the century when we are far removed from the primordial ways of life, small scale fishing with the minimum equipments, unassisted by modern technologies, retains the closest similarity to primitive hunting. And these two books, written in the fifties—depicting the same form of hunting, *i.e.,* simple fishing—in two different languages in two parts of the globe, distanced from each other by immense spatio-cultural removes, yet seem to present a common pattern of thinking and response on the part of their personae, and a comparative approach enriches our appreciation of both the texts which exploit a common heritage of the racial unconscious.

Hemingway's novella is the story of an old Cuban fisherman who had drifted far out into the sea, alone in his boat, while pursuing his big fish, had caught it, but could bring back only the long bone, the flesh having been eaten up by the sharks. It is his three-day long battle in the mythical world of the mysterious three days[7] with the 'strange' big fish that constitutes the story. Samaresh Basu's *Gangā* is spread over a period of four months, that is one-third of a year. It specifically deals with fisherman's life—its challenges, sadnesses, and the few joys—during the fishing season (that is the four months of the monsoon and post-monsoon) in the lower basin of the river Gangā.[8] *Gangā* focalizes on an old fisherman's prolonged pursuit of his fishes which come, allure and evade him in their strange ways. In the old man's imagination the fishes represent a fascinating, many-in-one mythical God, watching over the sea, the river, the hunter with "meenćakshu,"—the fish-god's inscrutable mysterious eyes; they are the fisher's friend-enemy-destiny, his life and his death. The stories are about animal versus man, and animal with man, depicting the paradoxical relationship of antagonists who are also allies.

Among the many instances of intertextuality perhaps the most notable one is connected with the two old men's attitude to the fish. They appear to talk a lot to their fish. Baker does not like it in Santiago. "This is painfully cute," he says, "like much of the aging Hemingway himself" (Sheridan Baker 131). However, this unique monologue may also be seen in another way. Since the hunt is, to the hunter's perception, his equal, and even superior, it may be reasonably talked to as an understanding listener. This is unlike the gospel assumption that implies the fisher's superiority to the fish; Frye underscores the importance of fishing in the gospels, the apostles being "fishers of men" who cast their nets into the sea of this world (Frye 191). Santiago and Panchanan continue all along interior monologues with the fish as the addressee, the imagined listener; they talk to the fish, sometimes silently, sometimes aloud, as if it were a conscious and receptive listener. Though both the texts are apparently in the third person objective mode, the narration often switches over to the tune of an intimate silent communique where the fisher is the speaker and the fish the silent auditor. Thus Santiago to his fish: "If you are tired fish...you must be very strange" (*OMS* 73). It is an intimate and friendly talk as if the fish would know and understand what he says and means. How do you feel fish... I feel good...Pull the boat fish" (78). It is, as it were, a fellow-human, an assistant. Panchu's address to his fish registers an imaginative apprehension of a profound kinship. Every year since his brother's death, the first fish of the season stirs and memories in Panchu. He looks into the eyes of the fish and silently says: "You see everything; nothing escapes your eyes. You have seen my brother. Now you see me. I have come for you" (*G* 117-18; translations from the Bengali text are by the present writer). While Santiago occasionally talks aloud to the fish amidst the vast silence of the lonely sea, Panchu's is mostly an unvoiced address, indicating his oriental reverence for the fish-cum-spirit.

As the two men talk to their fish, and remain engrossed in their contemplation of it fishing and myth get merged in their perception. The great fish unseen under water is thus characterized by a strangeness. Though it is literally and empirically a real fish, yet it is also strange like a fish in a mythical world. "Then when the fish (came)...out of the water...he was sure there was some great strangeness (*OMS* 95). In *Gangā* Basu adds an element of quasi-religious mysticism—quite befitting in his Indian context—in the fisher's envisioning of his fish. All fishes in Panchu's vision pertain the strangeness of "Meeneswarī," the fish-goddess with her inscrutable pisce eyes, "meenćakshu." The Mālos (fishermen of lower South Bengal) also invoke a boy god "Khokāthākur." In Panchu's vision the god and the goddess become one and the same as their "meenćakshu" stares at the hunter. It is present in the eyes of all the fish he kills. Thus he prays to Khokāthākur: "I do not know how you look like. When I kill fish with my own hands and look at its unblinking round eyes, I feel you are staring at me. O God, you are my hunt. This is the destiny of our life" (*G* 171). He feels that this spirit of the fish watches the fisher at moments of death and disaster; then the mysterious eyes seem to "laugh" (*G* 59). The fish is, as it were, a merciless death-god as well, pervading the air and the water. Panchu, as he gets old and weak, has occasional visions of the laughing eyes of the "Meen" (the spirit or god of the fish), glistening in the horizon; this seems to him a reminder that death is closing in (*G* 50). This "meencakshu," he knows, is "the fisher's ultimate destiny, which will embrace and strangle him in the form of turbulent waves, whirlpools, hurricanes" (*G* 60). Thus the fish also becomes part of the destructive elements from which it seems to float up and into which it disappears.

The narrator tells the story from Panchu's point of view; till his death it is either Panchu directly experiencing something, or reminiscing the past[9]; and the vision of "meencakshu" recurs in these experiences and reminiscences. Thus Panchu recalls the death of Abhay, the poor fisherman, who had desperately crept into the *bheri*[10] to steal fish when a sudden harpoon had run through him in the darkness. The fish he still held in his hand had unfathomable mystery in its round shining eyes; Panchu instinctively knew "what Abhay had failed to see—the laugh in the meencakshu which had stolen into this shallow water as his death" (*G* 97). According to the philosophy of Panchu, this "meencakshu" is an inalienable part of the fisher's existence, whether he is on land, or in water. Thus even when, during the days of draught and privation, he goes the ways of drink and women "someone watches everything; it is the meencakshu" (*G* 99). In his imagination the fish assumes the stature of an omniscient spirit, all-seeing and all-knowing, who also signalizes danger and death. On the occasion of the death of his elder brother Panchu had looked spell-bound into the eyes of the small fishes that had been caught and left on the boat by Nibaran; "As if they were watching everything with their unblinking, shiny, round eyes, the expressionless eyes of the Death-god" (*G* 21). Again, on the eve of the death of Thandaram, the young fisherman, by accident (he had struck against the iron pillar of the jetty in darkness), Panchu has the same vision: "around the turn of the river, innumerable "meencakshu" appeared on the crests of innumerable waves" (*G* 242). As Panchu is passing away he envisions and respectfully mentions the "meens," the spirits of all the fishes he had killed; "all, all of them I had killed have come" (*G* 262).

The fish is perceived in the two novels with desperation, love, admiration, respect, awe, humility, sympathy. The admiration and humility go hand in hand; behind them operates the awe that inspired the primitive hunter *vis-a-vis* his hunt, and made him feel humble and modest in relation to the animal world. Thus Santiago thinks: "Man is not much beside the great birds and beasts. Still I would rather be that beast down there in the darkness of the sea" (*OMS* 73-74). He feels "there is no one worthy of eating him from the manner of his behaviour and his great dignity" (*OMS* 79). It is humility and not insensitive pride that constituted the spirit of the ancient hunter, and the same humility characterises the old men's response towards their kill. Santiago is engaged with his fish in a desperate prolonged struggle, yet his feeling at this moment is: "I am with a friend" (*OMS* 64); "the fish is my friend" (*OMS* 79). He knows that they may not be "all intelligent as we who kill them"; but "they are more noble and more able" (*OMS* 70). With frank admiration he thinks, "I wish I were the fish, ...with everything he has against only my will and my intelligence" (*OMS* 70). Basu takes this empathy to another level of intuitive philosophy; for Panchu it is more than an easy friendship. It is an inseparable bond transcending ordinary human relationships. Thus Panchu talks to his fish: "My life and your life have been woven together by a single thread since the very moment of birth" (*G* 44). (The reader may recall Santiago's conviction that he had "to think of only one thing," the fish, "that which I was born for" (*OMS* 54).

The hunter-hunted relation had been depicted by both the authors as a paradoxical one where, in spite of the hunter's friendliness, his compulsion is to pursue, while that of the hunt is to evade. The old fishermen, even after their lifelong preoccupation with this work, never cease to wonder at the strange and saddening paradox. As Santiago ponders over his fish:

> "His choice had been to stay in the deep dark water far out beyond all snares and traps and treacheries. My choice was to go there to find him..." (*OMS* 61).

Though Santiago admires the fish he must also want its death.

"Blessed Virgin," he appeals, "pray for the death of the fish. Wonderful though he is" (*OMS* 71). Santiago knows "I will kill him though...in all his greatness and glory" (*OMS* 72). He remains unflinching in his painful wisdom: "The fish is my friend too.... But I must kill him" (*OMS* 79). Though he is "sorry" for the great fish "his determination to kill him never relaxed in his sorrow for him" (*OMS* 79). Nevertheless he also feels sad at having "to kill our true brothers" (*OMS* 70). Panchanan alias Panchu is haunted by the same wonder at the saddening paradox. Silently he tells himself: "If you are *Māchmārā* (fish-killer), you must come along following the fish's trail. It is in the water; you are on the bank. Its death is your life. This is the rule,—this co-existence of life and death side by side. You are to feel its moods and whims, its ways, its movement in the various currents, and tides, and layers of water. Wherever it goes, you have to follow there" (*G* 26). Santiago, in his simple way, registers his perception of the paradox inherent in the situation as he says, "Fish, ...I love you and respect you very much. But I will kill you dead before this day ends" (*OMS* 63). Even as he eats his food he is haunted by this enigma: "I wish I could feed the fish. He is my brother. But I must kill him and keep strong to do it" (*OMS* 67). When at last he kills the fish he is instantly sad; because, he feels, "I have killed the fish which is my brother" (*OMS* 92). He tries to assure himself that man is not born for defeat; yet he is sad at his victory; "I am sorry that I killed the fish though, he thought" (*OMS* 98). The sadness swells into an enormous empathy by which the hunt also becomes a fellow-traveller (*OMS* 57), a friend and a brother. After tying the killed fish to the skiff and starting homewards, Santiago feels, with the simple knowledge of the primitive mind, "We sail like brothers" (*OMS* 98). And "when the fish had been hit (by the sharks) it was as though he himself were hit" (*OMS* 98).

The old men of Hemingway and Basu are aware,—Santiago instinctively and Panchu intuitively, of the strange bond binding the killer with the killed,—the strong thread of death that binds the fisherman to his fish. In this game of death they are inseparable, and both the hunted and the hunter are at the end reduced to equals. Certain passages from the two texts may be read together in this context.

"You are killing me fish, the old man thought. But you have a right to. Never have I seen a greater or more beautiful, or a calmer and more noble thing than you, brother. Come on and kill me. I do not care who kills who" (*OMS* 91). This is Santiago's famous monologue. Similarly, Panchu, in his dignified humility before the fish, soliloquizes to himself: "You kill the fish, you are killed by another. This is the rule of life" (*G* 64). He feels with a sense of awe that death for the fishkiller is thus a bit different from the death of others. "With the fish lies your life; and the thread of your death is woven along with that very same fish. Whether you die outside your house or indoors, it is certain that you shall see that bleeding meenćakshu at the end" (*G* 31). It is an intricate pattern of life, living and death. And Hemingway's old man perceives it exactly like his Indian counterpart: "Everything kills everything else in some way. Fishing kills me exactly as it keeps me alive" (*OMS* 100). Panchu, again, has the same vision of the strange interrelationship, which he expresses poetically; this may also reflect a racial memory,—the memory of the fear that the ancient hunter felt of the spirits or souls of the creatures he had to kill. "This is the rule of the world.... If you kill someone, you also begin to get killed in the process. You may not realise it all the time. But as you kill fish the fish also kills you bit by bit" (*G* 64). Panchu can never really forget this apprehension; "I kill fish, and I know it is killing me day and night" (*G* 127). The knowledge that makes Santiago a resigned lonely man, makes a mystic visionary of his Indian counterpart. In Hemingway's story, there are moments when the separate identities seem to get blurred and merged. Santiago, in his utter fatigue, is not sure who is bringing whom in. He would even be happy at this confusion which, at least momentarily, seems to purge him of his sense of guilt and sadness. He feels, "We sail like brothers"; then wonders, "Is he bringing me in or am I bringing him in?..." The thought gives him a kind of happiness: "Let him bring me in if it pleases him. I am only better than him through trickery and he meant me no harm" (*OMS* 95). On the other hand Panchu, looking at the monsoon

Gangā, envisions (at such time the voice of Panchu and that of the third person narrator get merged): "The fish is coming with the rising tide in order to lay eggs. And you have come following its trail. This is the law of life. At your death it will come to see you; you will see it. It will then show you your entire life in flashback" (*G* 186). Panchu imagines in his characteristic Indian way that at the end it is the killed one who will come back as the killer. As Panchu ruminates: "You are the fish-killer. The fish may not kill you directly or instantly. But it is among the shoals of fish, along the line of its movements in its unfathomable that your death lies in wait. So long as you are destined to live it will sustain you. The moment your term is ended, it will come back in a different form" (*G* 37). And the hunters do not mind "who kills who." They know that neither of them can evade the other. With their primitive wisdom these killers know of the strange logic of this world where killing an animal is also a fratricide, and no Cain injures uninjured,[11] and one must pay back in consequence. So Santiago is not bothered that he may be killed by the fish. Rather he likes the idea of being killed by the admirable fish. He simultaneously pities and admires the great fish he has hooked. "He began to pity the great fish.... He is wonderful and strange and who knows how old he is, he thought. Never have I had such a strong fish nor one who acted so strangely" (*OMS* 59). What the "great fish" is to Santiago, is the "Meen" to Panchu,—epitomising all the small and big fishes, their mystery, strangeness, unpredictability, their admirable and pitiable aspects,—symbol of and spirit of all the fishes he has ever caught. Santiago even welcomes the possibility of death by this fish. "You are killing me fish," he says; but he admits, "You have a right to. Never have I seen a greater, or more beautiful, or a calmer or more noble thing than you, brother" (*OMS* 91). So he invokes the fish to be his noble killer: "Come on and kill me. I do not care who kills who" (*OMS* 91). On the other hand, Panchu, in his unceasing wonder at the mystery of his situation *vis-a-vis* the fish, sometimes even imagines it as a noble spirit which has "kindly conceded to come and die at your hand" (*G* 122); and which has not ceased to exist even after the physical death. "The soul of the creature you have killed is here, around, in this air, this water" (122); hence his warning against mentioning fish,—that "if you mentioned the name of the spirit of the dead creature might be displeased" (*G* 122).

Both feel their inseparable bond with the fish. What Panchu intuitively realizes as an abstract metaphysical perception gets concretized in Santiago's experience. Panchu feels that he was born to pursue the fish (*G* 44); this gives him the only meaning and explanation of life. "We do not know who is pulling the strings of the fishkillers' lives under this deep water. The one with whom I have my direct encounter is the 'Meen'" (*G* 202). And he has no respite: "I am born to move in the regions of the Meen" (*G* 44). Santiago too has no respite from the inseparable bond that ties the killer with the killed. "He thought, I can do it as long as he can" (*OMS* 62). And together he travels with his fish, together they begin to get exhausted. "'You're feeling it now, fish,' he said. And so, God knows, am I" (*OMS* 65). Even when he is almost at his tether's end, he cannot give up; instead he cries out: "Fish...fish, you are going to die anyway. Do you have to kill me too?" (*OMS* 90). He does not know what the fish is going to do. But the bond cannot be severed. "He stays down forever. Then I will stay down with him forever" (*OMS* 67).

In this way the two novels build around the archetypal theme of a hunter *vis-a-vis* his hunt, and since they grow out of the same archetype, they expectedly show remarkable similarities while making room for interesting variations as well,—variations that derive from their respective spatio-cultural contexts.

Besides this broad framework of ideational pattern which is common to both, there are also many intertextual echoes. Of course these echoes have a distinctive ring; if Basu had really read Hemingway's book, or learnt about it from his erudite friend Saroj Bandyopadhyaya,—which is not unlikely in view of their eager receptive mind and lively interest in contemporary literature,—it is clear from Basu's treatment of the details that he had personalized, poeticised, and completely Indianized the impressions, if any, that might have been left upon his imagination by Hemingway's book. It is indeed fascinating to follow this process at work. To cite just a few examples; first of all, the two old men, as they appear, may be noted. Their vocation seems to have left its indelible mark on their faces and hands. Both have seared, scarred hands and wrinkled faces. The wrinkles in Panchu's face are "like the watery pattern drawn by wimpling waves" (*G* 110; 117); his face is like a "fishing net" (*G* 117). Santiago is "thin and gaunt with deep wrinkles.... The brown blotches (marks left by the tropic sea)...ran well down the sides of his face"; but his eyes "were the same colour as the sea" (*OMS* 33). And Panchu feels "as if there were layers of moss and sediment of the river on his entire body" (*G* 148). Both the fishers and debilitated by old age, poverty, hunger, emaciation; they get less to eat than is necessitated by the nature of their hard and challenging work; the old men undertake a hard task, and they are scarcely equal to it because of ill luck, weakness, age. However both are characterized by the quality of endurance. So though Santiago—after his eighty-four days without taking a fish—returns only with the skeleton of the fish at the end of his unique pursuit, and Panchu dies empty handed in course of a frustrating pursuit of the fish during a prolonged *totā* (a bad season), both emerge as undefeated losers. For a long period both go out fishing and come back empty handed, with the disappointment and desperation of the frustrated hunter; yet they do not give up. What Gilbert Highet says about *The Old Man and the Sea*—a really "heroic" piece of narrative (Heyers 414) may be applied with equal validity to the other novel as well. Again, both Santiago and Panchu are basically lonely men; for all their courage and struggle they go unnoticed by the world around. Only the two growing boys, Manolin and Bilas, love their respective old men who have taught them fishing. This is the only relation that seems to survive and thrive in this life of the unceasing struggle with the elements. At the same time both the old men are basically lonely in spite of their beloved and loving boys. Santiago has to go fishing all by himself. Though Panchu has Bilas on the same boat, he has been immersed within his own loneliness since the day his elder brother had died on a fishing trip to the sea. Since then he has been carrying his loneliness like a load on his heart.

For both the fishers fishing is a professional compulsion, a way of surviving through extreme poverty, but also something more. It is their addiction, excitement, commitment, ecstasy. In spite of the uncertain future, the uncertainty of profit, and certainty of hardship and dangers, they cannot stay back at home when the fishing season arrives. They must come. And at the moment when they are engaged in the battle they do not remember the biting realities like poverty, price, money, money-lender, market, or anything. It is their epiphanic moment of grappling with a respectable entity when the question of victory or defeat, success or failure, seems to get blurred and become immaterial. Finally what emerges is their courageous, even joyous (quietly though) acceptance of the elemental life with its challenges, beauties, terror—an acceptance which dissolves the line between success and failure. It is the same simple feeling of Santiago that finds poetic articulation in Panchu's monologue as he stresses that fishing is his sorrow and it is his joy: "Who catches fish is filled with the joy of fulfilment just by the very act of catching" (*G* 141). At that moment it does not matter whether he gets a good price for it or not. It is the challenge and the joy of the game which a person outside this vocation will never appreciates, nor will he understand the sorrow of it: "The sorrow of the fish-killer can never be understood by the wholesaler" (*G* 195). Even one catch may fill him with joy, and failure to catch a single fish may depress him to death (*G* 195). This explains the irresistible call of the sea or the river for the fisher in spite of its dangers and possible frustrations (*G* 197; 204). They have got to go out whether they succeed or fail. As Panchu registers his sense of wonder at the compulsion: "What strong spell it is of the sea! What charm! Once it catches hold of someone, he cannot live in peace" (*G* 52).

Nevertheless, the lives of the fishermen, both on the Cuban Sea, and the lower Ganga and the coastal sea of Bengal, are similarly haunted by insecurity, unknown fears and unpredictable dangers. The shadow of death ever hangs low on the boats. One does not know how or when one may be carried too far out into the sea (*G* 30; *OMS* 58). The least carelessness could drag one directly into the far sea. At the moment the fisherman in Ganga pursues his huge shoal, he does not remember anything else, anything about the life he has left behind on the bank. Engrossed in the pursuit, he does not know when he has come away too far, like Santiago following his fish. Sometimes the entire Sābar[12] is killed, leaving no trace behind; only the empty boat may float up, signalling the unmistakable grim message. In this context, Basu's old man, with his oriental imagination perceives a vein of mystery behind the grim reality of his death-ridden life. He believes, like his fellow fishers, that "even those who have died, out on this limitless sea, might come back in unforeseen ways, to delude you into your death" (*G* 32). Death is the obsessive reality of this life; "here life and death go on hand in hand, side by side (*G* 33). The same cruciality marks the long three days of Santiago's travel with his fish in the sea.

Even the beasts that haunt the dream and thought of the two old men are two of the strongest and the most terrible. Northrop Frye holds: "The organizing ideas of the high mimetic area seem to be love and form.... The animals are those of proud beauty: the eagle and the lion stand for the vision of the royal by the loyal" (153). The animal figures that rule the consciousness of Santiago and Panchu are marked by this regal beauty and its accompanying terror in the latter's case. Arrived at the fag end of his life Santiago does not dream any more of storms, or women, of great events, or great fish, of fights or trophies, or of his wife. "He only dreamed...now...of the lions on the beach" (*OMS* 44). But they convey no terror for him. "They played like young cats in the dusk and he loved them as he loved the boy" (*OMS* 44). At the end Santiago is seen sleeping after his three exhausting days in the sea, and the narrator adds, "was dreaming about the lions" (*OMS* 113). He remembers them even when far out into the sea. While travelling together with the great fish day and night, Santiago falls asleep for a few moments, and in his dream "he saw the first of the lions come down onto it in the early dark and then the other lions came and he...waited to see if there would be more lions and he was happy" (*OMS* 83).

Panchu, on the other hand, pays his respect to Dakshin Roy, the tiger-god, and also Banbibi, the tigress-goddess, who are worshipped by the people of the Sunderban[13] region. Dakshin Roy is imagined to be a terrible god with the form of the royal Bengal tiger; he is the terror of the poor panicked fishers of the area, and is held to be the king of the Sunderbans, wielding magical powers. Panchu here shares the folk-belief of this part of the South Bengal when he stresses that all the delusions that trap the poor fishers into dangers and death are the work of Dakshin Roy's magic of which there is no end (*G* 7). His name is a taboo among the fishermen, foodgatherers, and woodcutters of this coastal zone. He is the fearsome demi-god of the forests where even the roaring wind through the trees sounds like an angry tiger (*G* 16). Banbibi is a female incarnation of the same. Panchu invokes the tiger deities on occasions and envisions them on the eve of his death. Santiago finds his lions almost lovable, distanced as they are from the actual reality of the fisherman's daily life. But in *Gangā* the tiger strikes real panic and awe as it is very much a part of the grim reality of the life of the poor fishermen of South Bengal, going seaward for fishing. Santiago dreams of lions he may have seen in his youth on African beaches; he dreams of them with love and affection. Panchu remembers Dakshin Roy, the ruthless tiger-god, who is also a real man-eater, with terror, respect, awe. However, these dreams/ visions of terrible grandeur also indicates the old men's nostalgia for their lost youth when they had their glimpses of this fierce beauty. These images of strong fierce beauty which are embedded in the consciousness of both, may also go back to the racial memory of a time when these were part of the primitive atmosphere of the ancient hunter's life.

Both the stories have very simple narrational style which reminds one of folk-literature. Edwin Muir observes that Hemingway's story is "told with a simplicity which shows that Mr. Hemingway has forgotten that he is a tough writer" (Meyers 408). Basu too, like Hemingway, knew about the sordidness of the grim modern life, and could write about this in the appropriate language of a tough writer through which bitterness seeped (*Bibar, Prajāpati*, for example). But in *Gangā* he wrote in a simple and mellowed poetical style that was in perfect tuning with the simple life and ways of the poor fishermen who still had a rich mental life, considered in its emotional-imaginative aspect. The personae of both the books, like the characteristic primitive mind living close to nature, inhabit the world of free poetic imagination to which they bring their simple perception and expression. It is the unassuming, unsophisticated man's imagination, rendered in an exquisitely simple and appropriate style that is not only befitting the protagonists, but also significantly contributes to the charm of the narration.

An epic, when primary, is necessarily folk-literature. And an epic pattern has been noted in *The Old Man and the Sea* by Gilbert Highet (Meyers 414). *Gangā* is also, in a sense, an epic of the fishermen's life in South Bengal. Indeed both the novels represent the infinitely repeated epic theme of man fighting and enduring in a mysterious hostile-friendly nature of which his hunt is a part.

* * *

A distinct mythical dimension may be perceived in the treatment of the above theme in the two texts. Whereas in Hemingway it is to be traced between the lines, in Basu it is vividly present with all the richness and colour of the oriental imagination, and the layers of associations that are accumulated over milleniums by an ancient culture.

In the context of his anatomy of myths Frye had underscored "the tendency to anchor spiritual vision in an empirical psychological experience" (154). This a precisely what Panchu goes on doing elaborately, and Santiago in a vague semi-conscious way. For both "the symbolism is an every day affair," as Dan Sperber would have said, "and not the cold material of the anthropologist" (72). The way the two protagonists look at their vocation and surroundings, evidence a mythical imagination. They live this imaginary world of myths and symbols in their own daily life. As Jung held: "The primitive mentality does not *invent* myths, it *experiences* them" (101). Thus the fish is a "brother" and a "strange thing" for Santiago, and is pertaining of the mystery of some god/goddess for Panchu (This corresponds to the Indian myths about Lord Krishna and Lord Buddha, both of whom were supposed to assume the form of the fish on certain occasions; "Keshava dhrita meen sariram," etc.).[14]

Their immediate surroundings also assume for them the

strangeness of spirits. The fish, as it is mysterious in its evasion and surrender, in its beauty and bounty, in its unfathomable ways, in its dignity and tricks, it is also seen as part of a greater mystery,—that of the river, the sea, the elemental nature facing the hunter. Panchu's death-bed invocation of all the spirits of nature envisioned by the fisherman reaches poetic heights: "O my Lord Dakshin Roy (tiger-god), I have glimpsed your terrible beauty. O mother Banbibi (forest-goddess), I have seen your deathliness and terror among the sea-going fishermen. Oh Great Sea, I have seen your amazing beauty of destruction. Oh demons of the forests (of the Sunderbans), I have trembled at your fearsome voice. O Mother Ganga, I have lived your terrors and received blessings in your bounteous bosom. Now you have come to stand at the head of my death-bed, with your long hair unwinded, my beautiful destructress! There was a time when I used to row about fishing surrounded by all of you. Now I leave my nephew in the hands of you all" (*G* 265). When day after day Panchu is afloat on Ganga in his narrow boat, Panchu realizes how his fish is part of a vast supernatural pattern: "I have come so far following the trail of someone who is not only under the water; it is my life and death; it is in the clouds, the thunders, the waves, the Southern wind" (*G* 63).

Santiago also envisages the sea as a living entity, which is ambiguous, unpredictable and extremely fascinating like an animated spirit. The sea appears to him "kind and very beautiful"; but, he knows at the same time, "she can be so cruel and it comes so suddenly..." (46-47). The old man's perception of the sea distinguishes him from the younger moneyed fishers with modern equipments like lines and motorboats who spoke of her as *el mar*,—a contestant or even an enemy. Santiago thinks of her lovingly as *la mar*. "The old man always thought of her as feminine and as something that gave or withheld great favours, and if she did wild or wicked things it was because she could not help them. The moon affects her as it does a woman, so he thought" (*OMS* 47).

This seems to illustrate Tylor's theory of animism. Tylor, the originator of the doctrine of animism, found that primitive men automatically translated their daily experiences into myths, because they believed that all nature was animated, and, as such, could be personified. He held: "To the lower tribes of man, sun and stars, trees and rivers, winds and clouds, become personal animate creatures, leading lives that conformed to human or animal analogies" (285). Tylor stressed that whereas the mythopoeic process could be active at all phases of culture, mythical creations among the primitives were essentially related to the understanding of natural phenomena. Indeed, the two old men, in course of pursuing their hard life, never cease to wonder at nature, and try to understand it in their charmingly simple imaginative ways; and this makes up to a large extent for the extraordinary charm of the two books.

Lawrence felt that myth had a salvaging function because the myths show the sense of wonder that governed primitive cultures of people who lived close to nature. The fishers in these novels have still retained their sense of wonder, so that even the fish is so much more than the fish, a kill, or food, and such a cause for wonder, ecstasy, reverence.

Frye defines myth as "an art of implicit metaphorical identity" (136). In accordance with the operation of this art the fish becomes "Meeneswari,"[14] the tiger "Dakshin Roy," the merlin a brother and a strange dignified noble thing, the sea *la mar*, the myserious beloved feminine spirit.

The basic characteristic of mythical thought consists in its concreteness. It works with signs that come midway between images and concepts. The many major signs (*Meenćakshu*, for example, or Ganga, the *rudrānī* mother, who destroys and preserves), so powerfully used in *Gangā*, are concrete like images, and at the same time have the power of reference like concepts.

Myths promote, as Cassirer would have put it, a tendency of solidarity and unity of all forms of life. "To mythical and religious feeling nature becomes one great society, the society of life" (Cassirer 110). Under the impact of such a feeling it becomes possible for the fisher to view himself and his fish as brothers or fellow-beings, bound to each other through life and death by an inseparable tie.

The hunter-hunted equation and their interlapping identities may also be seen in relation to Frye's theory of the apocalyptic conception of human life. According to this theory, at the one end of the pole there is the tyrant leader, while at the other is the pharmakas or sacrificed victim, who has to be killed to strengthen the others (Santiago's strange fish or Panchu's fish-god has to be killed). Frye shows how "in the most concentrated form of the demonic parody, the two became the same" (148). Seen in this perspective the fisher may be related to the ruthless yet melancholy tyrant, whereas the hunted fish may acquire the identity of the sacrificed victim, and the two become the same, so that one does not know "who kills who," and who pulls whom in.

Again, in the mythical imagination the cycle from birth to death is extended from death to rebirth. A similar vision of continuity gets reflected in the novels. Thus the dead Nibaran seems to have been reborn in Bilas,—in his appearance, temperament, and the final journey to the sea. Panchu is also proud and humble in his moments of sudden flashes when he has silent but firm conviction that Bilas is the first father of the *Malos* (a fishing community of South Bengal). Expectedly, the Bengal fishermen's myth about their community god or the first forefather is envisioned in terms of their own life-setting and vocation. Myth and life get merged and dissolved into each other in this vision of "a naked black man with curly hair like so many small snakes, and a harpoon in his hand, moving around in search of the sea-fish, all alone by the roaring sea, on the vast lonely wind-swept tide-washed beach" (*G* 24) reborn.

Again, Hemingway's story starts with a journey, and ends in return, thus completing the cycle. Yet there remains the unvoiced hope that such journeys will continue for the old man till he dies. *Gangā* starts with one journey, and ends with a renewed journey, the circle beginning anew. This myth of rebirth and an ever-renewing cycle seems to be suited to the oriental imagination. Frye also acknowledges this as he points out: "To this pattern of identical recurrence, the death and revival of the same individual, all other cyclical patterns are, as a rule assimilation," and, "the assimilation can be of course much closer in Eastern culture, where the doctrine of re-incarnation is generally accepted than in the West" (159).

However, it is not that myths are the exclusive property of the primitive mind and the olden times. The mythical imagination is constantly at work in the world. It is, to quote Charles Fiedelson, "the vindication of imaginative thought in a world grown abstract and material." Thus the two authors, both of whom had lost all illusions about the so-called civilized life of the modern times, restore us, through their protagonists, to a refreshing imaginative approach to nature and her small creatures.

Jung had been struck by the obvious similarities between myths, symbols of widely distanced societies—both spatially and culturally—and this led him to the theory of the collective unconscious which, he found, manifested itself through "archetypes." This could be compared to Bastian's *Elementargedanken* or Burckhardt's "primordial images" which were an impersonal collective possession of the race.

One may recall in this context what Allen Tate said with reference to Poe. "The imagination of any power at all often project its deepest assumptions about life in symbols that duplicate without the artist's knowledge, certain meanings the origins of which are sometimes as old as the race" (44).

To conclude with a quote from V.K. Arora's perceptive remark in his article on archetypal approach to literature:

> "It might be generally conceded that great works of art are rooted in some ultimate experience, the archetypal image or symbol. Sometimes the reader feels moved by a work of art, though he does not understand why. It may be that the work dramatizes some archetype, or its reflection or an echo of an echo. If the artist is a myth-maker, the function of archetypal criticism is to "decode the secret language" (Wilbur Scott, *Five Approaches of Literary Criticism,* p 249) so that the reader may comprehend rationally what he has perceived unconsciously."

Here precisely this attempt has been made to "decode the secret language" and trace the underlying universal pattern which alone makes comparison between the two books from so widely separated social-cultural-linguistic contexts worthwhile.

NOTES

1. The book has been enthusiastically acclaimed as Homeric, symbolic (Bernard Berenson); a world of free poetic imagination (Edwin Muir); perfect in descriptive details (Cyril Connolly); a classic (Mark Schorer); a moral fable, a parable (Schorer); an epic pattern (Gilbert Highet); a form suited to a folk-theme (Joyce Cary); the story of the fisher's alter-ego (Dupee); the story of the Undefeated (Delmore Schwartz); religious symbolism (Carlos Baker); R.W.B. Lewis had even expressed doubts if the book could bear the amount of critical weight already piled up on it. (J. Meyers, *Hemingway: The Critical Heritage* 47-48).
2. "In many ways Hemingway appears as pre-industrial man. He made his separate peace with America by opting out of it....(like) Natty Bumppo who in his old age plunged further and further into the prairies beyond the frontier, fleeing the settled communities—and their corruption...." (Walter Allen, *The Urgent West*, N.Y.: E.P. Dutton & Co., 1969, 206).
3. With reference to *The Old Man and the Sea*, American writer Delmore Schwartz claimed: "the experience of literature is always comparative" (Meyers 415).
4. Artemis (Greek); Diana (Roman—taken from Aricia, according to Will Durant, *Ceaser and Christ* 61-62), N.Y., 1944; various tribal gods among primitive people all over the world, who are also equipped with hunting weapons.

   The hunted animal has also been worshipped in various forms. "There is hardly an animal in nature, from the Egyptian scarab to the Hindu elephant, that has not somewhere been worshipped as a god...from the Indian tribes of North America to the natives of Africa, the Dravidians of India, and the tribes of Australia.... The Gallas of Abyssinia ate in solemn ceremony the fish that they worshipped, and said, "We feel the spirit moving within us as we eat." (Will Durant, *The Story of Civilization*, vol. 1., N.Y., 1942, 61-62).

   Durant even claims:

   > "Hunting and fishing were not stages in the economic development, they were modes of activity destined to survive in the highest forms of civilized society. Once the center of life, they are still its hidden foundations; behind our literature and philosophy, our ritual and art, stand the stout killers of Packing town." (*The Story of Civilization*, V. 1, 7).

   The heroes, hero-gods and culture heroes were often killed hunters.
5. In Surfacing the narrator wonders why did they kill the herons and hung up like lynch victims: "To prove they could do it, they had the power to kill. Otherwise it was valueless: beautiful from a distance but it couldn't be tamed or cooked or trained to talk, the only relation they could have to a thing like that was to destroy it" (117). She thinks: "Innocents get slaughtered because they exist...there is nothing inside the happy killers to restrain them.... It

would have been different in those countries where an animal is the soul of an ancestor or the child of a god, at least they would have felt guilt" (127-128).

6. Mergaret Craven in *I Heard the One Call my Name* gives extensive description of such practices in British Columbia. Also it has been claimed in *The Encyclopaedia of Religion and Ethics*, "In hunting cults... the species which receives honour is habitually killed...but not until it has...received divine honours, and...each individual of the species at its death by the hand of the hunter is propitiated and receives offerings, or whatever treatment is conceived to be proper to make its feelings predominantly those of satisfaction." (Ed. James Hastings, N.Y.: 1959, 488).
7. "He (Hemingway) does, of course, give the tale conscious touches of the mythical, changing the actual two days into the mysterious three of fairyland and Christianity" (Sheridan Baker 28).
8. Gangā is the name of the widest and longest river of North India; considered as holy and worshipped as a goddess by many.
9. Panchu for most of the time dwells upon past memories and remains absorbed in his own ruminations which come upon him like a stream of consciousness; so, when Panchu dies off the narration also seems to get a bit unhinged, with its focus shifting from the river and the fish to the romantic love between a young pair.
10. Bheri—enclosed marshy area used as fishery by moneyed proprietors.
11. "...no Cain
    Injures uninjured (in her best-aimed blow
    Victorious Murder a blind Suicide)...."
    (S.T. Coleridge, *Religious Musings, CPW*, I, 113)
12. Sābar—a group of boats which go together to the sea under the leadership of one fisherman, called *saidar*.
13. Sunderban—the dense forest on the delta of the Gangā, at the approach of the Bay Bengal, known for its maneater,—the royal Bengal tiger.
14. In the coastal area of Madras: there is a famous temple of the goddess known as "Meenakshi" (fish-eyed). Amitav Ghosh, in his well-researched book *In an Antique Land* (1992), has shown how the ancient gods of the fishing and sailing people of the Mangalore coast underwent changes in the recent past in order to enable them get a position in Hindu pantheon, and the worshipper in the Hindu mainstream. In view of this it may not be unlikely that the goddess "Meenakshi," whose name at least indicates an association with the fish, was perhaps originally worshipped by the fishing people who dominated the coastal area, and possibly attributed to their goddess some features of their hunt.

    English translations from the Bengali text are by the writer of the present article.

REFERENCES

Allen, W. *The Urgent West*. N.Y.: E.P. Dutton & Co., 1969.

Arora, V.N. "Archetypal Approach to Literature: An Analysis of Hawthorne's

The Scarlet Letter." *Twentieth Century American Criticism*. Ed. Rajnath. New Delhi: Arnold-Heinmann, 1977.

Atwood, M. *Surfacing*, London: Virago, 1979.

Baker, C. "Introduction." *Three Novels of E.H.*, N.Y.: Charles Scribners Sons, 1962.

Baker, Sheridan. *Ernest Hemingway*. N.Y.: Holt: Rinehart & Winson, 1967.

Barthes, R. *Theory of the Text*. Trans. R. Young. London: Routledge and Kegan Paul, 1981.

Basu, Samaresh. *Gangā*. Calcutta: Bengal Publishers, 1957.

Cary, J. Excerpt in Meyers (Ed.), *Hemingway: The Critical Perspective*. London: Routledge and Kegan Paul, 1982.

Cassirer, Earnest. *An Essay on Man*. 1944; N.Y.: 1956.

Eco, U. *Postcript to the Name of the Rose*. Trans. W. Weaver. N.Y. and London: Harcourt Brace Jovanovich, 1984.

Faulkner, W. Excerpt in J. Meyers, *Hemingway* 414.

Frazer, J. *The Golden Bough*. Hertfordshire: Wordsworth Reference, 1993.

Frye, N. *Anatomy of Criticism*. 1957; Jersey: Princeton UP, 1971.

Fieldelson, Charles. *Symbolism and American Literature*. Chicago: 1953.

Hemingway, E. *The Old Man and the Sea*. New Delhi: Kalyani Publishers, 1994.

Jung, C.J. and C. Kerenyi. *Essays on a Science of Mythology*. Trans. R.F.C. Hull. N.Y.: 1949.

Lawrence, D.H. "The Dragon of the Apocalypse." *Selected Literary Criticism*. Ed. A. Beal. N.Y.:1942.

Muir, E. Excerpt in J. Meyer's *Hemingway: The Critical Heritage*.

Riffeterre, M. *Semiotics of Poetry*. Bloomington: Indiana UP, 1978.

Schorer, M. Excerpt in J. Meyers, *Hemingway*.

Schwartz, D. Excerpt in J. Meyers, *Hemingway: The Critical Heritage*.

Sperber, D. *Rethinking Symbolism*. N.Y.: C.U.P., 1974.

Tate, A. "Our Cousin, Mr. Poe." *Poe*. Ed. Robert Regan. N.J.: Prentice Hall, 1967.

Tylor, *Primitive Culture*. 2nd ed., I. 1873.

7

Incommunicable Mythography: Thomas Wolfe's Novel *Look Homeward, Angel*

PREM PRAKASH

I

Man's attempts to create the structure of myth have been endless. Still the eternity has not been trapped. In his primary attempt, he created a mythical world which could neither be successfully fabricated nor yet communicated. This view is certified by the *Rig-Veda*[1] which says that the three-fourth of the *Purush* is invisible and only the rest visible and therefore it can neither be conceived nor structured. Lord Krishna says the same thing in the *Geeta,*[2] that He is not be found in words which are forms of time. He is beyond them. That is what incommunicable mythography means. Communicable mythography can assimilate and express human experiences from a transcendental perspective whereas incommunicable mythography falls short of expression because of its highly mystical nature. It is a realm of suggested metaphor and not expressed metaphor. It is the difference between timelessness of figurations and of temporality. Communicable mythography can be compared with the sounding of the bell which although stroked once continues to echo multiple times and is finally lost in the Infinite. Thomas Wolfe makes use of such workaday symbols as "(the stone, the leaf, the door)," and the prison of the earth and of flesh,"[3] among many others which are parts of a mythography under consideration.

This study mainly focusses on the genesis of incommunicable mythography which is deeply rooted in the psyche. Keeping this in view, the paper is divided into three parts. The first part of the paper would briefly outline the plot of the novel. The second part would analyse characters comparing them with their Biblical counterparts. The third and the final part shall focus attention upon the images and symbols which form a communicable mythography or fail to form it. This section will also gather findings and make necessary generalizations at the level of myth and vision.

Thomas Wolfe, born in 1900 at Asheville, lived in the small mountain town. He was frustrated with his parents and consequently developed adverse tendencies which are found in *Look Homeward, Angel.* In his wanderings, certain emotions are evoked within spatio-temporal contexts as numerous functional accounts impinge upon his mind, influenced as he is by James Jaycees's novels. As Pamela Johnson has pointed out:

> He set out in search of an impossible ideal—to communicate that which is incommunicable. He ended with a philosophy that is little more than a few vogue conclusions and a few verifications. What he did achieve was a portrait of the artist as a young man, and within this man the portrait of a continent "The whole thing's there—it really is."[4]

The incommunicable philosophy of life is based upon the recreation of Wolfe's own family, the Gants. The story in *Look Homeward, Angel* starts when Mr. Gant, the father of Eugene Gant, arrives in Altamont. Eliza, the mother of Eugene Gant, is the daughter of Thomas Pentland and wife of W.O. Gant. Her children are named Steve, Daisy, Helen, Grover Cleve-land, Benjamin Harrison, Luke and Eugene. Eugene Gant is the hero of this novel. He tells the story of his birth and then his departure for Harvard for learning the art of play-writing. At Harvard, he learnt a great deal and acquired wide experience. During this time he made long travels to Europe. Eugene Gant has to pass facing heavy social and psychological odds in life. These odds refer to the concept of spirit which is an embodiment of history. Hegel[5] believe that spirit manifests itself in terms of temporality, passing through a number of stages until the historical representation becomes equal to the nature of the spirit itself. Hegel finds a complete realization of this vision in Christianity where Jesus is the perfection as well as culmination of the human evolution in terms of history as an idea which is a spirit. On these lines, Wolfe wanted to create a world to people his characters, giving them a habitation which was central to his vision of life of the past. "The world, I create," he wrote to Mrs. Roberts, "is always inside me." Eugene Gant and George Webber always stand in the centre of his vision. Here, for example, is a passage which reveals the author's intention:

> ...The ghost of Ben Gant asks Eugene just before Eugene is about to leave Altamont for the North. Eugene admits that he is not sure of his reasons, that perhaps I just want a ride on the train. But Eugene unsure at the moment, both he and Thomas Wolfe are quite intent upon making the trip and merely to be in motion is response enough to go.[6]

The above passage reveals illusions which the author alone can destroy. In this illusion is involved the imprisement of the body and mind into the structure of time whose statutory forms are loneliness and death. William Blake used to say that whatever a man rejects errors and embraces truth a Last Judgement passes upon him. That is precisely what the angel has to do. He has to consider himself not as part of time but as part of the Eternity which is beyond time. That is what Adam and Eve enjoyed in the Garden of Eden before eating the fruit of knowledge. Man creates differential categories thinking that they are part of knowledge. In fact, they are forms of ignorance because they do not liberate but imprison. Thomas Wolfe seems to be offering *Vedantic* solution to the problems of existence.

नेति, नेति (Neti, Neti), not this, not this.

The reality is non-corrigible. One has to go beyond language, beyond phenomenalization, beyond forms of description in order to reach oneself. Knowing the home is *becoming* it.

लाली देखन मैं गयी, मैं भी हो गयी लाल। (कबीरदास)

(I went to experience the object, I became the object).

Berkley says the same thing; to be is to be perceived. However, empirical perception cannot go beyond the physical world.

The problem with the angel in the novel is that he has identified himself with those forms of time which are corrigible mainly with death. This is a "low mimetic" representation according to Northrop Frye of some thing which is far deeper, higher, and more mysterious. The forms that lead to inward journey are the forms of meditation upon time as timelessness, death as deathlessness. One has to create paradoxes in terms of understanding and then destroy those paradoxes in order to reach home. John Lane observes referring to Wolfe's paradoxes:

> ...these are but a few of the paradoxes Wolfe explores as he delves into the deeds and thoughts of Eugene Gant and George. Wolfe sought to learn why mankind behaved so much like a Janus, hoping to shed light on an ancient riddle: Why is it that really seldom equals appearance.[7]

Eugene Gant and George Webber are studies in paradoxes which can also be taken as mental states not necessarily contradicting each other but supplementing reciprocally. Wolfe's idea to present the complexity of existence in terms of situational paradoxes with the idea that each one of us as the agent of history has to resolve those contradictions for himself.

Home is beingness, loneliness is opposed to the world of becoming and relationships. It is precisely to this that Thomas Wolfe is referring while asking the angel to look homeward. It is interesting to note that Wolfe has not said "*Look Homeward, Man*" because he knows that man is the fallen form of angel. In his 'high mimetic' representation, man is the angel only and an angel is one who is part and parcel of God and this is another name for him. As Manroe M. Stears observed:

> The terms Wolfe uses in recurring refrains are symbols of other things than their direct referents. Thus 'home' is not only the Asheville boarding-house of Wolfe's Childhood or a pre-natal uterin existence; the word is also used in the wordsworthian sense for God. The door is the entrance both back to the protective maternal womb and to the heaven from which, in the platonic doctrine, we in our essence come. The "Stone, leaf, door" refrain symbolizes not only the pain of birth but also tokens (like Wordsworth's rainbow, rose, tree

and pansy) which remind the mortal of his immortal nature. The "Lost, and by the wind grieved, ghose" corresponds to the sense of the pre-existence of the soul which vanishes as the individual advances in material time down the river of corporeal existence.[8]

Closely examined, we find that Thomas Wolfe's concept of time is basically two dimensional—time as linear and time as psychological. Linearity is immutable, whereas the psychological time changes by transforming ideas, events and action. Wolfe is very much likely to be a part of a process of time where all forms of binarism and paradoxes exist in fragments and pieces. This Wolfe calls the world of fixity and change-fixed in the mechanical sense but in the sense of time, forming a destiny—a form of inevitableness—something which is bound to happen in spite of man's effort to avoid it. However, before form of time is realized, time is experienced as fragmentary, a form of pain, suffering and दु:ख very much in the Buddhist sense. That is one reason Wolfe asks the angel (human beings) to look homeward (beyond paradoxes) into a neutral world where concepts are exhausted and language does not constitute a block to the peace that passeth understanding. This is also the Buddhist *Nirvāna* and *Shūnya* which is Wolfe's home—the target to be achieved by the angel in the novel.

There are two kinds of paradigmatic strands in the structure of the novel as far as time is concerned. One strand is chronological, linear and historical. This captures and imprisons the human soul, body and mind. The other strand is trans-temporal or psychological, leading to the possibility of transcendence of the causal link which constitutes linear time. It is precisely in the conflict between these two forms of time that the structure of the novel rests.

II

The structure of *Look Homeward, Angel* has a tripartite division which runs parallel to the Biblical paradigm of Moses. In his early stage, Moses wandered in the wilderness and liberated the Hebrews from the Egyptian slavery and led them to the land of Cannan (Israel) and thus he reaches Jerusalem which is Thomas

Wolfe's home within. The early phase of Moses is one of search, for truth based on the collection of Torah and of authenticating it as law in the name of God. The authorship of Moses to the first five books of the *Bible* may be controversial, but the fact that he was the compiler is of little dispute. The search of Moses for truth parallels Eugene Gant's search for truth in the family, environment and social life. However, this search both in the novel as well as in the *Bible* results in a further wilderness of ideas, events and actions. The following lines from the *Bible* testify to the fact:

> Afterward Moses and Aaron went to Pharaoh and said, "Thus says the Lord, the God of Israel, 'Let my people go, that they may hold a feast to me in the wilderness.'" But Pharaoh said, "Who is the Lord that I should heed his voice and let Israel go? I do not know the Lord, and Moreover I will not let Israel go." Then they said, "The God of the Hebrews has met with us; let us go, we pray, a three days' journey into the wilderness, and sacrifice to the Lord our God, lest he shall fall upon us with pestilence or with the sword."[9]

Look Homeward, Angel develops complications around the figure of Eugene Gant in whom Moses as well as Thomas Wolfe are implicit. The implications are suggestive and far-reaching. The problems are related to complications which are unable to find a link with God-essential principle both in Moses and in Thomas Wolfe. Both are quest-heroes in search of a romantic and visualized world which is not on the surface of the world, but within one's own body. That is why Jerusalem is a symbol which Moses is trying to reach and attain as a part of himself. The transformation has taken place from Moses to Jesus—a transformation which shall make the wilderness fertile. That is what Eugene Gant is waiting for in the novel. He has to face opposition from a number of sources just as Moses has to face it from pagans and non-believers. In Wolfe's own words:

> ....in the modern bad manner (the pedagogic Neo-Greeky) were scattered around beyond the central design: beyond there was a thickly forested wilderness. There was still a good flavour of the wilderness about the place—one felt its remoteness, its

> isolated charm. It seemed to Eugene like a provincial outpost of Great Rome: the wilderness crept upto it like a beast.[10]

Eugene Gant faces complications and anxiety in his lonely life in which isolation and wilderness dominate greatly. Such complications are not widely rooted in his life alone, rather these are often found in the lives of great people and prophets. In Eugene Gant's method, ideas of one's father or one's mother have become events of appropriation and not simply events of history. These could be seen in case of the historicity of Jerusalem which is the body of Jesus. Later, if became the Christian Church and the Bride of Christ. Thus, acts become figures and figures become the writings of God which are manifest at the level of the soul which Thomas Wolfe calls the *Magnum opus* of the world. This world reflects itself in its binary, tertiary, and manifold oppositions. It is good to be intentionally (Biblical) in the wilderness, for the path to truth is only through these oppositions and not out of them. Referring to his own novel, Wolfe says:

> The past unrolled to him in separate and enormous visions, he built unending legends upon the pictures of the kings of Egypt, charioted swiftly by soaring horses, and something infinitely old and recollective seemed to awaken in him as he looked on fabulous monsters, the twined beards and huge beast bodies of Assyrian Kings, the walls of Babylon.[11]

Jerusalem is another name for integration as all spiritual states are. The structure of the *Bible* is Comic as Northrop Frye says and it abounds in contrapuntal symbolism in which one event is placed against another as part of the perennial conflict on the road to Eternity. Wolfe's images and symbols can be studied in terms of this phenomenal disintegration and integration.

Time is reliably the Cypher which is nothingness—a form of self-transcendence where the individual soul becomes a microcosm of the macrocosm and *vice versa*. This event is paralleled in the *Bible* in the vision of Ezekiel where the world is reflected in Ezekiel's body. The centrality of time means basically that all configurations of time are revealed to the simpleness of purpose and intentionality which is the world of God as *Logos* that is what Eugene Gant is trying to be, and it is precisely this which is the climax—both of the novel and of the character of Eugene Gant. As W.P. Albrecht has said:

> This process is dramatized in *Look Homeward, Angel.* Again the images of dark and light suggest lostness in time and being found. Alongwith his sense of time as a fading light, Eugene finds within himself a living pattern of certain experiences originally separate in time but fused by imagination beyond the distinctions of the time-space world, the many become one.... These images that burnt in him existed without beginning or ending, without the essential structure of time.[12]

Eugene Gant lives in a world where the distinction between time and space comes to an end. This conceptual thought clearly refers to the cyclic pattern of life where death becomes a form of renewed life in which there is neither beginning nor end as these are merged in the essential structure of time. This concept of cyclicity we find in *The Old Testament* when Moses tries to transform himself into the form of Jesus. At that time he has to forget that he is Moses. In the *Bible,* King Herod used to kill the children of Joseph. Joseph was worried about the death of his children. He was worried about his own death just as Thomas Wolfe is worried about his own. The reasons are existential in both the cases; the specific context, however, differs. Joseph has to produce Jesus not only to end his sufferings but also to end the sufferings of others, and ultimately Jesus came to represent a transformation as well as a creation both for Moses and for Joseph. Both Moses and Joseph have to transform themselves into Jesus which is a spiritual stage of mind. All transformations require death-psychological as well as physical. The fact that Thomas Wolfe is willing to die shows that he is very anxious to come out of the Mosaic wilderness of contradictions into the realm of pure ideas which Jesus represents. W.P. Albrecht discusses the cyclic concept of time as follows:

> The repetition of the archetype through numberless forms is a cyclic concept of time inherent in the pre-existence-and-return myth and in the metaphor of the buried life. With the cycle of time Wolfe frequently unites the earth symbol, which usually suggests permanence. Earth's cycle of growth

> preserves for Eugene something of past time, for after Ben's death Eugene knows that Ben will come back again...in flower and leaf." Growth as the solution to the time problem is further suggested by the "self" to which Ben Directs Eugene's search, a self of accumulated experience which has not simply been but which is always becoming.[13]

Civilization is a form of artificiality because it tries to supplement nature. All civilization and culture provide second nature which is an illusion. Man should finish this opposition between illusion and reality, only then shall he be able to embrace nature in all its primitive freshness and naked grandeur. In other words, binary oppositions can only be reconciled when there is a point of discovery within which cannot only be synthesized but also transcended. It is precisely this transcendence which is Thomas Wolfe's home inward. It is a home which integrates everything into everything else and belongs to every created object.

III

Thomas Wolfe realizes the significance of the symbolical meaning of the trio-recurring motif: "the stone, the leaf, the door." These symbols are never found, but Wolfe always remembers them. They not only symbolize the pain of birth, but also those tokens which remind him of his immortal nature.

The "Stone" symbolizes the angel. The symbol of the stone is related to one of the episodes associated with Mr. Gant who once saw in a Baltimore stonecutter's shop a big marble angel in which he found something dark and deep which is incommunicable. In the angel's head is expressed the possibility of life. In the same way "leaf" symbolizes life coming to an end; in October because of the annual recurrence of death, the leaf passes away. Likewise, the "door" becomes an obstacle for man because he is confined to a fragment of space and time. However, the author's continual need is to make at least a momentary escape through one of the doors which surround him. But one cannot pass through these doors easily because "stone" is too resistant for us to mould. These symbols enabled Wolfe to apprehend the universe and are deeply rooted in his sensuous perceptions. Wolfe says that if he had not found the symbols ("the door," "the leaf," "the stone") he could never have discovered America.

Thomas Wolfe says that "the door" is unfound for the simple reason that man has forgotten the eternal bliss of life. He is badly tangled in the corporeal existence which has corrupted his soul. An escape from the worldly affairs does not seem possible. The door thus has become a symbol of eternal and spiritual life in heaven from where he has come into this world. He does not recollect his past in which lies wisdom and heritage of his ancestors. For this reason the "door" remains closed for eternity. Death is the only way out, to open the door. This is what Thomas Wolfe has learnt from the deaths of several characters in the novel. Thus we find that is this novel death recurs repeatedly and has become the *leit-motif.* It dominates the major part of the novel, haunting the mind of the novelist. It has become an over-whelming presence everywhere. Every one submerges in the river of time.

We gather from the foregoing discussion that the images of darkness and devastation come before us related to passing time. At such moments, man becomes simply a stranger or a ghost quite different from others and his own self. In case of Eugene Gant, it is his past memory which links him with a better time. And it was found that while imprisoned in the dark womb of his mother, he lost his communication from the eternity. Ultimately, in his loss, he becomes a stranger in the insoluble prison of being—a "phantom" destined to wander homeless and friendless in a darkened world. This is what we find in the mystical world as W.P. Albrecht has noted:

> In *Look Homeward, Angel,* to dramatize the individual lost and then found in relation to time, Wolfe uses the myth of pre-existence—and—return and with it the usual Platonic contrasts of dark and light, many and one, isolation and union, imprisonment and freedom, shadow and reality.[14]

Thus we find that the contradictory images and symbols from polarity which enters very prominently in the psyche of Eugene Gant who has not recovered Ben and found himself representing two contradictory images—one of the ghost and the other of the angel. The ghost as well as the angel is an embodiment of a spirit lost in death and secured in eternal life. The angel directs Eugene "home." "You are your world," says Ben to Eugene, directing him to the bright world of fused experience. Eugene further says in such lines as:

> ...my unimprisoned soul haunts through the million streets of life, living its spectral nightmare of hunger and desire. Where Ben! where is the world?
>
> "Nowhere," Ben said, "You are your world."
>
> "Fool" said Ben "This is life," You have seen no where":
>
> "But in the cities"
>
> There are none. There is one voyage, the first, the last and the only one.[15]

Thomas Wolfe says that the last voyage brings Eugene to the end of his life because this is the longest and the best. At the end of life, Eugene finds himself nearer the unfound door, as is evident from Wolfe's own words:

> But in the city of myself upon the contingent of my soul, I shall find the forgotten language, the lost world, a door where I may enter and music strange as any ever sounded; I shall haunt you, ghost, along the labyrinthine ways until...until.[16]

On a close study, it is found that Wolfe's metaphysical theory is based on the Western and Eastern traditions. He has adopted the guest-myth in the novel, related to the *Bible.* In addition, Wolfe has derived mythical ideas from the Eastern tradition which is evident from *Look Homeward, Angel* in the following reference to an Indian god:

> I am Eugene Gant—the conqueror of nations, lord of the earth, the Siva of a thousand beautiful forms.[17]

Moreover, the concept of the original Sin is the backbone of this novel. It influences the conduct and destiny of the human race throughout history. It, at the same time, is very much responsible for the first journey of man from heaven to earth. This journey was considered the first and the last, that is, from the world of innocence to the world of experience as the *Bible* says. Thomas Wolfe was greatly influenced by this universal phenomenon which constitutes the central doctrine of this novel because he asks the angel to look homeward that is the kingdom of God which could solve all the problems of human life and society. Our mystic poet Kabirdasa has expressed similar views:

> कबीरा जब हम पैदा हुये, जग हंसा हम रोये,
> अब ऐसा कुछ कर चलो, हम हसें जग रोये।[17]

> (When we were born, the world laughed, we wept, Now let us do such things that we should laugh, the world weep when we die.)

Like Kabirdasa Wolfe tried to communicable an impossible ideal which is incommunicable at the same time. This ideal contains hidden springs in the wilderness of this commercial and cultureless society. About such as ideal Pamela Hansford Johnson says:

> The deepest search in life, it seemed to me, the thing that in one way or another was central to all living, was man's search for a father, not merely the father of high flesh, not merely the lost father of his youth, but the image of a strength and wisdom external to his need and superior to his hunger to which the belief and power of his own life could be united.[18]

Incommunicable mythography is the source of creativeness which requires mythological imagery to give it form. It is like a whirlwind which seizes upon everything within reach and by carrying them aloft assumes a visible shape. This incommunicable mythography refers to the substantial unity of the soul from which emerges a living tradition and which will continue unending in life and literature.

NOTES

1. *Rig-Veda* (10-90) 2-2.
2. *Gita,* Chap. IX, Slokas 4, 5, 6; p. 754. Pune: Gita Printers, 1993.
3. Thomas Wolfe, *Look Homeward, Angel* (Prefatory Prose-Poem), (New York, London: Charles Scribner's Sons, 1929).
4. P.H. Johnson, *The Art of Thomas Wolfe* (New York: Charles Scribner's Sons, 1963) 157.

5. Hegel, *The Philosophy of History (*New York: Dover Publications, 1956) 109.
6. Wolfe 619.
7. John Lane Idol, *A Thomas Wolfe Companion* (New York, London: Greenwood Press, 1987) 46.
8. Richard Walser, ed., *The Enigma of Thomas Wolfe* (1953) 203-204.
9. *The Holy Bible,* Revised Standard Version, Sec. Ed. Regency (Nasheville: Publishing House, 1971) 49.
10. Wolfe 396.
11. Wolfe 62.
12. Richard Walser, ed., *The Enigma of Thomas Wolfe* (1954) 242-43.
13. W.P. Albrecht, *The Enigma of Thomas Wolfe* (1954) 245.
14. Richard Walser, *The Enigma of Thomas Wolfe* (1954) 291.
15. Wolfe 624-25.
16. Wolfe 625.
17. Wolfe 585.
18. Johnson153.

8

The Alienated Self: Searching for Space in Morrison's *The Bluest Eye* and *Sula*

S.P. SWAIN AND SARBAJIT DAS

At no stage in his mortal life can man overcome the existential alienation caused by human conditioning, finitude and mortality. The experience of this sense of alienation is vividly illustrated by David Riesman's treatise *The Lonely Crowd*. The 'crowd' is made up of people so linked together as to give it its own organic life. In the 'lonely' crowd individuals are estranged from one another, so that the links become handcuffs, and estrangement and hostility replace communication and understanding. Individuals become 'alienated' not only from others but also from their own 'selves.' According to Geyer and Schweitzer, "*the loss of identity is alienation...it leads to powerlessness, the lack of control over various aspects of existence*" (Felix 1981: 251). Eric Fromm elaborates this point and states that:

> The alienated person does not experience himself as the center of his world, as the creator of his own acts, but his acts and their consequences have become his masters (The Sane Society 1955: 120).

The Africans, transported from their native country, uprooted from its rich traditions and culture, were replanted in a strange and hostile soil. Africans citizens, who enjoyed bliss and freedom, turned into lowly Niger and suffered the pangs of alienation. Slavery, dependence upon the ruling class, abject poverty and suppression of their own values leads to the 'loss of self.' Though the experience of the entire race in terms of identity crisis and alienation was common for men and women, the black women found themselves in a unique position altogether:

> There are three major circles of reality in American Society which reflect degrees of power and powerlessness. There is a large circle in which white people most of them men, experience influence and power. Far away from it there is a smaller circle, narrow space, in which black people regardless of sex experience uncertainty, exploitation and powerlessness. Hidden in this second circle is a third small enclosure in which black women experience pain, isolation and vulnerability. These are the distinguishing marks of black womanhood in white America (Wade-Gayles 1984: 3-4).

The paper aims to show how these alienated female characters search for space in an incarcerated milieu and flounder to achieve an authentic selfhood.

In African-American women's writing there is a recurrent pattern of concern with identity formation. Toni Morrison's novels revolve round the problems of isolation and identity. But the theme that cuts across her novels is that of alienation rooted in the most vicious form of racism and sexism. Here, Morrison depicts the African-American women's pain of being black and female. The characters are depicted as stifled and anguished being desperately groping for their genuine self. In dealing with the innermost recesses of the abandoned self, Morrison delineates the growth of her protagonist from self-alienation to self-assertion. The sequestered self in Morrison novels evinces a graded progress from neuroticism to moods of pollyannaism, from the realm of despondency to the world of resilience, from isolation to identity.

Most of Morrison's black women characters like Sula, Pauline or Pecola who suffer from agonizing alienation and remain fragmented and disintegrated at the outset attain integration and wholeness at the end. Thus the development of their self is slow but gradual, painful but definite.

Morrison's first novel *The Bluest Eye* probes deeper into the black woman's psychic dilemmas, oppressions and tribulations symbolized by the tragic life of Pecola literally affected by the dominant culture's beauty standards. It speaks about "*a little black girl who wanted to rise up out of the pit of her blackness and see the world with blue eyes*" (Morrison 1970: 137). Pecola believes that 'blue eyes'; the symbol of white beauty, would make her beautiful, acceptable and desirable. However, it couldn't be so in reality. So she is disgruntled about her beauty. Disgust drags her to the corridors of madness. Pecola encounters racial discrimination from white men and women as well as sexual violence from black men. She faces humiliation and pain when her own father rapes her, another victim of "double jeopardy" (Beal 1970: 90). Her deranged nerves say a lot about the socio-economic and political oppression of little black girls as they get isolated from the social milieu.

Pecola's tragedy is due to her alienation from family, friends and the black community of Lorain. All she has learnt about herself from school, from her friends and the world around is that she is black, poor and ugly. Trapped in a world of taunts and threats, Pecola craves for love, but there is none to convince or reassure Pecola of her-worth. Even, her brother Sammy is not a companion at home or outside:

> She had long ago given up the idea of running away to see new pictures, new faces, as Sammy had so often done. He never took her, and he never thought about his going ahead of time, so it was never planned (39).

Her isolation is further aggravated when she finds, even the cats and dogs are no playmates of hers. Pining for love and admiration but finding it nowhere. So she gradually lapses into the world of fantasy and fancies that she has the bluest eye in the world. She converses with her 'other' self and feels that 'blue eyes' will solve all her problems of being ugly and black. *"Each night, without fail, she prayed for blue eyes. Fervently, for a year she had prayed. Although somewhat discouraged she was not without hope. To have something as wonderful as that happen would take a long, long time"* (40).

Her alienation is complete when she withdraws into her own neurotic and insane world. The desire for blue eyes is an evidence of Pecola's frustrations with her racial identity, with her social milieu and of her longing for an authentic selfhood. Weever rightly observes: "*The desire for blue eyes is part of the inverted quality of her world; in wanting blue eyes Pecola wants, in fact, to be white*" (CLA Journal: 406). Here Pecola's nature of alienation is socio-psychic, somewhat reminiscent of Kafka's Gregor Samsa. Both Gregor and Pecola suffer from a tremendous sense of guilt, which is not of their own making, but prompts them to submit passively to the psychotic managing of the personality, an irretrievable damage.

The discordance of Pecola's girlhood could be attributed to Pauline's nonchalant and standoffish attitude. The intimate touch of a mother-daughter relationship was almost non-existent between Pecola and Pauline. This becomes evident when Pecola address her mother as Mrs. Breedlove, a most formal way of addressing one's mother. The source of Pecola's malady can be traced back to the childhood of her parents. Neither Cholly nor Pauline had grown up in an atmosphere conducive to the actualization and affirmation of the self. Neither parent could provide the child the means for a sense of self-assurance they themselves had never attained. Pecola is thus victimized by both parents who have been "*made incapable of nurturing her by the limiting phenomena of race, sex and class*" (Wade-Gayles, 1984: 77).

Acute alienation has plagued Pauline since early childhood. She feels an "*unsettling emptiness*" (Wade-Gayles, 1984: 74) within and longs for a man who will fulfill her carnal needs. Pauline marries Cholly, but he too fails to satisfy her since his own life has been one of emotional and economic deprivation. Besides, motherhood brings more trouble in her life: "*...the daily needs of her children are like lighted matches to the fuse of her disappointment as a black woman denied beauty and romantic love*" (ibid). Tormented and tortured by a sordid life, she plunges into a world of fantasy and derives great pleasure from identifying herself with white woman in the movies. Morrison observes:

> There the flowed became whole, the blind sighted, and the lame and half threw away their crutches...there the black and white images come together, making a magnificent whole (*The Bluest Eye* 1970: 90).

For Pauline, fantasizing becomes a crutch she could hardly

relinquish. Fantasies about men and love and touching has been drawing her mind and hands away from her work. Her alienation is the outcome of her struggle to achieve the white bourgeois social model which itself is produced by the capitalist system of wage labour. Ann Foreman observes that, alienation of a woman *"is profoundly disturbing because woman experience themselves only as the fulfillment of other people's needs"* (*Femininity as Alienation*: 65). In such a capitalist set up women like Pauline have no sense of self and they do not experience themselves as whole persons but only as fragmented or splintered beings. Their marginality confronts the world of Hollywood movies, white sheets and tender blonde children. They feel isolated at work where they separate themselves from their own *'kinky hair'* and *'decayed tooth.'* Right from her infancy, Pauline has never felt at home anywhere, or experienced a sense of belonging to any place. Rootless and alienated, she is hectored by the obsessive feeling of *'separateness'* and *'unworthiness.'* She feels de'trop. Thus, the tragedy of Pauline's alienation has its dire impact on her role as a mother. So she fails to develop a positive relationship with Pecola. She rejects her own daughter who is black, but is so much caring to the wealthy blonde girl-doll. *"By her discriminatory action, Pauline deepens Pecola's feelings of inferiority and steals her life beyond rescue, beyond salvation"* (Wade-Gayles 67). Her negative self-image alienates her not only from her daughter but also from the larger society. Hence her alienation is temperamental and dispositional.

Morrison's *Sula*, her second novel, shows a woman's leading *'an experimental life.'* Like Pecola, Sula too lives a solitary and isolated kind of life in her hose. Her mother Hannah is hardly aware of her only daughter of a distant mother. The conflict between Sula and Hannah represents the clash between the old and new; tradition and modernity; pride and prejudice. As her mother is an obstruction in her path to self-realization, she seeks refuge in Nel's companionship. So Sula and Nel are:

> Solitary little girls whose loneliness was so profound that it intoxicated them and sent them stumbling into techno-colored visions which always included a presence, a someone, who,

quite like the dreamer, shared the delight of the dream (Morrison 1982: 51).

Both resemble each other in their emotional isolation from other people. Prof. Anniah Gowda observes, *"Their friendship is based on a sense of alienation from community and family values, and a similar experiences of emptiness in their relationship with men"* (*Literary Half Yearly:* 29). Their alienation from the larger society paves the means for Sula's rebellion against the 'set norm' a woman is supposed to follow in the black community. She prefers to be a social outsider than to play any social role. After Nel's wedding, Sula searches for experience outside her town Bottom. This rebellious spirit of Sula alienates her from her only friend Nel. Here Sula's flight is self-directed.

After ten years away from Bottom, Sula comes back home. Eva, her grandmother suggests that she should marry and bear children. To this Sula responds: *"I don't want to make somebody else. I want to make myself"* (92). As she refuses to undergo the usual rites of marrige and becoming a wife and a mother, she is deemed as a Pariah. Here Sula's alienation is more psychological than existential. But for Nel:

> It was like getting the use of an eye back, having a cataract removed.... Talking to Sula had always been a conversation with herself (95).

Instead, the first thing Sula does is to make a successful attempt in seducing Nel's husband. She experiences a rare kind of pleasure and feeling in making love to a white man. But Nel fails to understand this aspect of Sula. When both Sula and Nel meet for the last time, Nel asks Sula why she has slept with Jude, and Sula can only answer that Jude temporarily filled up the *"space"* for her. Nel, however, demands a greater response : *"But what about me? Why didn't you think about me? Didn't I count? I never hurt you. What did you take him for if you didn't love him...?* Sula then counters with a similar question for Nel: "*what you mean take him away? I didn't kill him, I just fucked him. If we were such great friends, how come you couldn't get over it?"* (144). Sula's question reveals her perspective; she, too, had been abandoned. She too had suffered alienation. But Nel's isolation and estrangement are different from Sula's. Nel's isolation stems from her mother's attempt to obliterate her racial features, her loss of Sula (a female bonding, a bond to her own womanhood), and her trauma following Jude's betrayal. The most important of her psychic wounds is the loss of her feminine self—something Sula never relinquished. In this sense we see Sula as an epitome of feminine imagination set free. This prompts Sula to fill the empty spaces, both without and within. She wants to pursue and live her life, and make herself. The first experience taught her that *"there was no other that you could count on... there was no self to count on either"* (118-119).

Look how Morrison portrays her in the novel:

> Sula was distinctly different. Eva's arrogance and Hannah's self-indulgence merged in her and, with a twist that was all her own imagination, she lived out her days exploring her own thoughts and emotions, giving them full reign, feeling no obligation to please anybody unless their pleasure pleased her...hers was an experimental life (118).

In her quest for identity she realizes that *"no one would ever be that version of herself, which she sought to reach out to and touch with an ungloved hand"* (121). The monotony and malaise of modern life in cities make her aware of her loneliness in urban centers. Her searing experiences of the seamy side of city-life have been vividly portrayed:

> All those cities held the same people, sweating the same sweat.... They taught her nothing but love tricks, shared nothing but worry, gave nothing but money (120-121).

She finds that *"man love"* only serves to accentuate her alienation. The men with whom she sleeps are mere vehicles to bring her to her authentic 'self.' Thus, Sula realizes the dire consequences of alienation. Even in love making, which seems to her in the beginning a special kind of joy, she gradually feels that *"in the center of that silence was not eternity but the death of time and a loneliness so profound the word itself had no meaning"* (123). Slowly, Sula rejects the patriarchal social order, understands that there is no love left for the black woman. Therefore she must love herself. She must become a narcissist.

To acquire self-love, she does what pleases her and in the process she is completely destroyed. Yet she achieves a rare personhood which none of the Bottom woman ever dared to achieve by defying the role model set for them.

Fighting tooth and nail against the fragmentation of her 'self' by the double alienation of race and sex, she achieves a *'wholeness'* and a *'home'* for herself and for her community. Hence her journey is a growth from negation to assertion, from diffidence to confidence, from self-alienation to self-identification.

In the body of black American fiction, Morrison's characters like Pecola, Pauline and Sula try to create a space of their own where they could carve out a niche for themselves. Patricia Mckee says:

> In Toni Morrison's Sula, Spacing...that is, closing down or opening up distances between things and persons...has extraordinary urgency. Houses and bodies are the sites of hyperactive mechanisms of containment and expulsion working to effect identity and distinction: of inside and outside, of self and other. Spacing, moreover becomes crucial to issues of representation and meaning in the bottom, the place in which most of the action of the novel occurs (*Modern Fiction Studies*: 01).

According to Derridean deconstruction, spacing is the distance of representation, where the material signifier stands for something detached from it. Alienation in *Sula* manifests through *'spacing'* and *'missing.'* The alienational experience of 'missing' in Sula is a particular historical experience. Missing itself takes place in the novel, due to the missing of particular persons from particular places. Morrison presents both 'missed presences' (awareness of something that once was present) and 'missed absences' (missing of things that might have been but never happened) to portray alienation of her characters. *The Bluest Eye* postulates how the lack of a proper 'role model' wreaks havoc with the life of a black female child. It is the lack of feeling of self-worth that leads to the psychological abnormality and insanity of Pecola. Her madness is the off-spring of the influence of the dominant culture that is both white and male. Her longing for the 'blue eyes' eventually alienates her from her 'self.' In *Sula*, Morrison creates an entirely self-contained and women-centered universe where Sula disowns the traditional role ascribed to women by distancing herself from her community and seeking space for selfhood. Sula's suffering as a woman is the outcome of an oppressive economic system. Not men. She finds it impossible to negate them. Thus, to escape, to recreate self, Sula has but two options: to become a *'man'* or to *'die.'* She chooses death. While in *The Bluest Eye,* Morrison advocates the need for transcending the politically motivated definitions of beauty and ugliness, in *Sula* she asks people to overcome the narrow conceptualization of good and evil. The message she conveys is that for a successful quest for selfhood, one ought to depend upon one's own worth. She strikes a balance between Sula's wilderness and Nel's submissiveness for the betterment of society and growth of an individual. It was in *Sula* that Morrison has discovered a means to offer her people an insight and a sense of recovered self so majestic and resplendent that no mortal anguish would dull the final light, thus enabling one to see 'the clear light of day.'

REFERENCES

Beal, Frances. "Double Jeopardy: To be Black and Female." *The Black Woman: An Anthology*. Ed. Toni Code. New York: Signet, 1970.

De Weever, Jacqueline. "The Inverted World of Toni Morrison's *The Bluest Eye & Sula*." *CLA Journal* (1979).

Felix, Geyer R. *Alienation: Problems of Meaning*. Boston: Routledge and Kegan Paul, 1981.

Foreman, Ann. *Femininity as Alienation: Woman and Family in Marxism and Psychoanalysis*. London: Pluto Press, 1977.

Fromm, Eric. *The Sane Society*. New York: Fawcett Premier, 1955.

Gowda, Anniah. "Feminine Black Voice." *Literary Half Yearly* 25.1 (January 1994).

Mbalia, Doreatha D. *Toni Morrison's Developing Class Consciousness*. Selinggrove : Susquehanna UP, 1991.

Morrison, Toni. *The Bluest Eye*. New York: Pocket Books, 1970.

——. *Sula*, New York: New American Library, 1982.

——. "Rootedness: the Ancestor as Foundations." *Black Women Writers 1950-1980: A Critical Evaluation*. Ed. Garden City. New York: Anchor Press, 1984.

Wade-Gayles, Gloria. *No Crystal Stair: Vision of Race and Sex in Black Women's Fiction*, New York: The Pilgrim Press, 1984.

MFS Modern Fiction Studies 42.1 (Spring 1996).

9

The Element of Protest in Toni Morrison's *Sula*

MONIKA GUPTA

Far above the issues of 'identity' and 'belief,' the factors disintegrating the global unity are parochialism and individualism. Whether it is the effect of the political awareness born of the scientific, as well as the technological advancement, or a sense of rejection in a compatible world of trade and marketing, the individual has always induced frustrations at all levels of the society. It is often said that the racial atmosphere has produced the greatest rebels, particularly for not adjusting themselves to oppression and servitude. An approach like this generalizes the behaviour of the people of a country, or a community in regard to the social and the political values. But it is not always that the element of protest, or the psychology of an individual failure is induced by the general conditions of a racist society or atmosphere. The fact is that the projections of an individual in an atmosphere are more meaningful than the atmosphere itself. The wicked person needs the minimum reason to activate his viciousness whereas a virtuous person is unfaltered in his stance by any number of reasons. It has been possible with many African-American and South-African writers that they analyse the development of a being in the form of a character in the light of the racial conditions of a particular time and place. But seldom does Toni Morrison overshadow the individual characteristics by the general issues of political suppression and protest. It is different with her that the rebel characters dominate the political scenario, and that the demerits, or the merits at times are the result of the individual misgivings and not generally induced by societal issues. Morrison's women are in search of identity; they resent their oppression by virtue of which they are rebel beings, thwarting the protest spirit they cannot handle at a time. But the element of protest, of oppression, or of identification is individualistic, and we can say, also regional. The individual is more evocative than the general in all her novels, particularly *Sula*.

The remark that "contemporary Black Women writers have placed the black woman at the center of human experience, art and consciousness,"[1] envisages the true characteristics of Toni Morrison. Born in a family, which had suffered the racist atrocities, she brings to light the negative individualism to have been perpetuated by the white regime. Whether it is *Sula*, or *Jazz*, or *The Bluest Eye*, the thematic emphasis is laid upon reproducing "many of the dominant establishments' values,"[2] such that appropriation of a system, congenial to the 'blacks' is channelized down these. Morrison lets a non-African reader to understand that a reaction, or an individualistic attitude, is always the result of oppression, whether racial, or religionistic. A black woman, like Sula must be individualistic, partly as a reaction to the White rule, partly, for the deterioration in administrative approach to the meaning in native terms. Morrison's *Sula* is more of the expression of a black feminist identity under racial suppression than a female consciousness in an ordinary way.

The general truth about a colonial country is that the racial, as well as the societal restrictions affect the conscience, and also the African-American women indirectly. It can also be pointed out that the race is linked with class exploitation, implying that a capitalist power structure must be complementary to capitalist exploitation, as well as race oppression. The removal of the one cause is "the removal of the other."[3] Morrison designs the fate of a 'black woman' in terms of her relation with class, and also the race she belongs to. It is in a way to say that Morrison portrays the struggle of the 'black woman' not only against the oppression let loose by the White but also the Black ones. It is true that she presents woman as an oppressed creature, needing a humanistic approach. But it is more than a reality that Sula's grudge is not against the racial discrimination shown by the 'whites' alone. She as well reflects here dialectical relationship with African males, for the exploitation of African women. At least Sula establishes that the real racial axe is brought upon the black male by the 'white-regime' through whom the evils of exploitation reach to her door. It is true that Sula is "concerned with the exploited and oppressed condition of African people,"[4] but things are again true that the real exploiter of 'black' women is the 'black' tradition itself. Morrison's approach in *Sula* has been to delineate a trend in the life of 'black' women, which describes the 'black' chauvinistic atmosphere as an equal devil to the 'white' excess.

Morrison's class analysis, as reflected in *Sula*, manifests the creations of a female character, who, because of her oppression, makes individualism supreme over the collective rather than a female character, who struggles to change the oppressive nature of society in order to ensure the full development of each individual. The novel presents, as a theme, the oppression of African women in United States, especially in the first quarter of the 20th century. Traditionally, the African-women "suffer a triple oppression, if they are working women, as workers under capitalist-class oppression, national oppression and oppression because of their sex."[5] The misery attached to 'black' women's lot is that she suffers an abject position of a second citizen by having really no legal rights in a family dominated by the males. Far into the interiors of Africa, wherefrom she grows as an entity, woman has neither emotional, nor legal responsibilities. Of course, there are a few customs by virtue of which she feels attached to her family. Otherwise, the permissive society does make her a machine than the symbol of mother earth, procreating man and his race. The first oppression is in the hands of 'black' man that he permits her to be exploited in sex without any responsibility on the part of the exploiter. Once she is devoid of her rights and is let suffer her agony alone, her soul quivers for justice and comes out with reaction in a rebellious mood.

Sula's rebelliousness is manifested in her estrangement from traditional family organization. Unlike other Medallion women, including Nel, she refuses to marry, settle down and raise a family. It is explicitly in her mind that it is no use of being the mother of many children and finally being kicked out, like an animal to a destination which must be most imprudent in her thinking. She should definitely not feel any obligation to please some one unless she, in turn, gains pleasure. In spite of her non-conformist behaviour she is tolerated until she commits the queer deed of putting her grandmother in an old-folk's home. She is an explorer, perfect and "freakish, repulsive, or unattractive."[6] Sula is laid away from the sterile soil of the Bottom, coupled with her need for independence and a desire to transcend herself above everything. After years of travelling and pursuing education, she returns having discovered that the Bottom and Medallion are microcosmic of the world at large. She realizes the "one-sideness of her proposal," indicating the idea that the individual fulfillment is "dialectically related to group fulfillment."[7] It is all in view of the fact that Sula finds both Bottom and Medallion appropriate for her pursuit of the self.

The manner is which Morrison chooses to explore the nature of the women's oppression is unique. Often she chooses two compatible characters, neither of whom is complete in herself. Sula, in this light, struggles to enjoy herself as a human being against the Bottom community, and not capitalism. She is a rebel, without giving "a kind of revolutionary solution,"[8] so that her oppression remains individualistic, and not communal. Rebelliousness is, of course, in her betrayal, and also alienation from family, friends and neighbours, thereby causing her own death. Despite her deepest feelings, "deep enough to bring tears for the death of littlest things,"[9] she keeps her individualism supreme above all other things.

It is the quality of a rebel, a suppressed self, in search of her own identity that she watches her mother burn to death and keeps her grandmother in a nursing home. It is again true that she reacts to the place man has given to her in society that she seduces her best friend's husband. If she has to be exploited sexually in a society comprising her husband, children and in-laws, why should she not exploit man according to her own need. It is, of course, individualism above the attitude of a rebel, who has undergone oppression for decades and centuries together. Even the "post-coital privateness in which she feels herself relaxed in matchless harmony,"[10] is the mark of the beginning of rebellion against a society which makes her a little below the gambit of a sex symbol. It is Sula's sense of revenge, an expression of female identity, the feminist consciousness that she aims at exploiting men sexually, taking him as "the means to her end."[11]

Toni Morrison's each novel reveals the accuracy of her perceptions of a psychological motivation of the female, "especially of the Black in particular, and human, in general."[12] However, neither the 'black,' nor the general-human, is perfect. Morrison has conveyed her point of view through the contrast between two ideologically different female characters. On the one hand, it is Sula, who has broken away from both the family and its tradition, and the other, it is Nel, confined to a traditionally social life. In the contrasting characters of Nel and Sula, seen to retain their balance for years to come, the latter shows a kind of survival which is "independent and autonomous," and carries "individualism to an extreme."[13] She exerts the assumption that the "black people are the humans of the globes," having "serious doubts about the quality and existence of 'white' humanity."[14] Nel, on the contrary, sticks to the family traditions and shows how woman, "as helpmate, mother and housekeeper is connected to the sense of failure black men feel in a world that denies them status."[15] Sula is imperfect despite her spirit of a rebel and a conscious 'black' woman to whom meaning would be only she herself and nothing beyond. Throughout her life, she is alienated from everyone and remains confined to Eva's boarded up room, symbolizing that a person, outside of the collective, is like a head cut off from a body. In Morrison's fiction there is no place for an isolated individual; especially, the female protagonist seems to be struggling for her identity, however, she is a part and parcel of the community in general. No matter how cruel, tragic and futile are the operations and suppression of the society. For instance, Sula, after whom the novel is named, fails to flourish without her community. She is searching for her 'black' identity with Nel, Shadrack, Eva and the community itself. Her identity shines as it is the representative reflection of her community's identity, and, when she is away from the society for ten years she does not exist at all even within the text. She is visited by none except Nel. After death, she is prepared for burial by 'white' folks, since no one in the community would do all this for her.

The contrast is evident. Sula reacts to the existing order, and so is taken as conscious character in either way. She is discovered to be a creative creature intent upon searching an identity of herself. Nel, on the other hand, values duty and tradition more than self, believing that the virtue of self-sacrifice is above self-possibilities. She becomes dependent of others for life's meaning and remains responsible for her loneliness. The two characters are imperfect even in their contrast—one for alienation out of reaction, and the other, out of submission. The relationship of an individual with his racial identification is evident in *Sula*. Sula is questing for her identity and Nel is negating her quest for identity. Sula is not ready to be dominated by her circumstances; rather she masters them. Nel, on the other hand, is truly a feminine in her own activities. Her definition of 'Self' is not a part of collective consciousness, and, so, her identity cannot be seen in relation to the identity of a 'black' community, which is already in the process of a 'search' of itself. For Sula, reaction is a way of life, and, for Nel, submission is a fulfillment. Love is synonym for freedom for Sula, and under the shell of love, Nel wants to protect herself. Love is a security for Nel. Sula's alienation from the community has a purpose as she forces the community to re-examine its values. Although the community does not approve her way of life, and she, as a rebel, is considered to be a threat to the traditional and the conventional community. On the contrary. Nel despite loosing herself, has lost among the people of the community and cannot be treated as a rebel and a revolutionary.

Feminism is marked as a "self-conscious interest in the celebration of the values, beliefs, ideas and behaviour uniquely, or traditionally characteristic of women."[16] Morrison has presented the female protagonist as an advent in her cause for the uplift of women. It is true that black woman, out of suppression, wants to wage war against the standards the male has fixed for her. Whether it is the societal set up, or the family life, *Sula* is structurally designed on feminist cause. It not only shows the action and reaction in Sula's life, but as well portrays the tension between the opposite female typologies. The novel is rich in about both change and stability in women's bonds in various life stages, because each woman identity is, at least, partially forced, *vis-a-vis*, the masculine principle both within herself and as embodied in men; the male and female relationship also receive some attention. Morrison has put woman to an extent where she has even thought of establishing a family in which the male has no concern. Calling a spade a spade, Morrison puts Sula and Nel as lesbians, pushing themselves towards an ultimate, radical and isolated image of the individual female separated from society, family and friendship. Morrison describes:

> They never quarreled, those two, the way some girlfriends did over boys, or competed against each other for them. In those days a compliment to one was a compliment to the other, and cruelty to one was a challenge to the other.
>
> Nel's response to Jude's shame and anger selected her away from Sula. And greater than her friendship was this new feeling of being needed by someone who saw her singly. She didn't even know she had a neck until Jude remarked on it, or that her smile was anything but the spreading off her lips until he saw it as a small miracle.[17]

The relationship between men and women is vividly described by Morrison in *Sula*. Sula's quest for a woman friend invites discussion as well as contradiction. The search for the 'self' forces her to make friends with a woman, instead of a man. Men might take care of her physical needs as masters, providers and lovers; they can cherish her emotions to an extent, but they could not present a solution for her inner restlessness, tension, madness, pleasure, fears and depression that, being a 'black' woman, she is brimming up. She does not give importance to her beauty and body; instead, she is searching for someone who has willing, loving curiosity to explore her thoughtful mind as deeply as possible:

> During the love making she found and needed to find the cutting edge. When she left off cooperating with her body and began to assert herself in the act, particles of strength gathered in like steel shavings drawn to a spacious magnetic center,

> forming a tight cluster that nothing it seemed, could break. And there was utmost irony and outrage in lying under someone, in a position of surrender, feeling her own abiding strength and limitless power. But the cluster did break, fall apart and in her panic to hold it together she leaped from the edge into soundlessness and went down howling, howling in a stinging awareness of the ending of things: an eye of sorrow in the midst of all the hurricane of joy. Then, in the center of that silence was not eternity, but the death of time and a loneliness to profound the word itself had no meaning.[18]

It is mistake to accept *Sula* as a "lesbian novel."[19] It is true that Morrison however does not portray "her women characters' relationship as inherently lesbian, they nevertheless are so," not because women are lovers, but because they are central figures; "are positively portrayed and have pivotal relationship with one another."[20] Morrison opens the door of lesbianism to the African women as a mark of her consciousness; she has preferred a way for a black women in acquiring an identity which has been lost and is chaotic in racism, sexual atrocities and capital classicism.

As far as the psychology of woman goes all terms like identity, self, self-actualization and emancipation converge into the single possibility of her comfort. If she has ease in bending out herself into the world of reality she must definitely feel identified. Once woman has hesitation to vent-out herself in regard to the biological, the spiritual, and the meta-biological activities of this world, she feels suppression of either kind which, inadvertently, she calls the exploitations of her 'self' and misrepresentation of her 'identity.' All kinds of feminist reactions and demands for emancipation arise only with the unsettled, and also the uncompromising sexual, as well as social life. In Toni Morrison's novels, one change of the attitude is finally apprehended that the reason of dissatisfaction, or the suppression of the self comes into question only after the woman has failed to compromise and adjust with her personal peace and happiness. Once these two things are absent from her life, whatsoever be the reason, the innumerable and nightmarish confusions start surfacing. Such confusions, produced with individualistic failures take the shape of exploitation in the forms of identity, suppression and feminist reactions. The fact is, as shown by Toni Morrison in *Sula,* protest becomes the prime weapon of the woman to project and defend her failure, but exactly she needs to know that the identity crisis is more a result of her personal debacle than the making of society, or man who exploit her condition. Sula represents the spirit of protest without always knowing that the real matter of protest is her own attitude, and her own self.

NOTES AND REFERENCES

1. Joanne Braxton, *Wild Women in the Whirlwind; Afro-American Culture and the Contemporary Literary Renaissance* (New Brunswick, N.J.: Rutgers UP, 1990) XXIX.
2. W. Lawrence Houge, "Literary Production: A Silence in Afro-American Critical Practices," *Belief Versus Theory in Black American Literary Criticism,* ed. Joe Weixlmann and Chester J. Fontenat (Greenwood, Fla.: Penkeril, 1986) 41.
3. Kmwne Nkrumah, *Class Struggle in Africa* (New York: International Publishers, 1970) 27.
4. Doreatha Dwmmond Mbalia, *Toni Morrison's Developing Class Consciousness* (Selinsgrove: Susquechanna UP, 1993) 16.
5. Amiri Baraka, "Afro-American Literature and Class Struggle," *Black Literature Forum* 14: 1: 5-14.
6. Robert Stepto, "Intimate Things in Place: A Conversation with Toni Morrison," *Chant of Saints: A Gathering of Afro-American Literature, Art and Scholarship,* ed. Michael Harper and Robert Stepto (Urbana: U of Illinois P, 1981) 215.
7. Mbalia 48.
8. Karen Carmean, *Toni Morrison's World of Fiction* (Troy-New York: The Whitestone Publising Company, 1993) 16.
9. Toni Morrison, *Sula* (New York: Signet, 1973) 159.
10. Morrison 159.
11. Mbalia 39.
12. Mari Evans, *Black Woman Writers* (1950-1980) (New York: Anchor Press/ Double Day Garden City, 1984) 359.
13. Karla F.C. Holloway and Stephanie D., *New Dimensions of Spirituality, A Biracial & Bicultural Reading of the Novels of Toni Morrison* (New York: Greenwood Press, 1987) 75.
14. Toni Morrison's "Slow Walk of Trees..." *New York Times Magazine* 4 July 1976: 152.
15. Barbara Chirstian, *Black Feminist Criticism Perspective on Black Woman Writers* (New York: Pergamon Press, 1985) 76.
16. Elaine Show-Walter, "*Toward a Feminist Poetics,*" *The New Feminist Criticism: Essays on Women Literature and Theory,* ed. Elaine Show-Walter (New York: Pantheon Books, 1985) 131.

17. Morrison 111.
18. Morrison 158-59.
19. Barbara Smith, "Toward a Black Feminist Criticism," *Conditions* 2 (1977): 33.
20. Smith 33.

10

Post-mortem of Marriage in Harold Robbins's *Where Love Has Gone*

RAJESHWAR MITTAPALLI

Harold Robbins's *Never Leave Me* (1954) and *Where Love Has Gone* (1962) remind us of the popular novels occasionally written by the "serious" writers like Norman Mailer, Kurt Vonnegut, Jr., Saul Bellow, Scott Fitzgerald, Irwin Shaw and Katherine Anne Porter. These two novels of Robbins have a serious purpose and attempt to discuss, in the light of psychological and social realism, the all important question of the degeneration of the institution of marriage in modern America. The characters of these novels are primarily interested in their own personal happiness and they work out their marital problems mostly on the social and psychological planes. But the very ordinariness and familiarity of the problems faced by them make a powerful appeal to us. It may be thus understood that in the guise of a familiar tale they "reflect their own times preoccupations"[1] especially with the issue of marriage.

In spite of the obvious literary merit of these two novels some unimaginative critics of popular fiction[2] have done great disservice to them, carried away as they do by the popular image of Robbins. In order to set the record straight an attempt is made here to study *Where Love Has Gone*[3] within the tradition of popular fiction criticism.

After analysing scores of American best sellers dealing with ordinary life Karen Hinckley and Barbara Hinckley have come to the conclusion that a large majority of the crises faced by their characters are marital ones.[4] The chief theme of *Where Love Has*

Gone is, as has been stated earlier, the degeneration and disintegration of the institution of marriage in the sixties. The fifties and the sixties are known in American history for their optimism and prosperity on the social and economic fronts. Paradoxically, however, the institution of marriage seems to have received a rude set-back and got twisted out of shape during the same period.

Never Leave Me discusses, against the background of the romantic love affair of the hero, how a marriage endures in the face of serious threats. *Where Love Has Gone* critically analyses, albeit in retrospect, the reasons for the miserable failure of the marriage. It can therefore be said that the former constitutes the anatomy of marriage and the latter the post-mortem of marriage.

Where Love Has Gone in a way takes off where *Never Leave Me* ends. Brad of the latter novel has had a successful romantic experience with Elaine who belongs to a socially superior class. But ultimately he returns to his wife and family because that is where his roots lie and that is where he experiences security and comfort. His marriage has proved itself to be successful because of a combination of factors—his recognition of his responsibilities, especially toward his children, and his wife's steadfastness, spirit of sacrifice and a relative lack of jealousy.

These are the very things which are lacking in the marital relationship of Luke Carey and Nora in *Where Love Has Gone.* The continuing link between the two novels is that Brad's counterpart, Luke, marries Elaine's counterpart, Nora, a rich woman and social superior instead of limiting it to an affair. That is where everything goes wrong. Nora is beautiful, jealous, ambitious, talented and highly sensual above everything else. The chequered course of their marriage illustrates how if Brad did end up getting married to Elaine, it would have of necessity failed. The social and psychological adjustments which are essential to make a marriage work are woefully wanting in the Luke-Nora relationship.

Where Love Has Gone is termed a post-mortem of marriage because it opens many years after the marriage was dissolved and both have remarried and Nora has been divorced again. The entire story is narrated from Luke's point of view. Considerable time and space are devoted to the story of Luke and Nora's only daughter Danielle who is guilty of adolescent promiscuity and who in a fit of anger and jealously commits the murder of her and her mother's common boy friend. But even this phenomenon of juvenile delinquency is treated against the backdrop of the failed marriage and broken home. It is possible for a reader, lost in the tempo, to lose track of the importance placed on marriage in the novel and the disastrous effects of its dissolution on the children. Moral judgements are avoided but it is clear that Nora is held responsible for destroying relations and for setting herself as a bad example for her daughter. We will consider the question of the extent of her responsibility later.

Returning to the state of affairs at the opening of the novel, we find Luke broke and somewhat disturbed but happily married to Elizabeth who is expecting a baby any day. But the damage Nora has wrought on his psyche is so severe that he is still nursing the wounds caused by her both within and outside their marriage. He confesses: "Nora has a way of cutting me up, and it always took a while to get the pieces back together again,"[5] and adds that she has a way of "creeping into your mind and pre-empting thoughts that should be of someone else" (7). The laws Nora lives by are strange indeed: "the only thing important to her was what she wanted to do. What damage she'd do, whom she would hurt, didn't matter at all" (361-62). This is looking at her from his point of view. It may not however be the whole truth as we will see.

Luke does not want to return to Nora or San Francisco even if that means suppressing his love for his daughter. He has kept himself away from Nora and his daughter Dani for the past six years but the news of the girl's committing a murder now compels him to return to San Francisco. In a way, it is even a psychological necessity for him to go back because, as Elizabeth rightly understands, he has to exorcise the devils and break free of his guilts and tortures and have a catharsis of the accumulated bitterness in him by reliving the bad experience.

Several flash-backs keep taking us back in time to tell us the story of the marriage of Luke and Nora. Nora hails from the family of Spanish dons of old California. She has wealth, power and a "strange wild kind of talent that lifted her high above everyone else" (6). As an artist she has made a big name for herself. Whatever she touched, stone or metal or wood, "took on a shape, a life, of its own." But paradoxically, when she laid her hands on anything that "had a shape, a life, of its own, she destroyed" (6). One such thing she has destroyed is Luke.

Luke, the son of a friend of Nora's father, has a humble background. After entering the Air Force he rose to the position of a colonel but otherwise he is an architect by training. It has been his life long dream to build low cost homes for middle class people, which goes to prove that he is a practical man and that he does not fancy visualising himself greater than what he really is. But at the core of his personality there is self-respect which he zealously guards.

Nora gets interested in him partly because of his initial apparent unconcern for her and partly because his war hero image would help contribute to her own reputation. Having developed interest in him she does not wait for the relationship to mature but brings it to the point of marriage immediately. She thinks that she has everything expected of an ideal wife: "I'm the right age. I'm not hard to take. I've got all the money we'll ever need...." But when here manager Sam asks her a pointed question, "Do you love him?" her answer is a half-hearted, "Of course." She is not sure whether she really loves him. It is just that loving and giving things unselfishly are things very alien to her nature. Luke is someone who will fulfil her sexual and social needs and she must therefore have him. What she really thinks of him comes out much later when she is under the influence of drugs. "My husband?" she says to Sam. "He's just a watch dog my mother hired" (113).

Initially however she uses all her feminine wiles—playing the helpless maiden, confessing and soft-crying—on him to boost his ego and thereby win his assent to marry her. But right from the beginning it is clear to both of them that the marriage is based on lies and make-believe and not love. Nora thinks that she will be able to mould him, like she does the raw-materials of her art works, to suit her expectations and to fit him into her world without protest, in return to the financial favours she will be conferring on him. She seems to believe that given the right conditions things will automatically happen. She does not know that simple faith and unqualified love have greater power than temptations and threats. It does not occur to her that she is not dealing with inanimate objects but a human being who refuses to do her every bidding. The thought of failing to get him to fit into her world is intolerable to her; so she destroys him.

Luke has had no great expectations from marriage or Nora. In fact, he does some deliberate soul-searching before he gets involved with her:

> Then I knew what it was. I wasn't eager to get involved because I was afraid. Afraid that if I let myself fall for her, I'd really be gone. She was everything I'd ever wanted. Class and style and charm, all bright and shining with a veneer that only the years could achieve. All this plus an artistic talent and the wild fierce bitchiness that I sensed running deep within her. Life with a girl like that wouldn't be easy (87).

He also knows that she means a peculiar kind of reality, "like beating your head against a wall because it feels so good when you stop" (55). Yet the marriage comes about and almost immediately begins to show cracks. This is symbolically suggested through the image of the statue of *The Dying Man* which won for Nora a UNO prize. Appreciating the statue Luke says, "I'm like the man in that statue over there. For every moment that I live" (56). This he says referring to his work as a fighter-pilot before they get married. But it is soon clear that he becomes more a dying man after marriage. It is thus significant that on the day of winning the UNO prize Nora destroys Luke socially, financially and, yes, psychologically too. When Sam breaks the news to her, she wants to share it the first thing with Luke but he is away at the construction sight of low cost homes which he undertook in defiance of Nora's wishes and on borrowed money. To add to everything else he was taken their tiny daughter along on that fateful day. Nora always believed that Luke existed for her and if he is not around to share her happiness on such an important occasion he is as good as not there in the world.

She moves quickly and fills Sam's head with a host of lies: "you know perverted things. He makes me do them. It's the only way he can get stimulation. Without that he's almost impotent!...All he wants is for me to have babies so that he can prove he's a man!" (141). Then she goes to the construction site and declares to the ever present and ever inquisitive reporters:

> The American builder is completely contemptuous of the American home owner and housewife. Being completely unimaginative and inartistic, he is turning the American home into a conformity-ridden and tasteless cube for purely selfish economic reasons which enable him to secure greater profits.... Speaking only for myself, I would not even be found dead in so tasteless and styleless a structure, much less live in one (150).

When this statement appears in the newspapers the next day, all hell breaks loose. Luke's financiers and customers back away and he is discharged in bankruptcy. He drowns himself in drink and goes virtually impotent. And that becomes yet another reason for the ever strengthening wall of separation between them.

Unlike most Robbins heroes Luke is sexually not very active right from the beginning. The disastrous association with Nora robs him of whatever sexual enthusiasm he has had. Nora on the other hand is sexually hyper-active and for good reasons. In her manager Sams's opinion, "she needs sex the way some people need liquor," because she "is an artist. She finds both a certain stimulus and an escape in sex...it helped bring her closer to people, to know more about them, to understand them better" (70). Later she herself confesses:

> "Do you think all those things I do come from here?" She touched her forehead. "Well, they don't! They come out of here!" She touched her naked body. "That's where they come from, and every time I feel a little bit emptier. And I have to get something back to fill me up again!" (114).

Even when Luke is feeling weak, sick and disgusted nursing his wounds over the housing project episode and Nora's irresponsible behaviour, she forces him to make love to her. As can be expected, he miserably fails. She then tells him with utter contempt in her eyes, "Sometimes I wonder whatever made me think you were a man enough for me.... Even a boy could make a better job of it than you do" (150). True to her word she almost immediately starts an affair with a boy, but only to be caught red-handed and slapped across the face by Luke.

Perhaps Nora cannot be faulted for her adultery. She is not a nymphomaniac as Russel Nye thinks.[6] She is an artist and artists do have greater sexual appetites than ordinary people. Being an artist and a woman of special sexual orientation she is also jealous and selfish. Her jealousy and selfishness come out in relation to their daughter. She did not want to have the baby in the first place because pregnancy and child-bearing would make her look ugly. When the baby is born she wouldn't even look at her. By contrast, Luke's heart wells up with joy and love on first looking at the baby:

> Something inside me began to ache and I could feel the pain of being born, all the shock that that tiny body had known in the last few hours. I looked down at her, and I knew even before she opened her eyes and then her mouth what she was going to do. We were in tune, we were on the same wavelength, we were like locked-in to each other, and she was mine and I was hers. We went together and belonged together. And the tears came to my eyes for the tears she could not shed (31).

Nora has no such sentiments. Later, when they have moved out of the hospital, she keeps complaining that the baby is crying all the time and that she cannot sleep. When Luke takes care of the baby she cannot hide her jealousy: "You always think about the baby before you do me. Every time the baby cries, you're in there worrying about her. You never worry about me! I don't count, I'm only her mother. I've served my purpose!" (134). In a fit of anger born of jealously she removes herself into the next room and even insists that wife and husband sleeping in separate rooms is somehow more civilized. This same jealously, coupled with her illicit affair with the boy, contributes to the final breaking up of the marital, relation. On his return from service in Korea,

Luke is served summons for divorce, accused of mental cruelty, desertion and non-support.

The divorce spells a further disaster to Luke. He fails to win the custody of Dani because he is broke. Nora even goes to the extent of disowning him as the father of the child claiming that she was conceived before his return from service. The way Luke deals with the fact of divorce has something interesting about it. He removes himself to La Jolla where he has a boat and gets drunk and remains so for many days and months. He finds it impossible to reconcile himself to the fact of not being able to see Dani. It is in that state that he meets Elizabeth. He is so broken-hearted that he cannot get himself to make love to Elizabeth. As she rightly understands he loves too much and feels too much (like perhaps Herzog of Saul Bellow). Otherwise, like Robbins's most autobiographical hero, Joe Crown of *The Story-teller,* he would have tried to make love to the first woman he meets after divorce, even if that happens to be a bar-maid, or thrown a temper tantrum and found his anger and frustration extinguished. Luke takes it to his heart and allows himself to be eaten away by the memories of the bad experience. Elizabeth finds it impossible to go alongwith him in that mental state. In a letter therefore she tells him:

> If the time should come when you win enough of your war to come out of hiding and be the kind of man you really are, may be we can take that long trip together (179).

Luke does come out of his hiding but not before he has lost everything and has served a thirty-day prison term. He then works as a labourer on a housing project and having put by some money, he approaches Elizabeth and asks her whether she is willing to "take a long trip" with him.

At long last he finds a perfect companion in Elizabeth. She knows everything by instinct. A short talk with her has the effect of taking all his tension away from him. She is not colourful and flamboyant or talented like Nora but she is a true woman and wife and behaves like one. She loves Luke for what he is and not for what he does. This marriage is projected as a contrast to the earlier one where incompatibility led to its dissolution. It is a success because the partners concerned belong to the same social class, same frame of mind and finally cherish same values. It further proves that it requires both husband and wife to want to adjust and achieve mutuality. Nora's second marriage too fails because she fails to achieve mutuality even with Sam who knows everything about her and has no illusions at all. It prompts him to wonder why, being a great artist as she does, some of that understanding does not brighten her personal life.

The severest damage caused by the failure of the Luke-Nora marriage is borne by their daughter Dani. She becomes a living testimony for the devastating effects of broken homes and the failure of parents to act as role models. She develops an insane jealousy for Nora because she thinks that every time somebody loves her more than they do Nora, she sends them away. This list includes Luke, Sam, her nanny Mrs Holman and finally Anthony Riccio, their common lover. When Riccio is on the verge of being dismissed Dani gets so mad with rage that she rushes at her mother, armed with a sculptor's chisel. But Riccio somehow gets in between and is killed.

The trial of Dani at the juvenile court brings Luke back to San Francisco. The events in the course of the few days of the trial have a salutary effect on him. He almost relives the experience of marriage with Nora all over. In a feeble effort to secure the release of Dani, Nora even proposes marriage to him. She still works by her old rules. She offers to buy off Elizabeth and when Luke does not give in, she even stoops down to the level of blackmailing him. Luke however knows that life with her is going to be a life of pretence and destruction. He then coolly declares that he just does not like her. His catharsis is complete with this.

> And the ghosts are gone, the guilts vanish. This was the way it was, this is the way it would have been. No matter what you did.
>
> I put down all the windows of the little car as I drove back to the motel. The cool clear night air washed even the hate I

> had felt out of my soul. Nora didn't matter that much to me. Not any more (364).

Later he also tells Dani, "I don't hate here at all now. Not any more. I used to be afraid of her but now I just feel sorry for her" (405).

He goes home, to Chicago, with no ghosts haunting him, to start life afresh with a perfect wife. Back in San Francisco, Nora has to make do with her art because outside of that she has nothing else to share with anyone.

NOTES

1. William Darby, *Necessary American Fictions: Popular Literature of the 1950s* (Bowling Green, Ohio: Bowling Green State U Popular P, 1987) 2.
2. Russel Nye, *The Unembarrassed Muse: The Popular Arts in America* (New York: The Dial Press, 1970) 50.

   Nye thinks that Robbins combines topical interest with softcore pornography and thus produces "a steady series of massively sexual novels." He betrays his profound ignorance of Robbins's achievement in these novels by not exempting them from the above category.
3. I discussed *Never Leave Me* in an article in Volume 16 of this journal.
4. Karen Hinckley and Barbara Hinckley, *American Best Sellers* (Bloomington and Indianapolis: Indiana UP, 1989) 181, 184.
5. Harold Robbins, *Where Love Has Gone* (1962; New York: Pocket Books, 1963) 18. Subsequent references are to this edition.
6. Nye 50.

11

Sex and Property as Means of Tragedy in O'Neill's *Desire Under the Elms*

BASAVARAJ NAIKAR

O'Neill is one of the modern American playwrights who has tried to delineate different aspects of American life in different plays by employing a variety of techniques like symbolism, expressionism and realism. But his major contribution happens to be the field of tragedy wherein he tries to contemporise the Greek myths by giving them a modern, local, American setting. Tragedy, both as a philosophy of life and as a form of drama, has been very popular in the western society which has a tendency to emphasize extreme individualism and limitless freedom. O'Neill, who belongs to the materialistic society of the west, naturally perceives the tragic element in the life around him and tries to transform it into literary art, especially tragedy, two variant forms of which can be seen in his *Desire under the Elms* and *Mourning Becomes Electra.*

Desire under the Elms may be considered as a modern American tragedy in that its theme is rooted in the nineteenth century America. The setting is that of the Cabot farmhouse in New England in 1850. The main characters of the play are based upon the members of an agricultural family. The protagonist of the play Ephraim Cabot happens to be an old man of 75 who has already lost two wives and has three sons. The house of Ephraim Cabot is not a happy one, but that seems to be suffering from a sort of curse. It easily brings to our mind the house of Atreus suffering from the ancestral curse in Greek tragedy. The stonehouse is flanked by the two small elm trees which appear to participate symbolically in the human life of the house. They seem to have a deep influence upon the human life. O'Neill's introduction to the play contains a description of the elms which bears it out clearly:

> Two enormous elms are on each side of the house. They bind their trailing branches down over the roof—they appear to protect and at the same time subdue: there is a sinister maternity in their aspect, a crushing, jealous absorption. When the wind does not keep them astir, they develop from their intimate contact with the life of man in the house an appalling humanness. They brood oppressively over the house, they are like exhausted women resting their sagging breasts and hands and hair on its roof, and when it rains their tears trickle down monotonously and rot on the shingles.[1]

The dramatist's description of the elms offers a clear hint on the very close relationship between human life and Nature and provides a clue to the understanding of the nature of O'Neill's tragic vision of life as embodied in the play.

The main action of *Desire under the Elms* resembles that of the Greek drama especially *Hippolyta* by Euripides in that the protagonist and the other characters appear to be guided not by reason or discrimination but by some uncontrollable instinctive force. The tragic flaw of Ephraim Cabot, the protagonist of the play, may be understood to lie in his indulgence in instinctual pleasures and comforts and the concomitant negligence of his family responsibility towards his three sons who have already attained marriageable age. At the beginning of the play, we meet Ephraim Cabot who has already lost two wives. Ideally speaking one would expect him not to bother about his own comfort, but to think of giving some kind of security to his sons by arranging their marriages and by helping them improve their agricultural set-up so that he could easily and naturally earn their love and affection. But contrary to such an idealistic expectation from a good father, Ephraim Cabot does not bother to give his sons either a stable financial life or emotional security. He is almost killing them by his supreme indifference. The three sons are, therefore, deeply frustrated in their own ways and feel utterly helpless. They feel that their house which is built with stones is not an abode of peace and happiness but a sort of a prison. Peter's description of it makes the meaning explicit: "Here—It's stones atop o' the ground-stones atop o' stones—makin' stone walls—year atop o' year—him 'n 'ye 'n 'me 'n' then Eben—makin' stone walls fur him to fence us in!" (280)

The stonehouse easily symbolizes the petrification of human feelings and indicates how it has been converted into a prison. Another metaphor suggested by the dramatist for the house is that of a cage. His description of Eben, "His defiant dark eyes remind me of a wild animal's in captivity. Each day is a cage in which he finds himself trapped, but inwardly subdued," (279) clearly throws light upon the feelings of the character. Thus the metaphors of 'prison' and 'cage' symbolize the frustration, helplessness and suppressed anger of the sons under the tyranny of their father. They feel that their old father is not able to manage his farm on account of his carelessness and irresponsibility. Peter, therefore, suggests that "I calc'late we might git him declared crazy by the court." (281) They are very sore to know that he killed his two wives by forcing them to overwork. Simeon describes him as a murderer:

Eben: Didn't he slave Maw t' death?

Peter: He's slaved himself t' death. He's slaved Sim 'n' me 'n' yew t' death—on'y none o' us hain't died-yit (283).

The frustration of all the three sons is aggravated by Ephraim Cabot's third marriage with a young and impecunious widow called Abbie Putnam. Ephraim Cabot's third marriage clearly indicates his negligence of responsibility towards his sons and lack of self-control. His marriage does not show his desire for mere companionship in old age but his strong sexual desire for woman. His behaviour, thus, shows his inability to maintain a balance between instinct and reason. Consequently, his instinct begins to reign supreme over his reason thereby upsetting the smooth run of things in the family.

The frustration of the sons is caused by their inability to have full control over their shares of the farm from him as long as he is alive. He has not allowed them any freedom that is due to them, but made them slog almost in a thankless manner. The two elder sons of Ephraim's first wife have, therefore, planned to leave the house and go to California, the western part of America where they can earn a lot of gold and become rich in order to lead a comfortable life. Peter dreams, "We kin walk. It's an a'mighty ways—California—but if yew was t' put all the steps we've walked on this farm end t' and we'd be in the moon!" (283) But the youngest son (by Ephraim's second wife) Eben wants to fight for his share of the farm which belongs to him legally as it was bought by his own mother. He wants to stay back at home and manage the property. Thus the Marxian struggle for the possession of property happens to be the main caused of their frustration.

The Marxian problems are linked with the Freudian ones in the play. For example, all the three sons of Ephraim Cabot are worried about the materialistic security in terms of possession of land and gold. Eben, the youngest son, is bothered about his share of land which once belonged to his mother who happened to be the second wife of his father. Likewise, the elder and the eldest sons of the first wife of Cabot have been suffering from a sense of insecurity because of the thanklessness of their jobs on the paternal farm. They, therefore, have decided to leave their home and go to California in search of gold and other materialistic benefits and pleasures. But Eben, who has his own share of land, wants to buy the share of land belonging to his elder brothers also. Thus, their desire to achieve some kind of happiness through the possession of material wealth like land or gold has, obviously, a Marxian significance about it. The father, Ephraim Cabot, does not want to part with his land by giving it into the custody of his sons as long as he is alive. Frustrated by this experience, the sons tend to dislike their father. The struggle for material wealth sets the father against the sons thereby converting filial love into hatred. The Marxian principle that all the human relationships are affected favourably or adversely by money or wealth is specially borne out by the theme of *Desire under the Elms* showing the strained relationship between father and sons.

The Freudian interpretation that all the problems of human life are those of bed or sex (*d'alcove*) may be specially applied to the play. As per Marxian interpretation, even sex is subordinate to the problem of material wealth, but for Sigmund Freud, sex happens to be the central problem of life. Thus both Marx and Freud are correct in their interpretations separately, but human life is so large and complex that both the interpretations may be seen to be complementary in understanding it. Sometimes, the problem of material wealth may be predominant and that of sex may be subordinate and sometimes it may be *vice versa*. Many times both of them are interchangeable. Sex may affect wealth or *vice versa*.

In *Desire under the Elms,* the problem of sex occupies a very dominant role which is directly associated with that of property. For example, Ephraim Cabot has strong desire for a woman, a third wife, even at the age of seventy-five. His desire for marriage may not be said to be merely a desire for companionship, but one for a sexual partner so that he could produce a son even at such as advanced age, especially when he already has three sons of his own by his two wives. His desire for the third marriage is not only absurd and abnormal in itself but is closely linked with the problem of property. The arrival of the third wife *i.e.* Abbie Putnam creates new legal problems of property for his sons, especially his third son Eben who feels a new insecurity. He fears that he is going to lose his share of property belonging to his own mother to his new stepmother Abbie and rebels against her: "(Spitting with disgust) Her-here-sleepin' with him—stealin' my Maw's farm! I'd as soon pet a skunk 'r kiss a snake!" (290) Eben hates his father as much as his stepmother. His hatred expresses itself in his vindictiveness towards his father. He wants to take revenge against his father by sleeping with the same prostitute *i.e.* Minnie with whom his father used to sleep. Thus the revenge caused by the probable loss of property takes the guise of sexual revenge. As Eben says:

> Waal—when I seen her, I didn't hit her—not I didn't kiss her neither—I begun t' beller like a calf an' cuss at the same time, I was so durn mad—an' she got scared—an' I jest grabbed holt an' tuk her! (Proudly) Yet, sirree! I tuk her. She may've been his 'n your 'n, too—but she's mine now! (290)

The close link between sex and property could be seen in the later life of Ephraim Cabot. He has married the third wife Abbie as much for sexual companionship as for procreative purpose. The father's third marriage means loss of property for the youngest son. The birth of a child to the stepmother perpetuates the loss of property for the step-son. On the contrary, sex becomes a means of retention of his property for Ephraim Cabot. By marrying Abbie and by getting a child on her, Ephraim wants to have his land and house under his thumb:

> Cabot: A son is me—my blood—mine. Mine ought t'git mine. An' then it's still mine—even though I be six foot under. D'ye see?
>
> Abbie: (Giving him a look of hatred) Ay—eh. I see. (She becomes very thoughtful, her face growing shrewd, her eyes studying Cabot craftily).
>
> Cabot: I'm gittin' old—ripe on the bough. (Then with a sudden forced reassurance) Not but what I hain't a hard nut t' crack even yet—an' fur many a year t' come! By the Eternal, I kin break most o' the young fellers' back at any kind o' work any day o' the year!
>
> Abbie: (Suddenly) Mebbe the Lord'll give *us* a son.
>
> Cabot: (turns and stares at her eagerly) You mean—a son—t' me 'n' yew?
>
> Cabot: (his face growing full of joyous pride and a sort of religious ecstasy) Ye been prayin,' Abbie?—fur a son?—t' us?
>
> Abbie: Ay—eh. (With a grim resolution) I want a son now (311-12).

For both Ephraim Cabot and Abbie, sex in its procreative aspect (real or mythical) is a means of fortification of their property. In fact Abbie has married him only to get hold of his property although she knows that he is already seventy-five-years-old and perhaps not able to produce a son at that age. But her belief in the remote possibility of getting a son has compelled her to marry him. When Ephraim Cabot dreams of getting a son on her, she grows aware of the legal rights. She asks him, "Would ye will the farm t' me then—t' me an' it?" (312) Cabot easily agrees to comply with her desire. Thus legal sex in the form of marriage acts as a means of fortification of their legal rights of property for the father and the mother, it becomes a symptom of the possibility of loss of property for the third son.

Just as property is incomplete for Ephraim Cabot without sex, it is more so for Abbie, especially when she realizes that she can have only nominal sex with her old husband and cannot have real sexual satisfaction from him. Thus both husband and wife feel a sort of incompleteness in their life. Ephraim Cabot is eager to have a son and prays to God accordingly. But Abbie who knows that her old husband may not be virile enough to father a son on her, feels frustrated. She, therefore, wants to remove her frustration within the framework of legal marriage, by seeking it through the illegal, instinctive and animalistic channel. That is the reason why she sets about seducing her step-son, thereby achieving a double benefit for herself. She knows that her step-son being young has a natural attraction for the opposite sex because of which he has been visiting a prostitute called Minnie. She, therefore, wants to tease him about his nocturnal visits to the call-girl and tries to compromise with him by trying to be friends with him. She meets him privately one day and employs her wanton wiles of temptation thereby awakening his manhood:

Abbie: (at last painfully) Ye shouldn't, Eben—you shouldn't—I'd make ye happy!

Eben: (harshly) I don't want happy—from yew!

Abbie: (helplessly) Ye do, Eben! Ye do! Why d'ye lie?

Eben: (viciously) I don't take t' ye, I tell ye! I hate the sight of ye!

Abbie: (with an uncertain troubled laugh) Well, I kissed ye anyway—an' ye kissed back—yer lips was burnin'—Ye can't lie 'bout that! (Intensely) If ye don't care, why did ye kiss me back—why was yer lips burnin'? (317)

Although Eben hates Abbie as his stepmother and snatcher of his legal share of property, his latent sexuality is aroused by her systematically and with an ulterior purpose. As Abbie says:

> (quite confident now) I hain't a mite afraid. Ye want me, don't ye? Yes ye do! And yer Paw's son'll never kill what he wants! Look at yer eyes! They's lust fur me in 'em, burnin' 'em up! Look at yer lips now! They're tremblin' an' longin' t' kiss me, an' yer teeth t' bite (317-18).

After mentally arousing his sexual passion for her, Abbie invites him to the privacy of the farmhouse and tempts him physically so powerfully and systematically that Eben feels confused about his own feelings towards her. He does not know whether his love for Abbie at present is filial or sexual. Abbie is so clever that she understands his feelings towards his lost mother and promises to be his surrogate mother on the cordial level and his bedmate on the sexual level. Eben struggles quiet a bit mentally before deciding to choose either filial love or sexual love. Finally the animalistic instinct in him triumphs over his rational faculty. Nature achieves victory over the values of culture. He, therefore, declares his love for Abbie:

> (throws himself on his knees beside the sofa and grabs her in his arms—releasing all his pent-up passion) An' I love yew Abbie!—now I kin say it! I been dyn' fur want o'ye—every hour—since ye came! I love ye! (Their lips meet in a fierce bruising kiss) (321).

When the animal instinct is, thus, aroused in Eben, he forgets the apparent, legal relationship with her as his mother and enters into an incestuous relationship with her by making her his sexual partner. In the mythical sense, he becomes the secret husband of his own mother, thereby assuming the role of a modern Oedipus. As a result of this underground sexual union, Abbie conceives and is delivered of a male child. Thus incestuous relationship offers a multiple benefit to different people at the same time. For Eben, for example, it gives the secret and secure sexual satisfaction and a vicarious pleasure of taking revenge upon his father. For Ephraim Cabot, it offers the pleasure of having a son so that he could fortify his legal title to the property and maintain his dominating position as a father and master of the family. But it offers triple benefit to Abbie in the sense that it helps her to have secret sexual pleasure which is denied to her on account of her husband's old age; to cheat Eben of his own right to property and to strengthen her legal position and claim to property through her newborn baby. Thus the incestuous relationship between the step-son and the stepmother offers legal as well as illegal benefits to the parties concerned simultaneously. When Ephraim Cabot learns that he has become the father of a son even at the advanced age of seventy-five, he grows ecstatic and therefore arranges a birthday party and indulges in singing and dancing. Eben is not very enthusiastic about attending the party. He, therefore, stays away from it. The fiddler and the other invitees joke about Cabot's illusionary ecstasy over his so-called child. They have come to know through rumour that the child's father is Eben and not Ephraim.

The illusory satisfaction of having got a male child gives a false dignity to Ephraim and swells his arrogances. He taunts his son Eben and irritates him by saying that he cannot part with the farm as it belongs to his child. There ensues a physical battle between the two. The old father overpowers the young son. At this moment of crisis, Eben can no longer contain himself. He shatters the illusion of Ephraim by revealing the secret that the child is fathered not by the latter but by the former. Now Ephraim Cabot is shocked beyond measure in the matters of both sex and property. On the other hand, Eben also begins to doubt the authenticity of Abbie's love for him. He feels that he is cheated by Abbie and used by her only as a scapegoat to be cheated of his own share of property. He is disillusioned about the genuineness of her love for him. That is the reason why he accuses her:

> (unheeding) Ye've made a fool o' me—a sick, dumb fool-a-purpose! (Ye've been on'y playin' yer sneakin' stealin' game all along—gitting me t' lie with ye so 's ye'd hev a son he'd think was his 'n, an' makin' him promise he'd give ye the farm and let me eat dust, if ye did git him a son! (335)

When accused by Eben about her disloyalty, Abbie feels that she is in a quandry now. Though initially she established sexual relationship with him mainly with the intention of getting a child by him, now she realizes that she has really fallen in love with him and cannot live without him if he goes away to California abandoning her. She feels a new amorous insecurity in his would-be absence from the family, although she would very much have her legal husband with her. She is now on the horns of a dilemma. She has to choose between amorous security and legal security. Being a young lady full of desires, she decides to choose amorous security to the exclusion of legal one. In order to demonstrate her preference for her lover over her child, she kills the child by choking it with a pillow. Circumstances compel her, thus, to take a bold action. Indeed, she shows a great strength of will in proving her love for Eben through the murder of the child. Shocked by Abbie's inhuman murder of the child, Eben complains to the Sheriff against her. Old Ephraim is also shocked by the event and wants to complain to the Sheriff. His momentary and illusory bliss is shattered to pieces by the revelation of truth by Eben who declares that the child born to Abbie is not fathered by Ephraim but by himself. The knowledge of the incestuous relationship between his latest and third wife and his youngest son disturbs and hurts Ephraim very deeply and consequently he realizes the gravity of his own folly. He feels let down very badly by his own 'darling' wife, the Rose of Sharon and his 'dumb' son Eben who have shamelessly desecrated his marital bed. Ephraim Cabot suddenly develops a kind of *vairagya* or renunciation and wants to gift away all his material belongings and burn off his house by way of vengeance:

> (Stares at them, his face hard. A long pause—vindictively) Ye make a stick pair o' murderin' turtle-doves! Ye'd ought t' be both hung on the same limb an' left thar t' swing in the breeze an' rot—a warnin' t' old fools like me t' b'ar their lonesomeness alone—an' fur young fools like ye t' hobble their lust. (A pause. The excitement returns to his face, his eyes snap, he looks a bit crazy.) I couldn't work today. I couldn't take no interest. T' hell with the farm! I'm leavin' it! I've turned the cows an' other stock loose! I've druv 'em into the woods whar they kin be free! By freein' 'em, I'm freein' myself! I'm quittin' here today! I'll set fire t' house an' barn an' watch 'em burn, an' I'll leave yer Maw t' haunt the ashes,

> an' I'll will the fields back t' God, so that nothin' human kin never touch 'em. I'll be goin' to California—t' jine Simeon an' Peter (346).

Whereas Ephraim Cabot is totally disillusioned by the futility of his action and defeated by life, Eben and Abbie are bound more closely in their love—however illegal it might be—and decide to go to the jail together.

The play, thus, clearly demonstrates the ultimate triumph of instinct over reason; Nature over culture; the animal over the angel. Ephraim Cabot who tried to negate reason by his indulgence in instinctive pleasure of life is finally forced to see the negation of his instinct by Nature itself and made wiser now but alas, only after paying a heavy price for it. In this sense he becomes a modern tragic hero. The Marxian problem of property is finally subordinated to the Freudian power of sex expressed in the final union of Eben and Abbie and their joint departure to the jail. Ephraim Cabot's disillusionment is symptomatic of his tragic wisdom awakened in him only when it is too late in life.

NOTE

1. Eugene O'Neill, *Five Plays,* ed. E. Martin Browne (Harmondsworth: Penguin, 1970) 277.

12

The Streetcar Named Desire: A Tragedy of Passion

BASAVARAJ NAIKAR

The Streetcar Named Desire, which happens to be one of the most successful plays of Tennessee Williams, has been variously interpreted by critics as a tragedy, a problem-play, and a psychological play etc., simply because of the complexity of its theme. One may see it as a play depicting on the whole the conflict between class and mass cultures with their inherent limitations and contingencies. For example, Blanche Dubois who visits her sister Stella for a brief stay is compelled to do so mainly because of the circumstantial compulsions. She belongs to the Southern aristocracy and therefore has all the grace of the class and is endowed with aesthetic, poetic and romantic qualities. But the contingencies of her life have reduced her to the level of a pauper. Thus the financial insecurity caused by the recklessness of the ancestors had made her very helpless. She explains it to Stanley:

> There are thousands of papers, stretching back over hundreds of years, affecting Belle Reve as, piece by piece, our improvident grandfathers and fathers and uncles and brothers exchanged the land for their epic fornications—to put it plainly! (She removes her glasses with an exhausted laugh.) Till finally all that was left—and Stella can verify that!—was the house itself and about twenty acres of ground, including a graveyard, to which now all but Stella and I have retreated (Williams: 140).

The financial insecurity compelled Blanche to take up a job of a high-school teacher with a meagre salary, although such a poor living does not agree with the aristocratic upbringing in the past. The contrast between the past affluence and the present pauperism is too blatant to give her any sense of satisfaction.

The second strand of her sorrowful life is attributable to the emotional shock she experienced on account of a number of tragic deaths in the family, after Stella left for her husband's. She explains it to her sister,

> I, I, I took the blows in my face and my body! All of those deaths! The long parade to the graveyard! Father, mother! Margaret, that dreadful way! So big with it, it couldn't be put in a coffin! But had to be burned like rubbish! You just came home in time for the funerals, Stella. And funerals are pretty compared to deaths. Funerals are quiet, but deaths—dot always.... Death is expensive, Miss Stella! And old Cousin Jessie's right after Margaret's, here! Why, the Grim Reaper had put up his tent on our doorstep! (*Ibidem*: 127)

Thus the emotional shock and exhaustion caused by many deaths in the family had worsened Blanche's condition by adding up to her financial problems. She has become a victim of circumstances which have suppressed her joy of life.

The third reason for her suffering in life was special kind of personality itself. Being an ebullient type of girl endowed with a fine aesthetic temperament, she wanted to enjoy life to the lees. Because of her nymphomaniac nature, she fell in love with a seventeen-year old boy who was a poet. She believed that desire was another name for life. The desire for the pleasures and comforts of life was intensified by her frustration at the financial and emotional level. But the irony of life did not help her to lead a life of happiness and satisfaction. Unexpected things creep into her life and destroy her sense of fulfilment. For example, her discovery of her husband's homosexuality results in a shocking disillusionment. She feels a special disgust for him and expresses it to him:

> He was a boy, just a boy, when I was a very young girl. When I was sixteen, I made the discovery—love. All at once

> and much, much too completely.... But I was unlucky. Deluded. There was something different about the boy, a nervousness, a softness and tenderness which wasn't like a man's, although he wasn't the least bit effiminate-looking-still-that thing was there.... He came to me for help. I didn't know that. I didn't know anything except I loved him unendurably but without being able to help him or help myself. Then I found out. In the worst of all possible ways. By coming suddenly into a room that I thought was empty—which wasn't empty, but had two people in it... (*Ibidem*: 183).

Having seen her husband engaged in a homosexual act, she had felt deeply hurt and disgusted and later told him, "I know! I know! You disgust me...." As a result of being ashamed of his homosexuality and its discovery by his wife, Allan Gray had committed suicide by shooting himself into the mouth. Blanche was thus disillusioned even in the beautiful emotion of love on account of its being tarnished by ugliness. This event closed a major chapter in her life. Her frustration was complete.

Once the beauty of emotional life is marred by her husband's homosexuality and eventual death, she seeks refuge in sexual adventures. Again she becomes a victim of circumstances like the death of her husband which adds to her financial, sexual and emotional security. Her scandalous life is made much of in Laurel. Having grown notorious there, she leaves the small town and moves over to Flamingo. She stays in the hotel Flamingo and entertains a number of rich men, simply because she is in need of money and fun. But scandalous life being discovered by the manager of the hotel, she is chucked out from there. As Stanley describes it to Stella,

> Our supply-man down at the plant has been going through Laurel for years and he knows all about her and everybody elase in the town of Laurel knows all about her. She is as famous in Laurel as if she was the President of the United States, only she is not respected by any party! This supply-man stops at a hotel called the Flamingo.

* * * *

> She moved to the Flamingo! A second-class hotel which has the advantage of not interfering in the private social life of the personalities there! The Flamingo is used to all kinds of goings on. But even the management of the Flamingo was impressed by Dame Blanche! In fact they were so impressed by Dame Blanche that they requested her to turn in her room key—for permanently! This happened a couple of weeks ago before she showed here (*Ibidem*: 187).

Because of her desire for fulfilment, Blanche went in search of new experiences. As she herself explains it to Mitch,

> The opposite id desire. So do you wonder? How could you possibly wonder! Not far from Belle Reve, before we had lost Belle Reve, was a camp where they trained young soldiers. On Saturday nights they would go in town to get drunk—and on the way back they would stagger on to my lawn and call—'Blanche! Blanche!' The deaf old lady remaining suspected nothing. But sometimes I slipped outside to answer their calls.... Later the paddy wagon would gather them like daisies...the long way home... (*Ibidem*: 206).

But the sexual adventures finally make her disillusioned about men in general, lead her to the sad realization of the fact that men are not interested in her life, though they need her physically for their own fun. She has been deserted by many men callously after the sexual need is fulfilled. That is why Blanche craves for the kindness of strangers and some sort of emotional security. It is because of the grave need for security, she tries to deceive the young and innocent Mitch by attracting him into matrimonial bondage. Instead of accepting the holy institution of marriage, Blanche went on experimenting with a prostitutional life on account of her nymphomaniac personality. Though she had had her sexual fulfilment, she realised rather belatedly that it was not accompanied by financial, emotional security and social approval which is possible only through marriage. Thus she comes to have a belated realisation of the multi-dimensional significance of marriage. That is the reason why she turns her attention from the institution of prostitution to that of marriage. Instead of having an *a priori* respect for marriage, she has only an a *posteriori* regard for it which is not the sign of an enlightened person but on the contrary that of a benighted soul which Blanche is. Part of her tragic suffering is due to her far belated realisation. She explains it Stella,

> He hasn't gotten a thing but a good-night kiss; that's all I have given him, Stella. I want his respect. And men don't want anything they get too easy. But on the other hand men lose interest quickly. Especially when the girl is over-thirty (*Ibidem*: 171).

Blanche is thus disillusioned in her temporary sexual adventures with a variety of men. That makes her realise the momentariness of pleasure and long for a relatively lasting relationship with some man. That is the reason why she wants to marry Mitch who would be a suitable partner as he is also suffering from loneliness and in need of matrimonial settlement on account of his mother's imminent death. She tells her sister that "I want to deceive him enough to make him—want me..." (*Ibidem*: 171). Accordingly she tries to hoodwink Mitch by flattering him—about his strong bone-structure, imposing physique and gentlemanliness etc.

Thus the very fulfilment of her desires (which is another name for life) has been the cause of a chain of disillusionments (which is another name for death). The principle of death in life is amply realised by her. What the Buddha said about desire could easily be applied to Blanche's life. For her 'desire' is synonymous with life. But as the Buddha said, 'desire' happens to be the root cause of sorrow, as the fulfilment of one desire leads to the awakening of another desire in a chain fashion. If the process of fulfilment is stopped due to the contingencies of life, there is bound to be some sort of frustration. This is exactly what happens in Blanche's life. In pursuit of the fulfilment of her desires, she seems to have rejected the moral restrictions imposed by the institutions of family and society. Her artistic tastes and tendencies and frustrations have made her defy the moral restrictions.

But her defiance of the norms of society is not appreciated by lower-middle-class or proletarian class represented by Stanley Kowalski. Thus Blanche suffers the tragedy of exposure by the brute culture embodied in Stanley. There is a sharp contrast between Blanche's aristocratic culture and Stanley's brutish culture. That is the reason why there is no meeting between their levels of thinking. Blanche's tragedy happens to be the result of the lack of alignment between class-culture and mass-culture. It is on account of this dichotomy that she is not understood by people like Stanley. It is proverbially said that to understand somebody is to forgive him or her. Stanley, being an embodiment of brute culture, does not understand her point of view, although she can understand his. Being a sportsman, he is deeply interested in body-culture and does not have any respect for mind-culture or heart-culture.

Stanley's incomprehension of Blanche's life might be seen from the day when she comes into his house. Being a proletariat, he is deeply interested in her property, because according to the Napoleonic code, he believes that whatever belongs to his wife belongs to him also. He wishes to know from her as to what happened to the property at Belle Reve. When Stella replies that they have lost it, Stanley wishes to know about the sale-deed and the money gathered from that, "Now let's have gander at the bill of sale" (*Ibidem*: 132). He further explains his point of view to his wife:

> In the state of Lousiana we have the Napoleanic code according to which what belongs to the wife belongs to the husband and *vice versa*.... It looks to me like you have been swindled, baby, and when you're swindled under the Napoleanic code, I'm swindled *too*. And I don't like to be *swindled* (*Ibidem*: 133).

Stanley is bothered about the money earned from the disposal of property. He asks, "Where's the money if the place was sold?" (*Ibidem*: 133). He mistakes the artificial things like garments, stones and ornaments to be genuine ones and therefore thinks that Blanche must have invested or wasted her property-money in those things and feels retrospectively angry with her. He explains this anger to his wife?

> Look at these feathers and furs that she come here to preen herself in! What's this here? A solid-gold dress, I believe! And this one! What is this here? Fox-pieces! (He blows on them.)

> Genuine fox fur-pieces, a half a mile long! Where are your fox-pieces, Stella? Bushy snow-white ones, no less! Where are your white fox-pieces?
>
> *   *   *   *
>
> Pearls! Ropes of them! What is this sister of yours, a deep-sea diver who brings up sunken treasures? Or is she the champion safe-cracker of all time! Bracelets of solid gold, too! Where are your pearls and gold bracelets? (*Ibidem*: 134)

Stanley, thus, tries to understand Blanche from his own proletarian point of view and thinks that all the so called gorgeous garments and ornaments are unnecessary and redundant for her and a criminal waste of money that should have belonged to him finally.

Although Blanche has fallen on bad days, here aristocratic mentality cannot be changed. She is a lady with great gusto for life and an exquisite taste for her the things of beauty. For example, she cares a lot for her physical appearance, her hair style, dress, cosmetics. She likes to be complimented for those things. She enjoys wearing beautiful garments like fur-coats, silken robes and colourful gems and jewels although she cannot afford the real ones. She is contented with the imitation-ones. Similarly she likes to see the same kind of aesthetic taste in others. She, for example, has also the courtesy to admire such qualities in others. She describes the appearance of her sister Stella, "Look you sit there with your little hands folded like a cherub in choir" (*Ibidem*: 123). She flatters Mitch by telling him, "You have a massive bone-structure and a very imposing physique," and "You're a natural gentleman, one of the very few that are left in the world" (*Ibidem*: 179). But on the contrary, she does not like Stanley's beastly behaviour. When she sees him throw away the radio, or talk rudely to women, or whack his wife's thigh in the presence of her sister, or his general lack of manners. After observing all the details of his 'crude behaviour' she ramarks to her sister,

> There's something downright—bestial—about him! You're hating me saying this, aren't you?....

> He acts like an animal, has an animal's habits! Eats like one, moves like one, talks like one! There's even something—sub human—something not quite to the stage of humanity yet! Yes, something—apelike about him, like one of those pictures I've seen in—anthropological studies! Thousands and thousands of years have passed him right by and there he is—Stanley Kowalski—survivor of the Stone Age. Bearing the raw meat home from the kill in the jungle! And you—*you* here—waiting for him! May be he'll strike you or may be grunt and kiss you! That is, if kisses have been discovered yet! There in the front of the cave, all grunting like him, and swilling and gnawing and hulking! His poker night!—you call it—this party of apes! Somebody grows—some creature snatches at something—the fight is on! *God*! May be we are a long way from being made in God's image, but Stella—my sister—there has been *some* progress since then! Such things as art—as poetry and music—such kinds of new light have come into the world since then! In some kinds of people some tenderer feelings have had some little beginning! That we have got to make *grow*! And *cling* to, and hold as our flag! In this dark march towards whatever it is we're approaching.... Don't—don't hang back with the brutes! (*Ibidem*: 163-4)

Blanche, thus, understands the low level of Stanley and tries to alert her sister about it. But conversely Stanley is not able to understand her point of view or aesthetic approach to life. He tries to understand her from his own limited proletarian point of view in terms of simple things like sex and property. He hurts her feelings by making crude remarks about her both in her presence and in her absence. Blanche has thus to suffer the tragedy of incomprehension by others. Far from understanding Blanche's aesthetic sensibility and even without being able to discriminate between the genuine objects and the imitation-ones, Stanley attributes Blanche's possession of pearls and gems to her spendthrift nature and questions the very necessity of having them. He asks his wife,

> Pearls! Ropes of them! What is this sister of yours, a deep-sea diver who brings up sunken treasures? Or is she the

> champion safe-cracker of all time! Bracelets of solid gold, too! (*Ibidem*: 134)

Later he questions Blanche, "What does it cost for a string of fur-pieces like that?" (*Ibidem*: 136)

Although Stanley is a Lawrentian kind of womaniser of the lowest order, he never has a sophisticated Lawrentian kind of cosmic philosophy of sex. He has no mental capacity even to appreciate the physical beauty of a woman, as his need for the feminine body is very functional. He makes a shameless confession of it to Blanche:

> Compliments to women about their looks. I never met a woman that didn't know if she was good-looking or not without being told, and some of them give themselves credit for more than they've got. I once went out with a doll who said to me, 'I am the glamorous type, I am the glamorous type!' I said, 'So what?' (*Ibidem*: 136-7)

As he confesses, he is interested in a woman only when she is ready to lay her cards on the table. Except sleeping with a woman, he has no other interest in her—her mind or heart.

Stanley's pleasure in exposing Blanche's sex-scandals is caused by his limited understanding of her predicament. As he explains it to Stella:

> The trouble with Dame Blanche was that she couldn't put on her act any more in Laurel! They got wised up after two or three dates with her and then they quit, and she goes on to another, the same old lines, same old act, same old honey! But the town of too small for this to go on for ever! And as time went by she became a town character.... And for the last year or two she has been washed up like poison. That's why she's here this summer, visiting royalty, putting on all this act—because she's practically told by the mayor to get out of town! Yes, did you know there was an army camp near Laurel and your sister's was one of the places called 'Out-of-Bounds?' (*Ibidem*: 187-8)

Stanley further tells Stella how Blanche was chucked out of her school on account of her sex-scandals:

> She is not going back to teach school!.... She didn't resign temporarily from the high school because of her nerves!.... She didn't. They kicked her out of that high school before the spring term ended—and I hate to tell you the reason that step was taken! A seventeen-year-old boy—she'd gotten mixed up with! (*Ibidem*: 188)

It is because of his discovery of the scandalous secrets of Blanche's past life that Stanley prevents Mitchel from attending her birthday party or from marrying her. He does not want her to stay any longer in his house. He, therefore, has brought a "ticket! Back to Laurel! On the Greyhound! Tuesday! (*Ibidem*: 198)

Stanley's failure to understand Blanche is combined with his awareness of the possible threat to his own domestic security and happiness by the presence of Blanche. Thus incomprehension is combined with vindictiveness in Stanley who, therefore, tries to humiliate her by raping her. His innate animalism is expressed in his words, "We've had this date with each other from the beginning!" (*Ibidem*: 215). But Blanche is so cultured that she does not bring the incident of rape to her sister's notice in order not to spoil their matrimonial harmony. The mass man *i.e.* Stanley treats the class woman *i.e.* Blanche from his own limited point of view.

Another reason for the tragedy of Blanche happens to be the striking difference between Stanley's nature and her own. Whereas Stanley is a down-to-the-earth fellow with his pragmatic approach to life, Blanche is a dreamer and an idealist who delights in dwelling in the beautiful world of imagination. Hence there is no meeting between the two approaches to life. Blanche tells her sister Stella, "How pretty the sky is! I ought to go there on a rocket that never comes down!" (*Ibidem*: 141), which holds a mirror to her implicit disappointment with reality and her desire for escape into the ideal world of beauty. As her very name suggests, Blanche wants her life to be as colourful as lively. She explains to Mitchel the significance of her name, "It's a French name. It means woods and Blanche means white, so the two together mean white woods. Like an orchard in spring" (*Ibidem*: 150). But the paradox happens to be that her life is full of deaths, graveyards and cemeteries. She does not wish to see the naked ugliness but wants to see it covered with a beautiful veil. She tells Mitchel,

> I bought this adorable little coloured paper lantern at a Chinese shop on Bourbon. Put it over the light bulb.... I cannot stand a naked light bulb, any more than I can a rude remark or a vulgar action (*Ibidem*: 150).

Because of her disappointment with the ugly reality of the earthly life, she frequently stares at the sky to enjoy the ethereal beauty. She explains it to Mitchel,

> Eureka! Honey, you open the door while I take a last look at the sky.... I am looking for the Pleides, the Seven Sisters, but these girls are out tonight. Oh, yes they are, there they are! God bless them! All in a bunch going home from their little bridge party... (*Ibidem*: 176).

Similarly Blanche wants to escape from the trap of the world into the sea which is a symbol of boundless freedom for her. Before being taken to the mental hospital she expresses her dream,

> I can smell the sea air. The rest of my life I'm going to spend on the sea. And when I die, I'm going to die on the sea. You know what I shall die of? (She plucks grape.) I shall die of eating an unwashed grape one day out on the ocean. I will die—with my hand in the hand of some nice-looking ship's doctor, a very young one with a small blonde mustache and a big silver watch.... And I'll be buried at sea sewn up in a clean white sack and dropped overboard at noon—in the blaze of summer—and into an ocean as blue as my first lover's eyes! (*Ibidem*: 220)

Blanche commits the tragic mistake of not marrying another man. Had she gone in for a second marriage, she would have been able to repair all the damage done to her life. But her constitutional make-up also contributes to her sorrow. Although she is partially a victim of circumstances, she is also equally responsible for her suffering. Because of her early suffering in life caused by countless deaths and the abnormal husband and his unexpected death, she decides to take revenge against her fate by indulging in the fulfilment of her desires outside the institution of marriage. Because she tries to negate the holy institute of marriage, she is negated by the social and moral order of life in the guise of the animalistic Stanley who exposed her thereby causing disintegration of her mind and soul.

NOTE

Tennessee Williams, *A Streetcar Named Desire, Penguin Plays* (Harmondsworth: Penguin Books, 1974.

13

"Everything Becomes...Too Late Finally"—An Analysis of Edward Albee's *A Delicate Balance*

R. SARASWATHI

(1)

When *A Delicate Balance* opened at New York's Martin Beck Theatre in 1966, most of the reviewers noted the play's similarity to *Who's Afraid of Virginia Woolf?* praising or childing Albee for progressing or declining to a subdued version of his most successful work. Superficially the two plays are very similar indeed. They are both built around two couples who reflect and clarify each other; the two couples are both plagued by an anxiety, the *Angst* to which the title of the earlier play alludes and which triggers the conflict *A Delicate Balance.* In both plays the anxiety turns out to have its roots in the fear of sterility and annihilation, a fear which originates in a traumatic confrontation with death. Unable to face the threat of non-being, the characters try to evade reality by escaping, in different ways, into an inauthentic, death-in-life existence. Despite such similarities, *A Delicate Balance* cannot be considered as a milder rehash of *Who's Afraid of Virginia Woolf? If a Delicate Balance* is a more subdued, a quieter play, it is not so because Albee was tying to appease those members of the Pulitzer prize jury who thought *Who's Afraid of Virginia Woolf?* "a filthy play," but because Albee's vision has undergone an important change. Whereas every line of the earlier play is evidence of the character's fierce determination to reach the partner, in violence if necessary, *A Delicate Balance* is dominated by the paralyzing melancholy of

Agnes' insight that "everything becomes...too late finally."[1] To Albee "the point of the play was that we lose...we develop a kind of arthritis of the mind, of the morality, and change becomes impossible finally."[2] The possibility of change, however, is one of the basic premises on which Albee's plays have been consistently built. But in *A Delicate Balance* the characters do not change to any significant extent. The play thus departs in an important aspect from the pattern of Albee's previous plays. The dynamic presentation of the development of human relationships is replaced by the static presentation and analysis of a condition or gestalt in Albee's recent plays *Box-Mao-Box* and *All Over* where this static structural quality has become a defining frame of reference. The stagnation which is preserved with some effort in *A Delicate Balance* is not even endangered, but unveiled only in the later plays. But while *A Delicate Balance* thus anticipates the plays that were to follow it, it also looks back to its predecessors in its allegorical technique and its thematic concern with man's metaphysical situation. In *Who's Afraid of Virginia Woolf?* and *Tiny Alice* Albee has each of the characters represent one of the possible response to the play's central question. He continues this way of achieving universality and comprehensiveness in *A Delicate Balance,* and the play's central challenge to the characters and the responses embodied by them resemble those of the earlier plays. But although the four basic types of characters representing four basic ways of evading man's anxiety about the meaning and purpose of life in *Who's Afraid of Virginia Woolf?* and *Tiny Alice* reappear in *A Delicate Balance,* the drama that develops from their interaction is resolved differently in this play.

Among the characters, Tobias resembles George and Julian, as well as Jerry. Like them he has withdrawn from physical involvement with the world as much as possible in order not to be reminded of the inevitable indignity of the body's animalistic death. Agnes attempted to give structure and meaning to her own and her family's lives by substituting the limited, arbitrary structures and ends provided by metaphysical values. Thus she approaches reality very much like Nick or the Lawyer and the Cardinal, even though her awareness of her limitation and her comparative lack of selfishness and complacency make her the play's most attractively drawn character. Claire shares her sister's insight into the emptiness of their lives, but in contrast to Agnes she exemplifies the despairing resignation to the physical and its meaninglessness encountered previously in Martha and Miss Alice. Like them, Claire tries to wrest a desperate value from the physical and its degradation by pretending to herself and others that she chooses it deliberately. But like her predecessors, she finds that in reality she cannot choose what she despises without despising herself. Julia finally persists in a childlike (and at her age, childish) view of reality and thus evades the anxiety of being, by simply refusing to acknowledge the negation, the threat of nothingness as a part of reality. Thus she uses essentially the same escape that Honey and Butler had tried before her.

As the discussion of *Tiny Alice* and *Virginia Woolf* has shown, four responses constitute the four evasions that are logically possible. Faced with the absence of meaning in a physical existence inevitably terminated by death, man can reject the physical and attempt to remain aloof from the necessities of physical reality. Or he may try to impose a pattern on the patternless reality, structure it arbitrarily to an arbitrary meaning which has ultimate validity. A third possibility lies in embracing the physical and pretending that mere physical and material satisfaction yields ultimate significance. Finally, man may choose to ignore the question of meaning altogether and simply not ask what Tillich calls "the religious question."[3]—the question about the meaning and purpose of his existence.

Since Tobias, Agnes, Claire, and Julia exemplify and exhaust among themselves the four possible responses. Harry and Edna do not constitute an expansion beyond Albee's four basic types. The play's list of characters identifies them as "*very much like Agnes and Tobias*" an identification which the play repeatedly confirms. Harry is shown "being Tobias" (103) and Edna, "becoming Agnes," scolds Julia, her godchild, and insists, like Agnes, on "manners' (115). Thus Harry and Edna do not represent alternative ways of being but they are duplicates or palimpsests of Agnes and Tobias. "Our lives are...the same," Edna reminds Agnes and Tobias at the play's end (166), and the very fact that they can be duplicated is one of the ways in which

Albee suggests that they exist as types in a society of types rather than authentically as unique human beings.

(2)

For Tobias this existential inauthenticity stems, as suggested above, from his rejection of involvement with the physical whose meaninglessness he fears because he can offer no spiritual value against it. Early in the play Agnes sums up succinctly the principle of Tobias' life: "things get hot, move off" (6). Thus his whole life has been a sustained manifestation of the principle of flight exercised more spectacularly by Harry and Edna at the end of Act I. The ultimate cause of Tobias' flight is the confrontation with death when his son Teddy died. This negation of life's meaning and promise, in a way the negation of his "immortality," has so severely intimidated Tobias that he practised "withdrawal" from then on, both literally, as a means of birth control, and figuratively, as a means of protection from suffering and loss. Tobias' withdrawal from the risks of involvement with others protects him, but it must also result in spiritual void that the absence of male offspring symbolizes in *The Zoo Story, Who's Afraid* and *Tiny Alice*. The physical barrenness in *A Delicate Balance* is alike indicative of a spiritual sterility because it is wilful, *i.e.*, a chosen, not an inevitable condition of man's life:

> *Agnes.* ...I think it was a year when you spilled yourself on my belly, Sir? "Please? Please, Tobias?" No, you wouldn't even say it out: I don't want another child, another loss. "Please, please, Tobias?" And guiding you, *trying* to hold you in?" (137).

Agnes makes it clear in this passage that Tobias is responsible for the sterility of his life, that it was not inevitable, and that the physical sterility is only of secondary importance. For, the primary aim of her pleas is not a pregnancy for herself but a genuine unconditional commitment of love from Tobias:

> I can take care of it: we *won't* have another child, but please don't...leave me like that. Such...silent...sad, disgusted...love (138).

But Tobias, although he admits that he hates this kind of

relationship as much as Agnes, does not have the courage to risk a genuine involvement and "took to (his) own sweet room instead" (138), a retreat that corresponds to Jerry's voluntary imprisonment in the cubicle of his rooming house and to George's and Julian's flight into their asylums. Tobias' withdrawal from reality is the same kind of madness. Even though the term asylum is not explicitly used in *A Delicate Balance,* Tobias' withdrawal is perfectly described in Agnes' definition of madness as "the...becoming a stranger in...the world, quite...uninvolved" (6). In fact, Agnes later speaks of Tobias twice as "a stranger in my room" (123-124) and thus explicitly links him with her definition of madness.

These and other references to becoming a "stranger" evoke echoes of Camus' 'The Stranger.' Tobias does indeed resemble Meursault in his comfortable adjustment to daily routine and in his inability to feel any deep spiritual attachment. His withdrawal is therefore not just an estrangement from his wife, but, like Meursault's, a much more radical separation from human reality itself, from the reality of others and finally from his own reality, too.[4] Tobias has therefore, like George, no specific identity; like George he "sank to a cipher, and...stayed there...very nice but ineffectual, essential, but not—really—thought-of, gray...non-eminence" (63-64). He has become like an interchangeable and replaceable object among other objects, and he consequently thinks of people in the same way. The absence of others only strikes him as the "lack of bodies" (127) and under Claire's probing he admits that he and his "indistinguishable if not necessarily similar friends" are "an environment, I guess" (19). They have no really human presence, but are there only as part of the objective background.

When Tobias converses with them he therefore uses mostly those polite clichés that serve to keep them at a distance rather than bring him into genuine communication with them. This applies even to his daughter. He is not even aware of her marital troubles until Julia comes home (14), so that Agnes reproaches him for evading the responsibilities of his fatherhood. He does indeed not talk to Julia very much, just as he procrastinated at talking to her husbands (32). His explanation for his reluctance to talk, to enter into communication with others (reminiscent of Jerry's refusal to speak much to people), reveals the reasons for his withdrawal from living in general:

Tobias: (*Not rising from his chair, talks more or less to himself*): If I saw some point to it, I might...break through to her, and say, "Julia..." but then what would I say? "Julia...Then, nothing" (33).

It is this threat of his "Then, nothing" which paralyzes Tobias into inaction and withdrawal. Without the assurance of success for his attempt at communication Tobias does not dare to reach out for the communion which Albee sees as man's only way of confirming his worthiness as a genuinely human being. This is a failure of courage, for the communion requires a faith in the availability of individual worthiness, a trust that is courageous because it is beyond any certainties that human systems of thought or ritual can supply. Tobias, however, has lost this faith in the confrontation with death. The nothingness at the end of man's physical existence, with which the loss of his son confronted him has destroyed Tobias' faith that significance is possible, just as faith had left Julian when the pressure of the physical world "intimidated" him.

Tobias' concerns are not directed toward the reality of living in the present. Like Daddy in *The American Dream,* Tobias just wants to "get it over with." He wishes that everything would "just go into the past...forget itself" (22), and Agnes reinforces this suggestion by remarking that "Tobias and Harry's concerns can simply be summed up as making ends meet until they meet their ends" (56). Faced with the chaotic condition of his house (a term that the play consistently uses to symbolize an ordered, sheltered past when "[he was] young and lived at home" (129). Both his "death wish" and his dreaming of his youth—with Harry he drinks "to youth" (155)—are signs of his escape from the present. This retreat from the present has not only presented Tobias' own humanity but also that of his family.

(3)

Claire exemplifies the resignation to nothingness and submission to the threat rather than a defiant acceptance of it. This is, of course, very attractive to the meek Tobias' who is therefore always willing to excuse or overlook Claire's alcoholism. And her thinly veiled invitations to Tobias together with the suggestion that she may have been Tobias' partner in his adultery after Teddy's death indicate how tempting Claire's response to the threat of meaninglessness is. For Claire not only removes herself from the difficulties of existence but also makes this withdrawal seem a deliberate and admirable act of stoic courage. Tobias' withdrawal had been a half-conscious reaction, a flight into illusion away from the challenge of life and death. Claire, on the other hand, does not try to dodge the awareness of death. When the discussion turns to the plague that Harry and Edna bring with them, she claims to be immune because she had it already (152). She has been through the nightwatches, the "staring into dark" (119) she tells Tobias. Claire's detachment and passivity is therefore deliberate, which gives her a certain flamboyance that the meek and confused Tobias necessarily lacks. But this flamboyance cannot hide the fact that Claire's pose of watching from the sidelines as an "objective observer" (72) is an escape and a capitulation, too. It removes Claire from involvement with reality and simplifies life for her, for it relieves her of the necessity of making choices. Since ultimately nothing makes a difference to Claire, she makes no judgement, gives no advice, urges no action. When it comes to Edna and Harry's invasion, for instance, she claims to see no problem: "You've got two choices, Sis. You take 'em in, or you throw 'em out," (88) to which Agnes replies ruefully: "Ah, how simple it is from the sidelines" (88). Claire pursued an approach very similar to Martha's or Miss Alice's. Alcohol and sexual adventures are the ways in which their escape from authentic existence manifests itself. On the surface the choice seems courageous, but Claire has, after all, chosen her distractions to escape pain and anguish, and hence her stance is ultimately dictated by fear. Although she can see her wilful self-destruction as the ultimate expression of her selfhood, Claire does not have the courage to see living in the same way, and her seat "on the sidelines" turns out to be a selfish illusion. For in her insistence on self-sufficiency, in her arrogance, Claire cuts herself off from others, deserts them actually, and imposes more suffering on them in order to escape from them herself. With withering irony Agnes therefore attracts Claire's pretense that a special human reality results from her wilful alcoholism:

Agnes: ...We shall all rest easier to know that it [the drinking] is wilful; that the vomit and the tears, the muddy mind, the falls and the absences, the cigarettes out on the tabletops, the calls from the club to come and get you please...that they are all...willful, that it *can* be helped (*Scathing, but softly*).

If you are not an alcoholic, you are beyond forgiveness (28-29).

Claire scoffs at this attack by Agnes, but she cannot hide the fact that her pose of wilful detachment does not give her the permanent peace and commitment that she looks for. Again and again her need to be recognized, to be confirmed by others in dialogue, breaks to the surface and belies here claim to the position of a neutral observer. She goads Agnes until her sister turns on her, and then exults: Ooh, I am here, after all I exist!" (32). Her entrance with bursts of accordion and yodelling or her adventure of trying to buy a topless bathing suit are likewise designed to shock others into paying attention to her, into acknowledging her existence as a unique human being, for such confirmation could help her transcend the meaningless animal existence that she claims to have chosen so deliberately. She explains her search for the bathing suit with a hope that Tobias would take all of them away from their present life to a more vital primitive existence. She knows that this is sheer fantasy, but in her plea to be saved Claire is more serious than she does in fact admit. In the same way her explanation for her surprise entrance with the accordion as allowing "sister Claire...to do her part-pay her way, so to speak...justify" (84), draws attention to Claire's continuing need to find the confirmation of others.

The detachment of which Claire is so proud therefore remains a one-sided affair. It means that she refuses to confirm the significance of others but demands from them confirmation for herself. This is an immature, almost childish attitude, and the play compares Claire repeatedly to a child. At the A.A. meeting Claire performs with her "little-girl voice," making her "little-girl curtsy," and padding back to her chair on her "little-girl feet" (25). Her drunkenness regularly makes her as helpless as an infant and she uses baby talk repeatedly. To readers of *Virginia Woolf* this childishness is a familiar metaphor suggesting the failure to find an adult relationship to reality, and *A Delicate Balance* uses it in the same way. Accused to her authoritarian way of ruling the roost, Agnes justifies it as the proper approach "when we are dealing with children..." (79).

Agnes' remark implies that there is something "childish" in the other family members as well. The immaturity of Tobias' withdrawal, his yearning for his protected youth and the time before Teddy's death, has already been shown. That leaves Julia, and she is clearly the most obviously childish of Agnes' family. She herself speaks of her "angular adolescence" (63), reminding the reader that Albee describes her as "still angular" in his list of characters. Julia clearly has never grown beyond this "angular adolescence." She still depends on her parents for protection and comfort, so that Claire calls her the "perpetual brat" (149) and Tobias accuses her of always wanting to "nestle into being fifteen and misunderstood" (62). How right Tobias is becomes clear when Julia falls back on exactly this appeal in order to defend her claim to her room. She becomes "(suddenly a little girl; crying) "Mother!"? Mother!?...MOTHER? FATHER! HELP ME!" (97-98) and Tobias tries to calm her with a soothing: "Julia, baby" (113). As a "little girl" Julia strongly recalls Claire's little-girl antics, and the play emphasizes the affinity between Claire and Julia by showing Claire's particularly warm welcome for her niece and later Claire suggests that Julia has "come to take my [Claire's] place" (92) in Agnes' household. The statement also makes it clear that Julia had until then occupied a place different from Claire's. For while Claire's childishness results from the wilful rejection of a reality that she has faced and found to be unsatisfactory, Julia's childishness is the result of her ability to block out the negations involved in reality. Claire's childishness is therefore the result of a regression, while Julia has never gone beyond the level of adolescence.

Unlike Claire's, Julia's childishness contains an element of naive confidence in life. She has never retreated into the pose of an uninvolved neutral observer and has even found it easy to enter into one commitment, one marriage after another. But these commitments have not been made because she has had the courage to accept those negations that led to Claire's resignation, but because she could or would not see them as part of reality. Like Honey in *Virginia Woolf* Julia has managed to ignore the negations of human worth and this unrealistic, "childish" behaviour has led to the failure of her marriages. For whenever an uncomfortable reality surfaced, Julia, rather than trying to love in spite of it, had fled from it to seek protection in the room of her "angular adolescence."

Agnes, like Martha, is enraged by her family's death-in-life existence: "What I cannot stand is the selfishness! Those of you who want to die...and take your whole life doing it (28)." This selfishness makes her furious because the withdrawal of the others makes it impossible for her to reach them, so that her love must go to waste. Her brutality, she explains to Claire, is therefore not brutality at all, but "the souring side of live" (13). When Agnes shouts she is only continuing her efforts to penetrate the isolation of the others, "to be heard...above the awful din of your privacies and sulks" (81).

But Agnes does not shout very often, for such a loss of control endangers the position in which Agnes has found a measure of comfort and security. It is a position of compromise and retrenchment where the seemingly purposeful order of social rules and conventions has been substituted for the precarious life of unpredictable human encounters, *i.e.*, for the only life capable of giving human significance to existence. Agnes has always considered this a temporary position, a "holding action" till the time when the others, particularly Tobias, would abandon their withdrawal and make real communication possible. As her efforts to force Tobias back into an involvement with life show, Agnes regards the prevention of the family's physical break-up only as the minimum basis necessary if spiritual and truly human contact is to develop eventually. "We are all together...which is something," she reminds her family and although her efforts to maintain the family balance cannot by themselves give meaning to their existence, these efforts to combat the "madness" of total withdrawal from reality. Agnes does see the superficial advantages of such a withdrawal, as her speculations about the attractiveness of insanity show. But she firmly concludes that she "could never do it—go adrift—for what would become of you [Tobias]?" (3-4). Agnes' decision to stay "same" and maintain at least the outward forms of human communication is thus motivated by a genuine care for the rest of the family. She is the only one who is not like the others, "unconcerned, or uncaring, assuming that [they] are on level ground...by divine right, I gather, though that is hardly so" (81-82).

But Agnes' sincere concern for the other family members cannot conceal the fact that she too has failed. Where unconditional trust and love, a dynamic and continuous reaching out toward the others, is called for, she has become discouraged and settled for the easier alternative of preserving a *status quo,* even though she recognizes its limitations:

> *Agnes:* "to keep in shape".... Most people misunderstand it, assume it means alteration, when it does not. Maintenance. When we keep something in shape, we maintain its shape and whether we are proud of that shape, or not, is another matter—we keep *it* from falling apart. We do not attempt the impossible. We maintain. We hold (80).

It is, however, just that attempting of the impossible, that is, persisting in loving even the deluded individual, that would make it possible to overcome the spiritual sterility of the balance. But Agnes also lacks the trust out of which such a commitment might come. Again and again her suspicion and jealousy of Claire alienate her from Tobias. He has perhaps helped to destroy her ability to trust by his rejection of Agnes and his infidelity after Teddy's death; but although this humiliation may explain Agnes' attitude, it does exonerate her. For the trust she lacks is exactly the trust that survives such confrontations with a negation of one's worth. It is that "absolute faith which says yet to being"[5] that Jerry, and Albee's other protagonists, demonstrate.

Agnes, however, has settled into the comfort of the limited

security offered by the arbitrary patterns maintained by her. So settled is she that she has, in fact, "stopped (missing Tobias), I believe? (127). Her "wonderful control" has protected her from outright suffering so that Tobias has not "seen her cry in...for the longest time...no matter what" (23). But this control has also screened out of her life all joys. "There are no mountains in my life...nor chasms," she observes wistfully. "It is a rolling, pleasant land" (9). The only time that Agnes does show real agitation is when Claire threatens to upset the balance by once again flaunting Agnes' rules of order; then "there is true passion here; we see under the calm a little. I will not tolerate it: I will not have you!" (28). Her fierceness is plausible because Claire, without offering any affirmation to take its place, threatens the fragile security that Agnes has built up for herself. This security consists in her temporary importance and identity as "the fulcrum" (82) of the equilibrium in which she holds the family. Her place in the family hierarchy defines her and assigns her a definite purpose as "ruler of the roost, maitre d,' and licensed wife" (149). Claire even suggests that Agnes may have contributed, though not necessarily consciously, to Julia's marital difficulties in order not to break up the family structure which provides her with a young-mother identity: "(*Texas accent, or near it*) Iswar! Ef I didn't love much sister so, Ah'd say she got yoh hitched fur the pleasure uh gettin' yuh back" (72). Julia's hint that her husbands were "whatever man her parents thought would hold the fief together best," (65) reinforces the suggestion that in order to keep her "baby" Agnes has either undermined, or at least not helped the marriages.

That such an identity as "the youngest older woman in the block" (136) is so important to Agnes points to the ultimate nature of the threat against which she tries to defend herself by creating and maintaining the balance. Like Martha, Agnes is greatly concerned about her aging. She insists, half-seriously, that she is "as young as the day I married" (6); she is reluctant to listen to the recital of Julia's marital failure because, as she says, "I see myself...growing old each time" (110), and she protests with "(*Qufet anger*) I am not an old woman" (86). It is thus the fact of growing old, the denial of man's significance in aging and death, that has precipitated Agnes: flight into the shelter of the rigid equilibrium that she maintains. But her aging only reinforces the ultimate reason for her life in the balance, the substitute for, and therefore a barrier to, a dynamic existence. For it is the death of her son that has permanently shaken her hold in reality, in the same way that it shook Tobias': "It [the time after Teddy's death] was an...unreal time...for a number of us, for me," she remembers, unreal because it undermined all the confirmations, of her life's significance on which she had relied until then: "(Not explaining, and to none of them, really) Ah, the things I doubted then: that I was loved—that I loved, for that matter!—my mind, you see. That Julia would be with us long. I think...I think I thought Tobias was unfaithful to me then. Was he, Harry?" (102).

The same confrontation with death that led to Tobias' withdrawal has destroyed Agnes' faith and her trust in the values of life. Although she has not withdrawn from life as complacently as Tobias, her withdrawal is as real and as sterile as that of her husband. For she has substituted the superficial certainties of a life of rules and routines for the risks of those genuinely human encounters, love and compassion, which in Albee's plays affirm the unique significance of the individuals involved. But Agnes, like George, finds herself dissatisfied with her escape from the difficulties and ambiguities of reality. For her consciousness, like that of Dostoevski's Underground Man, is a "superior consciousness," it keeps her aware that her life is as meaningless as that of those whom she condemns. Thus the delicate balance that she maintains is a dual one: she lives not only in the equilibrium of the established patterns of her family, but also in the balance between her commitment to this pattern and her constant awareness of its ultimate meaninglessness. Her existence is characterized by her "double vision, the great balancing act" (83) between her pretense of an ordered and meaningful life and her recognition of the pretense as pretense. She herself remarks somewhat wistfully: "I am the one member of this...reasonably happy family blessed and burdened with the ability to view a situation objectively while I am in it.... The double position of seeing not only the facts but their implications..." (87) Agnes' character therefore constitutes a significant variation of the "rule oriented" type represented in the earlier plays. She tries to control the chaos of reality by strict arbitrary rules like Nick or the Lawyer and the Cardinal. But unlike them, Agnes does not complacently mistake her ordered world for reality. Her bitterly ironic remark "whether we are proud of that shape [the equilibrium she maintains] or not is another matter" (80), clearly reveals her deep dissatisfaction with the balance in which she keeps her family and herself. She maintains this balance nevertheless in order to give her life at least a semblance of identity and purpose as well as to keep alive the possibility of eventual confirmation. It is this anguished and precarious affirmation (that is it worth caring for the significance of life, even while she recognizes her own insufficiently) that makes Agnes the most attractive character in the play. It clearly distinguishes her from her sister who shares her insight into the emptiness of their present existence. While Claire responds to this awareness by negating the value of life, Agnes fiercely insists on its worth.

This does not mean that she cannot understand and even sympathize with the inauthentic existence of others. At times her painful awareness of the hollowness of her own life makes her envy the apparent simplicity of lives like those of Tobias and Claire. But since Agnes is "concerned with peace—not mere relief" (10), she rejects both Claire's repeated escapes into alcohol (or the drugs suggested by Tobias) and Tobias' more radical and permanent estrangement. She sees the insufficiency of these escapes, too, and when the arrival of Harry and Edna threatens the escape routes by upsetting all the established patterns, Agnes does not hesitate to exploit this threat by trying to force Tobias into making a choice that would replace the deadening balance with a dynamic commitment to reality. The urgency of this attempt is in itself indicative of her dissatisfaction with the rules and patterns which she, at other times, seems to defend so fiercely; and her persistence in pressing Tobias for a decision shows that her primary concern is to bring Tobias back into an involvement with reality through an involvement with other people. In this endeavour of restoring Tobias to life and reality, Claire is Agnes' most formidable opponent. Since Tobias has been frightened into his withdrawal by the threat of nothingness, Agnes tries to bring him to an acceptance of that threat and to an affirmation of the value of being, his own as well as that of others. The manifestation of that affirmation is the ability and the courage to love and trust in the face of the threat of nothingness, and that is what Agnes tries to restore in Tobias. With Tobias, Agnes, Julia and Claire the familiar set of characters is complete. Faced with the uncontrollable threat of the negation of life's significance, the threat inherent in man's physical nature, Tobias has withdrawn from the physical. Claire has embraced it in despair and resignation; and Agnes has tried to evade it by restricting reality to the world contained by her rules. Julia, finally, has refused to acknowledge the threat of negation altogether. As in Albee's earlier plays, these responses exhaust the possibilities of responding inauthentically to the existential situation of modern man as Albee sees it.

(4)

A Delicate Balance thus closely resembles Albee's earlier plays in theme and technique. It now remains to be examined in which direction *A Delicate Balance* develops from the familiar basis. Albee's earlier plays all start with a collapse of the characters' established escape mechanisms and end with the destruction of these illusions and the affirmation of the possibility of authentic being either for all the characters, involved, as in *The Zoo Story* and *Who's Afraid of Virginia Woolf?* or at least for the main character, as in *Tiny Alice.* In *A Delicate Balance* the inauthentic responses of the characters are also challenged early in the play. When the guests carry the negation, the "plague," right into the delicately balanced lives of Agnes, Tobias, and Claire, the accustomed defenses are severely shaken.

The carriers of this disease are Harry and Edna as well as Julia. This is immediately suggested by their contest for the possession of Julia's former room, a room which is more than a convenient place to sleep. As Claire points out, Julia's room is "a special room with a night light or the door ajar so you can look down the hall from the bed and see that the Mommy's door is open" (92). What both Julia and her god-parents are looking for is therefore a psychological and religious protection from the encroaching terror of darkness. Since both Julia and the guests are after the same remedy, the implication is that their afflictions must be very similar. Both have been made homeless by the confrontation with nothingness. Julia has it pointed out to her several times that she is also "a visitor" or "a guest" (95). Thus one of Julia's functions in the play is to shed light on the nature of Harry and Edna's fright. For Julia has returned home also because she has been frightened and, as Claire suggests, so severely that this time she may be "home for good now...home for ever, back from the world" (92). Julia, Claire suggests, is now ready to join her aunt and her father in their total withdrawal from the risks of reality.

Julia's first three husbands had disappointed her with specific failings. These failings shock her, but she eventually absorbs them into her world-view. For the weaknesses of Phil, Charlie and Tom do not bring any change in Julia's view of reality. Doug confronts Julia with a deliberate, radical and sweeping denial of the value of life *per se.* With Claire he is against *everything* and would even welcome the annihilation of the world in a nuclear war. "HE IS OPPOSED! AND THAT IS ALL! TO EVERYTHING!" (76), the terrified Julia screams of her parents. It is this fundamental negation that makes, Claire suspect that Julia, if she resigns herself to it, will not have the courage for further involvement in the world. In the last scene, Julia joins Claire and Tobias, after a significant moment of hesitation, in their early morning drinking (165), a gesture of escape that implies that Claire's expectation may have been right.

But Julia's first reaction to the *Angst* that the confrontation with Doug has caused is to flee home. There she had once overcome that threat with the help of her father when Teddy's death brought her face to face with an equally radical negation. Now she calls on her father again for help, and the ensuing dialogue clearly implies the similarity in the situations:

Julia: (A terrified pause; runs from the room) Daddy? Daddy?

* * *

Agnes: (As if very little had happened) Why, I do believe

that's the first time she's called on her father in...since her childhood.

Claire: When she used to skin her knees?

Agnes: (Chuckles, but it covers something else) Yes, Teddy had just died, I think, and it was an...unreal time... (100-101).

It remains ambiguous whether Julia is helped by her father; for, her parents merely try to re-integrate Julia into the established family pattern in which Julia is the little girl who can be reassured by motherly care. When Julia arrives she is taken into the house not for her own sake as a uniquely valuable individual, but primarily on the strength of her place in the established routine. Her predictable returns—"each time that Julia comes, each clockwork time" (136)—have made her a part in an elaborate mechanism in which there are "quite a few people...whose lives are...moved—if not necessarily touched—by [her] actions" (95). In order not to disturb these predictable movements, Julia stays and plays her part: "YOU BELONG HERE!" (100-101). Tobias shouts at her and Agnes confirms that Julia is home because "it is where she belongs" (74).

But the security of this "belonging" is deceptive, and an illusion. Rather than reflect a spiritual and emotional commitment by her family, the "belonging" is based on chance and on the arbitrary convention that blood holds together a family even without love: "But blood binds us," Agnes remarks sarcastically, "Blood holds us together when we've no more...deep affection for ourselves than others." All of them, including Julia, are therefore in reality strangers to each other and Julia's "belonging" is ironic: it makes her on object possessed, a part of a stagnant and sterile world governed by mechanical routine.

Since this routine life has been constructed as a protection against the constant threat of nothingness, the confrontation with the negation embraced by Doug could destroy it. But nobody wants to hear about Doug's views and Julia fails twice in her talk about them (74-76, 88-89). Since her parents have failed to create in their marriage the love that would be an alternative to Doug's negation, they cannot reassure Julia of the possibility of love and life's value. They fail her again as they had failed her earlier when Tobias did not "tell her: 'Julia, go home to your husband and try it again!" (136). Such an advice would have required a faith that meaning is available in the acceptance of, and a dialogue with, the negative, a faith that Tobias and Agnes have not dared to achieve. Tobias has quickly withdrawn his timid offer of talking to Doug, of taking up the challenge of his views, so that Agnes can only try to put off Julia till "perhaps after dinner" when it will be time for the familiar adolescent ritual: "...the soothing recapitulation" of Julia's past and of her other marriages,

> "each one of them, the fear, the happiness, the sex, the stopping, the infidelities..." (109-110).

This progression from "fear" to "stopping" and "infidelities" is also a fairly accurate description of the marriage of Tobias and Agnes, and every one of Julia's failures therefore reminds them anew of the waste of their lives. "Each time, (I) see my own life passing," Agnes complains (110) for the sterility of Julia's life is a direct extension and reflection of her parents' sterility. They see themselves "repeated by those we bring into it all" (82). Agnes' hope for eventual motherhood for Julia is therefore a hope for an end to the barrenness of all their lives. But her wish to overcome their sterility remains futile; Tobias' withdrawal makes it impossible. When Julia brings home Doug's negativity she briefly raises the possibility that Tobias might come to grips with the reality, and thereby abandon his remoteness from life and confirm the individual significance of his daughter and wife: "Julia might, at the very least, come to think her father cares..." (32). But he dodges the challenge quickly when he retracts his offer to speak with Doug and misses his chance of creating meaning once again. Harry and Edna, however, reintroduce the threat of nothingness, of insignificance, and Agnes gets another chance to make Tobias face it.

Harry and Edna come to the house of their "best friends" to find shelter from a sudden, nameless terror. They are attacked by it one night when they fail to keep up the delicate balance of their lives, the protective routine that so far has preserved the lives of Agnes and Tobias. The country club activities, the perfunctory language study, Edna's needlepoint, all of a sudden fail to sustain their lives and they are left to face the terrifying emptiness of their existence:

> ...it was all very quiet, and we were all alone...and then....nothing happened, but.... WE GOT....FRIGHTENED... ... ...There was noting...but we were very scared.
>
> ... ...
>
> It was like being lost: very young again, with the dark, and lost. There was no...thing...to be frightened of, but.... WE WERE FRIGHTENED... AND THERE WAS NOTHING (45-47).

What Harry and Edna do not fully express, because they do not fully comprehend it, is that they are frightened *because* there is nothing. The final nothingness that is at the root of their anxiety is the inexorable approach of their physical annihilation. When Harry compares their experience to a child's terror at being lost in the dark, he is using the same imagery that Julian, in his dying speech in *Tiny Alice,* employs to express his fear of the nothingness of death. Edna herself suggests that it is indeed the fear of approaching death of at least old age that brings on the attack of anxiety. The reason why they are home, along and without the protective routine, is that "Harry's been having his shortness of breath again" (39), and they do not want to go to club because "Harry's been tired this whole week" (44). When their affliction is referred to later as "a disease" and "the plague," the suggestion that the threat of nothingness posed by death is at the basis of their anxiety gains greater force.

In referring to the affliction of Harry and Edna as a "Plague," Albee uses the same metaphor as Camus, in his novel of that title. For both authors, the "plague" signifies the indignity and meaninglessness of death, and it is the confrontation with this "plague" that they see as the source of the existential crisis in the life of every individual. The experience of anxiety, with which Harry and Edna infect the household of their friends, is analogous to the existential shock which Camus describes as the crucial experience in *The Myth of Sisyphus:*

> It happens that the stage sets collapse, Rising, streetcar, four hours in the office or the factory, meal, streetcar, four hours of work, meal, sleep and Monday, Tuesday, Wednesday, Thursday, Friday and Saturday according to the same rhythm—this path is easily followed most of the time. But one day the "why" arises and everything begins in that weariness tinged with amazement. "Begins"—this is important. Weariness comes at the end of the acts of a mechanical life, but at the same time it inaugurates the impulse of consciousness. It awakens consciousness and provokes what follows. What follows is the gradual return into the chain or it is the definitive awakening... ... . Mere "anxiety," as Heidegger says, is at the source of everything.[6]

Although the routine that dominates the lives of the characters in *A Delicate Balance* may be more upper-middle-class than that described by Camus, it is clear that Harry and Edna have experienced the same collapse of the stage-set for their mechanical lives.

When Harry and Edna turn to Agnes and Tobias, in this calamity, they upset the mechanical lives of their hosts, too, for the illusion that they are all very intimate, close friends is an important prop in the stage sets of both families. The source of agitation on the part of Agnes and Tobias over the invasion of Harry and Edna is the threat to this illusion rather any genuine concern for their well-being. There never has been such a concern between them: "...they're just passing through," Tobias insists and Claire adds: "As they have always been...all these years" (88). After the collapse of their stage-set Harry and Edna are faced with necessity of rebuilding their lives, and since they are so "very much like Agnes and Tobias" that "[their] lives are...the same," (166) they force same necessity on their hosts. Agnes and Tobias have a family and therefore more elaborate and diversified defenses, which is perhaps the reason why the fear has surfaced first for Harry and Edna. The fear has, however, always been present in the lives of both couples; "...now and then—you are frightened and you don't know why," (21) Claire reminds Tobias early in the play. Once this fear has surfaced for one of the couples, it replaces the same anxiety in the other couple, too.

Faced with this anxiety both couples have the choice of either going on to what Camus calls a "definitive awakening," *i.e.*, a life of defiant affirmation in spite of the negations inherent in being, or to "the gradual return into the chain," the mechanical object-existence out of which they have been shocked. As usual in Albee's plays, it is the man who has to make that choice: "we let our...men decide the moral issues" (132), Agnes tells Tobias. This does not necessarily imply male chauvinism on Albee's part. *A Delicate Balance,* like other Albee plays, merely exploits the two meanings of the word "man" as "male" and as "human being," Agnes' ironical pause before "man," indicated by the ellipsis, implies that Tobias, because he has not made the moral decisions, has not realized his manhood or is humanity.

Agnes therefore presses Tobias to make a choice: "what did you decide?" she keeps asking Tobais with increasing urgency (128, 130). The Harry and Edna arrival has already disturbed the balance of their lives enough to bring Tobias out of the asylum of "his own sweet room" back into their common bedroom. But this physical closeness needs to be complemented by the emotional and moral recommitment to life on Tobias' part. Without it he will remain the stranger Agnes and discovered in her room that night (213). Pushed by her, Tobias makes a sincere attempt to bring himself to such a commitment. "I tried...I was honest...didn't I?...Wasn't I?" (169), he afterwards appeals to the others and they agree. But he fails, nevertheless, because his withdrawal into the balanced life has become too firmly established. As he could respond to Julia's trouble only by assigning to her the familiar role of the adolescent daughter, he can likewise think of the present invasion only in terms of the balance.

Tobias' effort to remain detached is designed to avert a re-evaluation of himself and to preserve the sterile equilibrium of his life. He wants "to look at it all, reconstruct, with such...detachment,...play it out again, watch," (127), but that is merely a delaying tactic; for after he has "looked at everything, all of it" (133), he makes no decision or judgement. This is exactly the technique of evading the true problem that Claire had ridiculed earlier: "we live with our truth in the grassy bottom, and we examine all the interpretations of all the implications like we had a life for nothing else, for God's sake" (151). By thus continuing to think too precisely on the event, Tobias preserves the balance and lets the chance for living in a dynamic reality slip way.

Agnes, however, recognizes Tobias continued evasion. She sees that he is keeping Harry and Edna, in a familiar, safe pigeon-hole of his world by defining them and his responsibility toward them only in terms of their role as "best friends" and Agnes is resolved to block that evasion. She emphatically reminds Tobias that their visitors do not merely represent a limited practical problem but a confrontation that challenges the foundation of Tobias' whole life: "It is not Edna and Harry who have come to us—our friends—it is a disease." Tobias' restriction of Harry and Edna to their roles has been an example of the typical modern response to the "mortal illness" as Agnes described it: "...we merely isolate; we quarantine, we ostracize," and therefore his "reasoning in the cold, pure hours has been over the patient, and not the illness" (151).

Agnes therefore immediately directs the discussion away from the question of what to do about Harry and Edna to the question of the "mortal illness" that they have brought into the house: "The plague, my darling, the terror sitting in the room upstairs?...if we're not [immune]...(Shrugs) well why not be infected, why not die of it? We're bound to die of something...soon, or in a while" (162).

Although Tobias, catching the direction of Agnes' suggestion, makes a sincere effort to accept his friends and their disease into his life, he is only capable of offering the appearance of love and acceptance, the ritual that has been substituted for the reality. Tobias does plead with Harry to stay; thus he cannot reproach himself that he "might have tried longer," as after his failure to love his cat. But Tobias' invitation is only half-hearted. Rather than an unconditional affirmation of his friend's uniquely human worth, the invitation is a response conditioned by the same mechanical quantitative categories that have determined Tobias' life in the past. He begs Harry to stay because: "YOU'VE GOT

THE ENTREE, BUDDY! FORTY YEARS!" This shows that for Tobias the reality of their human encounter, for instance the reality that he does not want Harry and Edna, is irrelevant. He can respond to the situation only with reference to rights earned through habit, or accumulated through the investment of forty years of mechanical existence. "YOU'VE GOT THE RIGHT: DO YOU KNOW THE WORD? THE RIGHT"! Tobias shouts at Harry.... You've put nearly forty years in it, baby; so have I, and if it's nothing, I don't give a damn, you've got the right to be here, you've earned it" (162). Tobias desperately tries to preserve rather than to transcend the paralyzed balance. Tobias wanted Harry and Edna to stay because they had "the right"; Harry decides to leave because he feels that Agnes and Tobias wouldn't have "the right" if the situation were reversed (159). They both see the situation in the same mechanical, legalistic terms, in the categories that have structured their lives in the past. They cannot see in the acceptance of the other an occasion for the affirmation of man's freedom but only the necessities of quantities that are to be weighed against each other.

Thus Harry and Tobias miss the chance of giving their lives a new direction. Just when a new and free approach to life and interpersonal relationships is most necessary, they prove that they can see and think only in the terms and categories of their stagnant way of life. Even the confrontation with its vacuity no longer leads to a transformation. Their mutual confession that they do not really love and want each other, that there is no spiritual basis for their friendship, is simultaneously buffered by assurances and pleas for the preservation of the balance. As the visitors leave, all of them therefore return to the familiar routines of shared country-club activities, trips to town together, and the exchange of polite clichés and inconsequential socialities.

The crisis has proved the balance to be delicate and the protection it gives precarious and incomplete, for the nothingness, of all their lives has surfaced nevertheless. They know that their friendship as well as their marriages are without love, without genuine communication. "You must...coexist.... This is want is you have meant by friendship," Edna remarks and "Friendship," she points out, "is something like a marriage, is it not?" (117).

They sadly realize that they persist in the isolation of inanimate objects and are, in effect, living death-in-life existence. Agnes has seen this early in the play when she says of their mutual separation; "that is taken care of, and in life: the gradual...demise of intensity, the private preoccupation, the substitutions. We become allegorical, my darling Tobias, as we grow older. The individuality we hold so dearly sinks into crochet" (82). This judgement of their lives is confirmed in the end when Edna, speaking for all of them, remarks wistfully that "it's sad to know...the one body you've wrapped your arms around...the only skin you've known...is your own—and that it's dry...and not warm" (164), a remark reminiscent of Miss Alice's description of the Lawyer's body whose rubbery, non-sweating dryness reflects his failure to be alive in any but an animal way.

The confrontation with the essential deadness of their lives is something that the characters in Albee's earlier plays also experience. But for them the realization that they are not alive as humans becomes the basis for a deliverance from their life-in-death existence, an exorcism of their illusory reality and a break-through to an authentic existence. No such change occurs in *A Delicate Balance.* The confrontation with nothingness briefly disturbs the balance of their lives; the result, however, is not a new life of constant defiance of the threatening nothingness but what Camus calls the "return into the chain" of their mechanical, objective, inauthentic, lives.

(5)

Thus *A Delicate Balance* departs considerably from the cautiously hopeful endings of the previous plays. The possibility of a meaningful life, the play suggests, is also determined by time. Julian and Jerry could achieve a redemption even in the last minutes of their lives, and middle-age did not preclude the possibility of meaning for Peter or George and Martha. In *A Delicate Balance,* however, the characters have to realize the truth of Agnes' remark about time:

"TIME.
(*Pause. They look at her*)
Time happens, I suppose.
(*Pause. They still look*)

> To people. Everything becomes...too late finally. You know it's going on...up on the hill, you can see the dust, and hear the cries, and the steel ...but you wait; and time happens. When you do go, sword, shield...finally...there's nothing there...save rust; bones; and the wind" (164).

The scene that Agnes evokes it that of a wasteland but a wasteland that, like Eliot's, was once alive with struggling and perhaps sacrifice. The "hill" may even contain a suggestion of Calvary and the crowds of soldiers and spectators. In any case, there was life on the hill and the characters of *A Delicate Balance* have missed it irrevocably. While they have waited, watched from the sidelines, or examined all the possibilities without making a decision, the chance to create meaning for their lives has slipped away. They have failed to realize that meaning which is created by defying nothingness and confirming one's fellowman's worth in love. Now they must acknowledge that it is too late in their lives for this redemption. "*Le temps perdu,*" Agnes muses, "*...perdu* means lost, not merely...past" (124). Without the strength and the time to alter this reality, the characters find the pain of this truth too much to bear, and they return into the fragile protection of the delicate balance of their lives, even through they now realize that its elaborate forms and rules are empty.

The play ends with Agnes' return to her opening speech. Since none of the characters has been able to transcend his inauthenticity, the play must end where it started. Again we hear the long, convoluted, but carefully controlled sentence reflecting the complex balance maintained by Agnes. She expresses astonishment at the wonder of daylight, and taken by itself this might sound reminiscent of the hopeful note of the dawn rising on George and Martha at the end of *Who's Afraid of Virginia Woolf?* But although the sun rises on the last scene, Tobias suggests that no real "enlightenment," no true change has occurred. He advises that is would be more appropriate to "just think of it as very late at night," for the dawn does not appear after exorcism of the "demons" which they had let out in the preceding night, but after their regression. With daylight the demons have merely retreated to their lairs, ready to return any night: "I wonder if that's why we sleep at night, because the darkness still...frightens us?" (69) Agnes asks. There is, then, no reason to expect their eventual rejection of the illusory escapes and their acceptance of the anxiety of living.

On the contrary, the habit of retreating from reality seems to be more firmly entrenched than ever. Whereas *Virginia Woolf* ends with the clear rejection of escape (for the first time in the play Martha refuses a drink), *A Delicate Balance* ends with Agnes sadly accepting the fact that she has "*three* early morning drinkers now" (169). Tobias and Julia have both adopted Claire's despair and resignation. Thus the movement from despair to salvation, suggested by the play's expressly specified progression from Friday night to Sunday morning, is permanently arrested. Instead of achieving the triumph of the Easter Sunday, Albee's analogy argues, the characters find themselves trapped in a never ending Saturday night, the time of darkest despair. The hour is getting later, but the Sunday morning never comes. The ambiguous twilight between illusion and reality establishes itself as the governing metaphor of lives encapsulated in the modern existential anguish.

NOTES

1. Edward Albee, *A Delicate Balance* (New York: Atheneum, 1966) 164. All further references are to this edition.
2. Interview with Rutenberg, in Michael E. Rutenberg. *Edward Albee. Playwright in Protest* (New York: Arm Books, 1969) 250.
3. "The Lost Dimension in Religion," *Adventures of the Mind* (New York, 1960). Reprinted in *Thought in Prose*, eds., Richard Beal and Jacob Kong (Englewood Cliffs, N.J.: Prentice Hall, 1966) 576.
4. Tobias, of course, never finds the courage to accept death and the "benign indifference of the universe." Albert Camus, *The Stranger* (New York: Random-Vintage, 1946, 154]. He is therefore never reconciled with existence and is, in that respect, different from Camus' protagonist.
5. Albert Camus, *The Myth of Sisyphus and other Essays* (New York: Alfred A. Knopf (1955) 53.
6. Camus 10.

14

Edward Albee's *Tiny Alice*: A Reinterpretation

R. SARASWATHI

Of all the plays of Albee, *Tiny Alice*, is most clearly concerned with the metaphysical theme involving an examination of the difficulties underlying modern man's quest for a transcendental, meaningful self in a world of finitude and anxiety. The nature of the quest as well as its dramatic analysis is perspectivized in terms of illusion versus reality. The ostensible subject matter of *Tiny Alice* is the conspiracy of the four "nameless" characters against Julian. The Lawyer, the Cardinal, the Butler and Miss Alice are de-individualized and identified only by their function and together constitute a mandala of symbolic figures as in a Morality play. Even 'Miss Alice' turns out to be the title of a role she must "PLAY ACT"[1] rather than a real name. But Albee has not simply adopted a convention of the morality play, but has imparted to it a decpth, urgency and immediacy that compel attention to the contemporary predicament of Man. The characters have chosen to think of themselves, and of others, as objects or things. They exist not in accordance with the human way of being; they lack "authentic existence," as Heidegger would call it. "Instrument! is the ultimate "malediction" Julian hurls at the Lawyer" (178). He and his band are objects and tools having no purpose or significance—beyond the immediate function that defines them. This is a modern human condition which Paul Tillich has typically defined as "the loss of the dimension of depth," or the reduction of reality to the "horizontal dimension" where "religious" questions about the meaning and purpose of life, are not answered or even asked. Modern man, Paul Tillich claims, living only in the horizontal dimension, "transforms everything he encounters into a tool; and in doing so he himself becomes a tool. But if he asks, a tool for what, there is no answer."[2]

The Lawyer and his co-conspirators find themselves in exactly this position. They lack the courage to ask the "religious" questions and instead try to restrict reality to the material, and the understandable, to the recognizable fetishes of "horizontal dimension." "We must...represent, draw pictures, reduce or enlarge to...what we can understand,"[3] says Miss Alice. Their reality, and initially Julian's too, is therefore a "tiny" reality, reduced to human scale. It is in this that the significance of the title lies: A "Tiny Alice" implies the existence of a "great Alice" or a "full-size Alice" that would consist not only of the understandable, reduced, tiny reality of matter available to man through his senses, the reality of physical appearances, but also a dimension beyond the physical, a metaphysical dimension of mystery and meaning. Although this dimension may be withholding itself, it manifests itself as a reality through the pain that its absence causes in man. Since this mystery is part of the identity of Alice, an exact definition of the meaning of Alice must necessarily be impossible. The vagueness of Alice is therefore part of the play's meaning (just as the vagueness of Godot contributes to the total meaning of Beckett's play). Perhaps all that can be said is that Alice is the "totality of reality" of an "ultimate reality" which is by definition unreachable for man. The suggestion of "All is" that the name carries and the Greek meaning of Alice is truth—even if disallowed by Albee—support such an explanation.

Although 'Alice' defies complete understanding and definition, it is clear that a partial Tiny Alice can only be the illusion and perversion of Alice when it is mistaken for the complete Alice. Miss Alice reminds Julian that she is only representing Alice: "I am the illusion" (161). All members of her "team" are "representing" and, since they claim ultimate reality for the representation, they are perverting reality. The suggestion of perversion is reinforced by the homosexual connotations of "Tiny Alice,"[4] as well as by the repeated intimation of homosexual relations between the servants of "Tiny Alice," for the preversion of reality must also lead to a perversion of interpersonal relationships.

The totemic image of this tiny or perverted reality is the model of the castle dominating the stage. It is the model of a neat and orderly world, airtight and dustfree, according to Butler the model of a world that seems to be totally within the grasp of human understanding. As such, it is the concrete embodiment of those collapsed "moral, religious, political and social structures man has erected to 'illusion' himself of which Albee has once spoken in a different context.[5] Like those structures the model gives the inhabitants of Miss Alice's castle the illusion of belonging, of understanding their position in relation to the rest of reality. It becomes in effect a substitute or surrogate deity, an ideol to which Miss Alice prays and to whose worship Julian is to be converted or, if conversion proves impossible, sacrificed. For successful dissent would affirm the existence of a reality beyond that defined by the model. It would destroy the model's efficacy by testifying to an explainable reality, the mystery which Miss Alice and her companions have tried to evade. For, as becomes clear in the course of the play, the conspirators are converts themselves who at one time had accepted the reduced reality, the mouse in the model, which Julian, in the last act, refuses to accept. Their evasion can only temporarily be successful, however, for the model, their idol, is not a transcendent deity. It is part of the world experienced by man and therefore suffused with the same mystery that pervades all of reality. As the play develops the model which initially is perfectly understandable becomes increasingly enigmatic. It is endangered by the same fire of irrational passion that threatens Miss Alice's world of controllable accommodations. "The great presence" that Julian encounters in death manifests itself in both the castle and the model. The hope for the security of a world reduced to understandable dimensions proves illusory; the final reality remains a dimension of mystery.

Underlying the play is then the following definition of Realit: Alice/Reality = Tiny Alice/Physical appearance PLUS Mystery A/R = a/r+M. This allows Miss Alice and her followers four basic ways in which they can bring about the removal of the mysterious dimension and the reduction of reality to a "tiny" understandable version. Each possibility is exemplified by one of the conspirators:

1. One may ignore the distinction between Alice and Tiny Alice (Butler).

   If one does not, three more possibilities of reducing reality remain:

2. One may despair of reaching Alice and settle for Tiny Alice (Miss Alice).
3. One may declare that Alice is merely physical reality plus illusion, that the distinction is a mere failure of reason (Lawyer).
4. One may pretend to have supplied a dimension of meaning by ritual and thus to have realized Alice (Cardinal).

These are the four logically possible ways of evading the uncertainty of the metaphysical dimension proposed by the play. There remains, of course, a fifth possibility, exemplified by Julian: the possibility of genuinely trying to penetrate the mystery, to resolve the tension between man's limited vision of reality and his yearnings for a comprehensive understanding of himself and the world. Julian's attitude exhausts the number of logically possible responses to the problem posed by the play. Albee has thus achieved a comprehensiveness possible through the allegorical mode where the characters make sense only in terms of their typal or modal significance.

Butler's response to the problem of Alice/Reality is the simplest. He will not or cannot make a distinction between the world of physical appearance and a world of meaning. Appearance *is* reality for him. He appears to be the Butler and also *is* Butler. When Julian asks: "What does it mean if the pain...ebbs?" Butler flatly answers: "It means the agony is less" (174). A rose is and means a rose for him. The Lawyer's distinction between Alice and Miss Alice (102) (a pun:mis-Alice, *i.e.*, false Alice?) or Julian's corresponding awareness of the "Chasm between the nature of God and the use to which men put...God" are only artificial semantic distinctions for him (43). Compared to the pretensions and the duplicity of the other conspirators his lack of deceptiveness makes him attractive. But his unproblematic existence is not the result of a resolution of the tension between meaning and matter; it merely indicates his ignorance of the distinction. That this ignorance results finally in a betrayal of his humanity becomes clear in his Judas-Kiss in the last act.

Miss Alice offers another possible reaction to the mystery of Alice. Unlike Butler, she is painfully aware to the distinction between Alice and herself, but she offers no resolution. Paralyzed by the uncertainty of meaning, she merely vacillates. She knows that she is being used only to represent Alice but at no time admits that she does not understand the force that she is representing. So she continuously escapes into roles, tries, out different and contradictory symbols, nonc of which can satisfy her. She alternately an old crone or a Young Woman, the Lawyer's loyal accomplice or his fierce enemy hating him now for his impersonal, cold efficiency, the next moment for his sensitivity to emotional pain (74-75). Only once in the play is she revealed as what she really is: a lost vulnerable little girl trying to "obey what I have not understood" (90). This scene, in which Miss Alice confesses her metaphysical loneliness, with only the continuance of pain to assure her of her existence, anticipates the last scene where Julian finds himself in the same situation. He, too, becomes a lost child certain only of the fact suffering: "*Julian* (Rueful, laugh): Consciousness, then, is pain" (174), while Julian, however, keeps crying out for "God-Alice," Miss Alice despairs in the face of the uncertainty of meaning and, as soon as her physical survival is assured, returns to the relative, temporary security of the Lawyer and his dedication to matter and reason.

For the Lawyer, equally aware of the difference between Alice and Miss Alice, (or mis-Alice) has thrown himself, as he says, "into the arms of reason." Despairing of the uncertainty and inaccessibility of the mysterious dimension of reality he tries to destroy it by reducing everything to the rationally understandable. Thus he represents the third possible reaction to the problem of Alice, and as his "unsatisfied union (is) quite respectable these days" (12), probably the most common. His alliance with reason gives him power, power over matter, for matter can be manipulated according to reasonable laws. His profession is symbolic of his attempt to control the world by a set of rational rules. He is therefore interested in reducing everything to the rational and material. He tries to do this although he is aware, unlike Butler, that his vision is only a partial one, that reality is not all material and rational. His own irrational jealousy forces him to admit: "I, too: human," (97) so that Butler concludes: "You're acting like the man you wish you were" (97-98), *i.e.*, like a totally rational man, an impossibility.

But the insight into the insufficiency of his vision does not result in humble acceptance of a dimension for which the intellect does not account. It results in stead in proud defiance. With some justification, therefore, the Cardinal calls him "Satan" (17), for like Satan the Lawyer tries to destroy the significance from which he is excluded through his own pride. Thus he is the natural opponent of Julian who is overtly identified with Christ and whom the Lawyer tempts with the security of the model of the comprehensible material world represented by the model. At the same time, the Lawyer and his espousal of reason are reminiscent of Nick and his attempt at rational control of man is *Who's Afraid of Virginia Woolf*? Nick's name, suggesting "old Nick" Nikita Kruschev, and the allusion at Faust link Nick clearly to the devil, materialism and a world controlled by reason.

As reason can control only the reality of physical appearances, it makes every effort to eliminate or deny any other dimension of reality which would endanger this power. Only as long as Miss Alice remains the appearance of Alice, a symbol rather than individual essence, can the Lawyer retain his power over her. What worries him most is that appearance, the merely physical, could become reality in her relation to Julian. The fire that their non-rational attraction to each other kindles threatens the carefully constructed "model." It is threatened the because what is intended as a merely physical relationship begins to turn into a relationship in which each partner meets in the other a person of ultimate individual worth. What Butler calls an I—It relationship threatens to turn into an I—Thou relationship. Thus they threaten to overcome the objectification of the world of matter and to escape from the Lawyer's power.

But the escape fails. It fails because neither Julian nor Miss Alice is ready for it. Miss Alice is frightened by the "fire" that she has kindled in the neglected "chapel," the realm of spiritual significance in the model that "lacks resonance." She is frightened because the fire might deprive her of the relative security of her material existence, a danger that only Julian faces courageously in the end. But at this point, Julian actually saves her model and her world. His withdrawal from the world of matter makes it impossible for him to transcend it.

While the Lawyer tries to explain away the phenomenon of man's metaphysical aspirations by offering the rational explanation that all images of God are only man-made personifications of a non existent abstraction, the Cardinal uses a different method of bringing the religious impulse down to the level of human understanding. Ostensibly he believes in a dimension of meaning but in reality he has substituted the *appearance* of meaning for the *reality* of meaning. The appearance, the well-established ritual, is something that he can control and manipulate and therefore something that protects against the uncertainty and risks of questions about the meaning of these rituals. The irrational rules of the ritual offer the Cardinal and same kind of security that the rules of reason offer the Lawyer. Both use human rules to control what is beyond human control. The basic similarity between the two approaches is suggested in the last act when it is actually the Lawyer who conducts the ritual, the "ceremony of Alice" (149-51), which is to commit Julian to quarters in the model.

As the Lawyer has fallen into the arms of reason, the Cardinal "embraced the Church; and now we *know* our true father" (9) (Albee's emphasis). Faith, which includes doubt, has thus been replaced by knowledge, which excludes doubt, just as for the Lawyer "It is what we believe, therefore what we know.... Faith is knowledge" (159). This certainly becomes possible only because the Cardinal has also tried to reduce reality to the corporal world. The true father that he knows (in contrast to Julian's outcry for his "true father" to reveal Himself—is "an august and revered...body" (159) that he himself represents. It is therefore very much a part of the physical world of *carpe diem* instead of something transcendent. As the Lawyer implies, the Cardinal does not believe in God, he believes only in the Church (13).

Thus the Cardinal, like Dostoevsky's Grand Inquisitor, has betrayed the precarious but vital uncertainty of the faith for the comfortable pretense of knowledge. The ultimate aim of this betrayal is the same as that of the Lawyer's denial: to attain and exercise temporal power over men. In the last analysis, therefore, the Lawyer and the Cardinal and brothers in this perversion of their humanity, symbolized by their homosexual love-hate relationship. Their roles are inter-changeable: both talk gibberish to the birds and in Act II, Scene 2, the Lawyer "plays Cardinal" with Butler. And as the Lawyer is made aware of the insufficiency of his rationalistic-materialistic visions of reality by the irrational "human" forces within him, so the facade of the Cardinal's ritualistic security, his pretension to spiritual superiority over the Lawyer's materialism, is shattered when the prospect of more material power makes him abandon the symbol of his pretense: the majestic "we." With his lapse into the first person singular, reserved "for intimates...and equals" he admits that he and the Lawyer are indeed "of the same school..." "And in the same class" (6, 7).

While the kinship between the Cardinal and the Lawyer is the closest, the repeated intimations of sexual relationships among all the members of Miss Alice's "Family" suggest that they all have something in common: objectification, the imprisonment in matter. Faced with the unanswerable question of the meaning of reality they try to evade it by retreating into the temporary and temporal security of the "horizontal dimension." They thus correspond to the personifications of temporal, secular temptations of the traditional Morality play, who try to lure and intimidate Julian/Everyman into abandoning his faith which acknowledges that, beyond their offerings, "there is something. There is a *true* God" (104). It is this insistence that radically distinguishes Julian from the other characters. Although, he may yield to their temptations temporarily, he always remains aware that their alternatives are illusory situations, that they deepen rather than bridge man's alienation from the realm of meaning. Julian's insistence on something beyond the purposeless existence of matter, even if this can never be understood by man, constitutes the last of the five logically possible responses to the question of the nature of reality, and to the problem of man's relation to the transcendent.

Of these responses only Julian's response gives man a genuinely human reality. In the play this is immediately indicated by the fact that Julian is the only character with a name. He is furthermore the only one who does not share the air of unreality surrounding his opponents. They all "represent"; the Lawyer represents Miss Alice who in turn represents Tiny Alice or Alice "and that does not exist" for the Lawyer (105). The Cardinal represents the Church which in turn is supposed to represent God, who, for the Cardinal, is only the symbol for something he does not believe in. Therefore, since no ultimate reality exists for them, they are merely "agents, everyone of us," (154), or "surrogates" (156). What had been an attack on "the substitution of artificial for real values" in *The American Dream* has been developed into a much more radical exposure of the substitution of artificial, illusory "reality" for reality itself in *Tiny Alice*.[6]

Albee therefore has called *Tiny Alice* "a morality play about truth and illusion,"[7] a theme which is concretized most clearly in the protagonist of this morality play. Julian is "dedicated to the reality of things, rather than their appearance" (132), and his problem is how to achieve this reality or truth in a world dominated by the unreality of the Cardinal and the Lawyer. It is a world that the Lawyer describes accurately as "the great machinery" (142), a world in which "we all serve" according to the laws of cause, effect and probability, where reality and truth are only relative and provisional. The only way Julian can hope to achieve reality in such a world is by revolting against it. But this revolt is not possible in retreat from the world of matter but only through active involvement in it. Albee's praise of Christ as "one of the most exciting revolutionaries"[8] suggests that Julian's identification with Christ in the last act marks the fulfilment of his revolution.

When the play opens, Julian has withdrawn from the world of matter rather than rebelling against it. The Lawyer speaks of him as one of the "removed people" (31) and Miss Alice calls him "little recluse" (66). Enraged by the "chasm between the nature of God and the use to which men put...God" (43) by man's worshipping of the human symbol instead of the essence, Julian has rejected all physicality to the degree that he can no longer communicate with a human being, a renunciation symbolized by his voluntary celibacy, as well as his dreams of martyrdom and immortality. As the characters in *The American Dream* substituted the American Dream for the reality of living, Julian has substituted the dream of an other worldly life for "real" living. Thus his reality is, at the very beginning of the play, a reduced, Tiny reality devoid of fullness of an authentically human existence. In the end, he has to fear that he may have "accepted half, for nothing" (160). Achieving full reality, *i.e.* realizing "all," therefore means for Julian accepting the other half, the reality of his imperfect physical nature, not instead of his spiritual dimension (as the conspirators want him to), but in addition to it. This acceptance is an act of courage of which he has not been capable so far.

When the play opens, Julian is timid. He has been intimidated by the world around (him) (59), into losing his faith, (an intimidation which the Lawyer tries to repeat) and he has actually tried to flee into an asylum.[9] But the asylum has offered no security from the meaningless and therefore humanly unreal reality of matter. Divided into orderly section the asylum corresponds to the exactly fashioned, dust tight model of the castle representing Miss Alice's residence, "the entire...establishment" (53), the world, and the whole society, which has become oblivious to the question of meaning. This suggestion that the asylum is actually the modern world is reinforced when the Lawyer says that Julian comes "from the heartland of the country, from the asylums" (138), thus equating the two. It appears therefore that the asylum is not a retreat from "the world" but rather a retreat into the world. For, with the loss of his faith and the retreat to the asylum, Julian experiences the same alienation and the same loss of the sense of reality from which the residents of Miss Alice's castle suffer: "I...shriveled into myself; a glass dome...descended, and I went out of reach, unreachable, finally unreaching, in this paralysis of sorts (43). Thus his flight from the precariousness of faith does not result in a renewed sense of security. On the contrary; he "began...to hallucinate, and to withdraw," to feel "that (his) grasp on reality was...tenuous—occasionally" (58). Miss Alice points out the similarity between Julian's life in the asylum and life in the castle, suggesting that he is only "describing what passes for sanity" (60) in her world but might very well be the peculiar madness caused by matter: "Might not vast wealth, the insulation of it, make one quite mad?" (180).

The loss of his sense of reality is parallel to his loss of freedom, in the regimentation of the regulated asylum life. But the loss of freedom is a more fundamental one. Julian becomes an object like the others, a driven instrument, so that as intimate a human contact as the physical *contact* is not a matter of conscious choice but the result of blind driving forces and mutually contradictory illusions which lead to further self-deception and death. It is the absence of conscious choice, the fact that his encounter with the woman in the asylum is merely a matter of one object meeting another object, that gives the experience its feeling of unreality so that neither Julian nor the audience sharing his point of view can be sure it has happened. It is a little consequence whether a real female inmate is hallucinated that she is the Virgin Mary pregnant with the son of God, or it is Julian who has the hallucination of being a divine impregnator. Either case would exemplify the desperate attempt of asylum inmates to make the asylum bearable by denying their human mortality and escaping into an illusion of divinity.

When Julian leaves the asylum, he has not dealt with the challenge of the world of matter, the Lawyer's world that has intimidated him. He has settled for a compromise, "persuaded...that some (hallucination) was inevitable and a portion of that—even desirable (64). Instead of trying to resolve the conflicting claims of the physical and the metaphysical, he tries to live in a split reality. He has granted men the "blasphemy" of "God as older brother, scout leader," which has "let them, but cannot accept" (103-104). A fusion of the two concepts, a union that would be more than the sum of its parts, is as yet unthinkable for him because it would not meet his quest for purity and perfection. While the Lawyer demands and expects no ideals from anybody, including himself, Julian will not allow himself his human imperfection. He attempts to be perfect, be it in serving, or in "purity," or in his knowledge of God. What he does not realize is that the rejection of human imperfection, of his physical limitations, is at the same time a rejection of his human reality. His desire to serve, to be used, makes him as much a tool as Miss Alice and her accomplices.

Thus, although he professes the utmost humility, Julian is actually guilty of pride in his condescension toward mankind and their delusions. Miss Alice reminds him of the pride of many martyrs who court death in order to eradicate the greatest imperfections of humans: their physical morality. Julian is guilty of the same pride in rejecting his physicality, especially his sexuality, and in substituting for it a fantasy about immortality in martyrdom. In the seduction scene this fantasy disintegrates, and what is sacrificed to "Alice" is his vision of himself as the divine Christ:

> "A wound in me, the warm dark flow...runs down my belly...to...bathing my groin (Cleansing him of his sexuality/physicality; also proof of divinity). You see? I have come...bloodstained and worthy" (122).

In his submission to Miss Alice's seduction, Julian's physicality is affirmed; he becomes a man in a double sense. But his acceptance is only partial; he accepts his physicality, but not its limitations: death and the separation from meaning. The overtones of death in the reduction scene are all outside of Julian's consciousness: Miss Alice's great black wings, pointing to the all engulfing "great presence" of the end (also reminiscent of the physically beautiful Angel of Death in *The Sandbox*), the repeated references to Julian's "sacrifice" and his final "sort of dying cry" as he moves into the arms of Miss Alice (124). The seduction scene thus takes a middle position between the illusory encounter in the seduction scene, where hallucinations had totally replaced reality, and the death scene where illusion is totally destroyed by reality.

In the Third Act Julian gradually and reluctantly comes to accept the fact that his death, his own non-being, is a condition of his being and therefore part of the definition of his humanity. By yielding to the physical temptation of Miss Alice, he has been "pushed...over, back to the asylums" (103), the world of matter, as Butler has predicted. But this time, he turns to matter not as an escape from the quest for a human reality but in search of it. He successfully resists the attempt to intimidate him, to push him "over...to the (Lawyer's) Truth" that since matter has no meaning, life has no meaning either.

After his marriage to Miss Alice, Julian again experiences the loneliness and isolation which he had felt in the asylum and which the other characters experience constantly. "I was...one moment married, flooded with white, and...then...the next, alone. Quite alone, in the...echoes" (126). It is an isolation that anticipates the utter loneliness of his death. Julian shares this feeling of alienation with the other characters. Confronted with his isolation, he tries momentarily to return to his former escape mechanism; he tries to flee to the asylum again. But the Lawyer has seen him escape from the asylum before and is resolved to force Julian to make an irreversible decision. The Lawyer hopes that death, the ultimate proof of his physical nature, will convince Julian that matter is the only reality the meaninglessness of which he must partake. But contrary to his expectations, Julian finds in his death the strength to transcend mere physical being. As in the case of Jerry and Peter in *The Zoo Story* and George and Martha in *Who's Afraid of Virginia Woolf?* the experience of death brings about an authentically human reality for Julian. As in the asylum he again meets "the Virgin Mary," he and Miss Alice "create something of a pieta" (167). But this time there is no doubt in his mind as to the reality of the situation.

Although he shares the feeling of alienation with the other characters, Julian does not share their loss of freedom, which makes him radically different from them. His refusal to accept the meaninglessness of matter is a manifestation of that freedom. Again and again, he violently rejects the Lawyer's tiny model of reality where God is only a man-made abstraction, "the mouse, the toy. And that does not exist...." Although Miss Alice, Butler, the Cardinal and the Lawyer urge him to accept that "THREE IS NOTHING THERE!" (158) and try to convince him that there "is no choice here Julian... No choice at all," Julian insists on making a choice; "I...choose...*not* to accept" (161-162).[10]

This decision "not to accept" and Julian's last words, "I accept thee, Alice, for thou art come to me. God, Alice...I accept thy will" (184) seem baffling and contradictory only if one fails to realize that the Lawyer's "Truth," unacceptable to Julian, is the tiny Alice of the model, while the Alice that he does accept is the "great presence," an Alice that resides also in the model, of course, but only because it pervades and surpasses everything. What he accepts then is a notion of Alice/God as unlimited mysterious being.

This development toward a view that subsumes and transcends the Lawyer's materialism as well as Julian's earlier rejection of the physical is prepared by Julian's reaction to his seduction and marriage: he experiences *it not as a conversion* to belief in Miss Alice's view of the world, but as an *addition* to his own world view. The result of Julian's submission is not the replacing of one illusion by another, not a mere reversal of his earlier rejection of physicality, but a generically different concept of himself and of reality. He experiences a mystery, the "coming together of disparates" (155), "not losing God's light, joining it with my new [in a feeling] of EXPANSION..." (135). These images of expansion and addition contrast markedly with the tininess of the Lawyer's mouse-god and the images of enclosure, imprisonment, and limitation that define the world of Miss Alice's castle and the asylum.

Julian's marriage thus marks his transcendence of his former limited view of reality into something like a "sacramental" vision, where "God," a reality beyond the physical, becomes available in the material world, "that joy I thought available only through martyrdom" (135). Albee himself confirmed the Last Supper allusion in the "Ceremony of Alice," but the parallel is of course an ironic one: while the ceremony does mark the "coming together of disparates," Julian is at this point not the equivalent of Christ because he does not see that the ceremony is his "Last Supper." He still entertains the illusion that there is a "clear plan [in] that which we call change" (151). It is the illusion that the meaning of life, that God, though at times difficult to understand, will explain himself eventually, so that man will know instead of having to believe.

Only death can purge away this last illusion and bring Julian the complete humility that must precede the unconditional acceptance of reality as a mystery. Death is of course the Lawyer's most powerful argument to convince Julian of his material nature and its meaninglessness. To affirm meaning and dignity while accepting this radical denial of being is the ultimate test of Julian's courage. Confronted with death, Julian admits that he is alone in the attic, that everything that happens to him is inexplicable and takes upon himself the anguish of "I DO NOT UNDERSTAND, OH LORD, MY GOD, WHAT THOU WILT HAVE OF ME!" (181). Thus he experiences, for the first time without protective illusions, the mystery, darkness of the ultimate reality of man, and by accepting it *i.e.*, by relinquishing his hopes and efforts of knowing God and reality, he partakes of this ultimate reality and thus "becomes real." In Heidegger's terms, Julian's "authentic existence" can be said to result from his acceptance of the darkness of death and of the anxiety that accompanies it.

It is the same acceptance that the Speaker of Eliot's "East Coker" in *Four Quarters* tries to achieve when he sees the vanity of man's pretensions:

> I said to my soul, be still, and let the dark come upon you which shall be the darkness of God. As, in a theatre,
>
> The lights are extinguished, for the scene to be changed with a hollow rumble of wings, with a movement of darkness on darkness,
>
> ... ...
>
> I said to my soul, be still, and wait without hope
> For hope would be hope for the wrong thing; wait without love
> For love would be love of the wrong thing; there is yet faith
> But the faith and the love and the hope are all in the waiting
> Wait without thought, for you are not ready for thought
> So, the darkness shall be the light, and the stillness the dancing.[11]

Both Eliot and Albee use the image of the theatre to give form to the sense of the unreality of the corporeal world where the only certainty available is the certainty of death, and for both writers the transcendence of this negation of being is only possible after it has been accepted in humility. This humility is a long way from the pride that led Julian to dream of being like God, like Christ appearing to the disciples after the Resurrection (122). In his dying speech, Julian is again connected with Christ, and he dies in the position of a crucifixion, somewhat like John Loving in O'Neill's *Days Without End*. But this time all the references are to Christ's humanity; to his suffering, to his doubting, to his dying. This does not mean, however, that "Julian dies finally...accepting a martyrdom which has nothing to do with Christ."[12] For the significance of Christ in this context is exactly his radical acceptance of humanity. This means, above all, the acceptance of death and the separation from God expressed in the outcry repeated by Julian: "MY GOD, WHY HAST THOU FORSAKEN ME?" (183). With this outcry Julian, like Christ, realizes, in both senses of the word, the essence of his humanity, and it is immediately after this outcry that "a great presence" manifests itself. For in realizing the essential nature of all humanity and becoming one with it, Julian transcends his limited individual existence. Ursula Brumm's observation on the many Christ figures in contemporary American fiction applies also to Julian: they "are shown to fulfill the passion of Christ, while Christ signifies not only his own individual fate but that of all humanity."[13] Thus is becoming like Christ, Julian also becomes Everyman.[14]

(3)

The question whether the "great presence" at the end of *Tiny Alice* is real or is just another of Julian's illusions has engaged critical attention. A good many critics do not seem to have responded fully to the significance of the play's ending. For the play does not, and indeed must not, try to answer this question because Julian has at this point overcome the dimension of *Tiny Alice* where alone such a question is possible. His vision of "God, Alice" marks his transcendence of the "horizontal dimension" in which God is considered as an object among objects subject to a scientific inquiry into His physical existence. The great presence is real enough for Julian and constitutes a reality that cannot be ignored by others either. Gabriel Marcel has spoken of "a desire for the unconditional which is the requirement and the very mark of the Absolute in us," and has claimed that "to bear witness is to contribute to the growth or coming of that for which one testifies.[15] In the last scene of *Tiny Alice*, Julian's unfailing desire for the unconditional "bears witness" and thus "contributes to the growth of the Absolute" in himself. "Once Julian accepts what does not exist (*i.e.* physically), his concept (his faith) exists for him," Albee commented on *Tiny Alice*.[16]

Thus the protagonist emerges victorious from the battle with the secular and temporal forces bent on destroying his soul, on denying a metaphysical reality to his existence. This victory is won because the protagonist preserves his faith in a spiritual reality even through the confrontation with death. In the light of this victory his trials become steps toward tragic self-transcendence instead of remaining acts of absurd senseless suffering. Julian's life can therefore be said to have gained a dimension of meaning created by Julian in the confrontation with meaninglessness. It is not a supernatural dimension, separate from and above the human dimension, but one available, and available only in and through this life.

But although Julian's life gains a dimension of meaning, his victory is won on a completely personal and subjective level. The answer that he generates is not an abstract, general answer on which everyone can rely. For although Julian "bears witness," his testimony to a spiritual dimension is not generic or universal capable of being shared or corroborated by others. His victory is won in loneliness and therefore must remain ambiguous. In this respect *Tiny Alice* moves away from the two plays that preceded it. In *The Zoo Story* and *Who's Afraid of Virginia Woolf*? the characters find a dimension of meaning in an act of mutual confirmation. With that act the significance of their lives is no longer merely subjective since at least one other individual has accepted them as uniquely valuable. No such support comes forth for Julian who must create the meaning of his life *Sola fide*; and an inevitable consequence of this reduction to faith alone is the prevalence of a large measure of doubt and ambiguity.

Albee, like many contemporary theologians, insists that transcendence is only available in and through this world. In a discussion of *Tiny Alice* Albee has once called himself a Christian while at the same time asserting: "Why we are here is an impenetrable question."[17] In the light of his play these claims can only be reconciled if one assumes an interpretation of Christianity that remains secret to a great extent. Instead of manifesting itself in overtly religious symbols and rituals in all the paraphernalia of religion, it reveals itself in active, humble and courageous participation in the world. *Tiny Alice*, in projecting this variety of religious experience, dramatises an epiphemic response to the manechaen subject between illusion and reality.

NOTES

1. Edward Albee, *Tiny Alice* (New York, Pocket Books, 1966) 75. All further references are to this edition.
2. "The Lost Dimension in Religion," *Adventures of the Mind* (New York: 1960). Reprinted in *Thought in Prose*, eds., Richard Beal and Jacob Kong (Englewood Cliffs, N.J.: Prentice Hall, 1966) 574.
3. Albee 155.
4. Ruby Coh, "*Tiny Alice* is Homosexual Slang for a Tight Anus *Edward Albee*" (Minneapolis: U. of Minn. P, 1969) 29.
5. "Which Theatre is the Absurd One?" *New York Times Magazine* 25 Feb. 1965: 30, 31, 64, 66.
6. Sam Zolotow quotes from Albee's prospectus to the backers of *Tiny Alice*: "*Tiny Alice* is essentially an attack on modern institutions, modern materialism and the illusory nature of modern life." "Box Office Que for *Tiny Alice*," *New York Times* 31 Dec. 1964: 14.
7. Interview in *News Week* 4 Jan. 1965: 51.
8. "Tiny Alice mystifies Albee, too" *New York Times* 21 Jan. 1965: 22.
9. Cf. the use of the "madness" and "asylum" metaphors in *Virginia Woolf*? and *A Delicate Balance* to suggest modern man's failure to exist in an authentically human way.
10. A striking parallel to Melville's "Bartleby, the Scriviner" which Albee at one time converted into an Opera libretlo.
11. *The Complete Poems and Plays 1909-1950* (New York: Harcourt, Brace and World, 1962) 126-27.
12. C.W.E Bigsby, *Edward Albee* (Edinburgh: Oliver and Boyd, 1970) 86.
13. "The Figure of Christ in American Literature," *Partisan Review* 24 (1957): 403-13, 410.

14. Edward Albee, "Brother Julian is in the same position as the Audience," quoted in "Broadway: A Tale within a Tail," *Time* 15 Jan., 1965) 68.
15. *Homo Viator* (Chicago! Regnery, 1951) 135, 213.
16. "Tiny Alice Mystifies Albee, too," 22. The parenthetical identification of "his concept" as "faith" is Albee's.
17. "Tiny Alice Mystifies Albee, too," 22.

15

The Dramatic Art of Tennessee Williams with Reference to Lyrical Sublime Elements in his Plays: *The Glass Menagerie* and *A Streetcar Named Desire*

ABHA SHARMA

Tennessee Williams (1911-1983), the distinguished American writer, is considered by many to be the nation's finest dramatist on the post World War II era. Williams wrote about 30 full-length plays, some 35 short plays, an equal number of short stories, two volumes of poetry, and a volume of essays. He also wrote two novels—*The Roman Spring of Mrs. Stone* (1950); and *Moise and the World of Reasons* (1975). Some 15 of his works were made into films, and two of his plays have served as librettos for operas. His output though prolific, may be uneven, but the overall quality of Williams' works has assured him a lasting place in American drama.

His dramatic world is replete with emotionally charged characters, who while being compassionate and sensitive to the demands and challenges of the surrounding milieu get psychically wounded at different levels of human experience. Because of the life-long estrangement sustaining between his father and mother as well as on account of his loving sister remaining invalid as also unmarried, his creative expression got coloured with his personal suffering. He remained sour throughout his life on account of sister's unenviable condition. His sister's name being Rose Williams, "rose" remained as a recurring symbol in his writings. In fact, one of his plays, *The Rose Tattoo* as title is a way of commemorating his love for sister. This lingering association of his sister, Rose in his creativity contributed substantially in making him draw his female characters with understanding and sympathy. Since it coloured his feeling pattern, it naturally got expressed in a lyrical fashion. After all, a sizable number of great lyrics in the world have been composed to memorialise the image of lovingly tender women. The image of his sister haunts him in his first major play, *The Glass Menagerie* (1944) expressed in real identity whereas in *A Streetcar Named Desire* (1947), his sister's image is symbolised at a distance withal true in identity, though more complicated.

In *The Glass Menagerie*, Williams drew on his life in St. Louis to create a throbbingly intimate picture of a mother who lives on memories of her romanticized Southern past and on hopes for the future of her children, especially for the painfully shy Laura (real life sister, Rose), who seeks refuge from reality in her menagerie of glass animals.

The Glass Menagerie is essentially a "Memory Play" in which Tom Wingfield (Tennessee William, in real life) recalls his life in St. Louis with his mother Amanda, a former Southern belle deserted by her husband, and his sister Laura, a shy, slightly crippled girl. Amanda attempts to keep her children up to the social level to which she aspires. She sells magazine subscriptions by telephone, tries to make her daughter learn stenography in order to be economically independent, and nags Tom Wingfield to bring 'gentleman callers' that is, prospective bridegrooms, for purpose of establishing marital ties with his crippled, yet extra-sensitive sister. To pacify his mother, he invites Jim O'Connor to dinner. Amanda is so excited over the prospect of a gentleman caller that she practically redecorates the apartment in preparation.

When Mr. O'Connor, a gentleman caller, arrives, he proves to be everything Amanda could have desired: he is attractive, personable, and ambitious. He also turns out to be a former high school classmate of Laura's, someone she has quietly pined over for six years. After dinner, he and Laura talk, play, music and even dance. Their dancing is awkward and they stumble into her animal collection, breaking the horn from a glass unicorn. It has its own repercussions on the mood of Jim and Laura. Gaiety between the boy and the girl turns into tenderness, though Laura gets astir a little about her future. The breaking of a unicorn horn brought a passing foreboding in her. All the same what began as Jim's attempt to build Laura's confidence becomes an expression of genuine admiration, ending in a kiss.

Apologizing, Jim makes a clean breast by explaining that he cannot call Laura again because he is engaged to be married. His rather abrupt departure is followed by Amanda's railing at Tom for the cruel joke he has played on his family. Amanda is in consternation; for her cherished desire to get her daughter Laura settled in a marriage has come to nothing. Frustrated and angry at the causing remarks of her mother, he decides to leave the house. In the final lyrical monologue, it is revealed that soon after the fateful dinner he left his mother and sister to begin life afresh. Tom's mental perturbation is similar to Lawrence's Paul Morel in *Sons and Lovers*, to some extent.

Now, as the bare outline of *The Glass Menagerie* is already known, it is possible to elaborate on the thematic argument of this research article. It is concerned with the lyrical and sublime aspect of William's dramatic art. It is strikingly so because this distinguished dramatist wrote out of his deeply felt experience. "My chief aim in playwriting is the creation of character. I have always had a deep feeling for the mystery of life, and essentially, my plays have been an effort to explore the beauty and meaning in the confusion of living". In this respect, Williams stressed the importance of autobiographical art. "All work is autobiographical if it is serious. Everything a writer produces is sort of inner history transposed into another time.... It is simply not in my nature, as a dramatist, to work without humour no matter how dangerous may be the fates and situations of the protagonists."[1]

By and large, sublimity of thought and lyricism of expression are interwoven with a dramatist's creativity: at what altitude he expresses life and reality. It depends upon the multi-dimensional flow and movement of diction. Aristotle underscored the importance of diction: "By diction I mean...the expressive use of words, and this has the same force in verse and in prose. Of the remaining elements, the music is the most important of pleasurable additions to the play.[2] According to Longinus, sublimity in a piece of literature springs from the grand conception of thought and nobility of emotions.[3] In the light of these two eminent observations, it is possible to say that Tennessee Williams had the adequate force of subjectivity to make his dramatic art lyrical and sublime, as it is borne out by the undernoted excerpts taken from his play, *The Glass Menagerie*: Right at the beginning of the play, the narrator, Tom Wingfield reminds the audience and the readers that the great American depression of the 1930s affected all sections of Americans in different ways; and necessarily, it made a lasting impact on the narrator and his family. As *The Glass Menagerie* is a memory play, Tennessee Williams records his impression of the economic debacle of the 1930s in a spirit of comprehensive assessment of the frightful event.

Tom Wingfield in this prefatory remarks to the play says that he has things up his sleeves, but he is the opposite of a stage magician:

> He gives you illusion, the appearance of truth. I give you truth in the pleasant disguise of illusion.
>
> To begin with, I turn back time. I reverse it to that quaint period, the thirties, when the huge middle class of America was matriculating in a school for the blind. Their eyes had failed them, or they had failed their eyes, and so they were having their fingers pressed forcibly down on the fiery Braille alphabet of a dissolving economy.
>
> In Spain there was a revolution. Here there was only shouting and confusion. In Spain there was *Guernica*.[4] Here there were disturbances of labor, sometimes pretty violent, in otherwise peaceful cities such as Chicago, Cleveland, Saint Louis.... This is the social background of the play. The play is memory.[5]

This extract is in prose; but it has the movement of finely composed lyric. An epoch in which a great economic disaster took place is imaged vividly to show that by and large even men of commerce and industry were nonplussed. Their helpless condition was like the blind men were groping in the dark, for 'their fingers (were) pressed forcibly down on the fiery/Braille alphabet of a dissolving economy. From the standpoint of the figurative use of language, the expression 'the fiery Braille Alphabet' is meaningfully linked to a dissolving economy. As is the case with the first class poets who compose their lyrics in verse on the strength of inner cohesiveness and flow, so it is in Williams' prose rendering of the dissolving American economy caught in the vortex of the great depression in the 1930s.

The last paragraph in the extract is equally revealing; for Tennessee Williams in covering the global impact of the economic depression was different from country to country. If in Spain, there was violence and civil war, in America, there were labour disturbances in different industrial towns. Nonetheless, the economic depression was world shaking. The dramatist shows not only this acumen in understanding the American confusion during the economic depression and thereafter, but he also takes into account the depressive effect on the psyche of American people, as a result of the economic upheaval. At that time, American people by and large were on their tenter-hooks.

Williams besides being a conscientious dramatist was also a poet as well as a fiction writer with the added advantage of being a critic. 'A poet trapped in a mundane existence, he works days in a shoe factory and spends his evenings writing or going to the movies. His sister Laura, whose crippled leg is symbolic of her psychic deformity, is so painfully shy that she avoids reality almost altogether, creating her world through playing old phonograph records and tending a collection of glass animals—which is the basis of the title of the play, *The Glass Menagerie.* Their mother, Amanda combines obsession with her romanticised Southern debutante past and a fierce determination to survive a grim present.'[6]

This extract is largely autobiographical; and it depicts the painful situation in which Tom Williams (or Tennessee Williams) found himself in his childhood period. Apart from the early life economic difficulties, arising partly out of economic depression and partly out of temperamental estrangement of one parent to another, the life for Amanda as well for Tom Wingfield had become really grim. It made the narrator Tom all the more saddened. It makes Tom to say sorrowfully about his father in the preface to the play. 'There is a fifth character in the play who does not appear except in this larger-than-life-size photograph over the mantel. This is our father who left us a long time ago. He was a telephone man who fell in love with long distances.... The last we heard of him was a picture postcard from Mazatlam, on the Pacific coast of Mexico, containing message of two words: 'Hello—Goodbye! and no address.'[7] This is how a sensitive son, with a pinch of irony, sums up his attitude towards his father who betrays his lack of personal feeling towards his family.

In order to sustain dramatic interest among those who view the or read the play, Williams also uses the device of legend or motto—as part of the drama spectacle, which Aristotle has also recognised in his *Poetics*. By using legend device on screen: *Ou sont les neiges d'antean'* or 'Where are the snows of bygone years'[8] Tom Wingfield heightens the dilemma and agony of his mother, Amanda Wingfield. With one foot in the past, and one in the present, Amanda as woman and mother acquire well in terms of the dialogue which shows how deeply and minutely she was solicitous of the well being of her son, Tom:

Amanda: (to her son) Honey, don't push with your fingers. If you have to push with something the thing to push with is a crust of bread, and chew-chew: Animals have secretions in their stomachs which enable them to digest food without mastication, but human beings are supposed to chew their food before they swallow it down. Eat food leisurely, so and really enjoy it. A well-cooked meal has lots of delicate flavors that have to be held in the mouth for appreciation. So chew your food and give your salivary glands a chance to function.

(*Tom deliberately lays his imaginary fork down and pushes his chair back from the table.*)

Tom: I haven't enjoyed one bite of this dinner because of your constant directions how to eat it. It's you that make me rush through meals with your hawk like attention to every bite I take. Sickening—spoils my appetite—all this

	discussion—animals' secretion—salivary glands—mastication.
Amanda:	(lightly) Temperament like a Metropolitan star. (*Tom rises and walks toward the living room.*) You're not excused from the table.[9]

It is a scene centered around dinner table and the living room. The atmosphere is homely with mother trying to introduce in her son the basic truth about the gustatory approach for body-growth. As her son takes exception to mother's advice, Amanda attempts to tickle Tom's vanity, 'Temperament like a Metropolitan Star': She says so in good humour and affection. Williams captures the homely atmosphere right at the beginning of the play to set the pace for the dramatic plot in terms of emotive intensity of a mother, estranged from her husband, trying to pace up the future prospects of her son and crippled daughter as much as she could out of her motherly concern and affection. Here, it is worthwhile to observe that wherever there is the presence of affectionate feelings, one's mental attitude is attuned to appreciate the silent ecstasy of life. Then, the human experience gets lyrical and sublimatory. This is how Tennessee Williams builds up his dramatic text.

In continuity of the extract cited earlier, the remaining part of the dialogue runs as under:

Tom:	I'm getting a cigarette.
Amanda:	You smoke too much.
	(*Laura rises*).
Laura:	I'll bring in the blanc mange.
	(*Tom remains standing with his cigarettes by the portiers.*)
Amanda:	(*rising*) No, sister, no sister—you be the lady this time and I'll be the darky.
Laura:	I'm already up.
Amanda:	Resume your seat, little sister—I want you to stay fresh and pretty—for gentlemen callers.

Laura: (*Sitting down*) I'm not expecting any gentlemen callers.

Amanda: (*Crossing out the kitchenette, airly*) Sometimes they come when they are least expected. Why I remember one Sunday afternoon in Blue Mountain.

(*She enters the kitchenette.*)

Tom: I know what's coming.

Laura: Yes. But let her tell it.

Tom: Again?

Laura: She loves to tell it?

(*Amanda returns with a bowl of desert.*)[10]

From this part of the dialogue, to be continued a shortwhile here after, it would be noticed that Amanda as mother is humourous enough to see that her son (Tom) and daughter (Laura) do not show intransigence to her affection-filled prodding, from time to time, to improve their conduct, mainly for the sake of their better future. Knowing that her daughter, Laura was very much shy; and as such was not very much forthcoming towards her marriage. Williams has very intelligently defused the frayed temper of Tom when he took exception to his mother's suggestion of eating food slowly, with due mastication. Amanda also changes her tactic, by addressing her daughter, Laura as sister, saying 'you be the lady this time and I'll be the darky (which means, her daughter Laura) would be the mistress of the house for a while and the mother would be playing the role of a negro maidservant.[2] This changing of the role was done with an intent.

Amanda wanted to tickle her adolescent ego in order to make her more receptive to the compulsions of her being a female, in need of a male partner for her life. Further, when Laura said that she was not expecting any gentlemen caller, her mother, Amanda chose to point out that sometimes they come when they are least expected. I remember one Sunday afternoon in 'Blue Mountain.' Then, in the unquoted text, she made her son and daughter know that her company was sought by some of the eligible sons of big planters in the Mississippi Delta. This was because she was sociable and good conversationalist. Amanda as mother to the two children tried to romanticise her Southern past. It was partly done to soften the rigour of the grim reality in which she was placed; in doing so, she wanted to inspire her son and daughter to be more sociable to get going in the world. If *The Glass Menagerie* is a symbolic representation of Laura, the disabled sister of Tom, the narrator, he also underscores the axial role of Amanda in managing the small-well-knit family in the face of the economic difficulties of the depression era; and that too, when she has been estranged from her husband. In this way, the overall impression of the play is that its plot is elegantly simple; and that there is a due play of elemental emotions. As such, taken together, the play is closely textured in terms of mother's longing to see her son and daughter settled well. The family lingers in the gathering shadow of sorrow owing to the estrangement of their father and the persistent lack of adequate money. The son, Tom (the narrator) in the play, being extra sensitive remains dissatisfied with the warehouse job; and he finds relief from his dismal surroundings in his absorbing interest in literary reading and in developing his creative talents through the writing of poetry, fiction and plays.

Through the use of 'legends' and other descriptive dramatic devices, Williams has sustained not only the theatrical movement, but has also increased lyrical and sublimely effects, which vary from one situation to another. For example, in the course of the dancing sequence, when the gentleman caller, Jim stumbles himself to utter: ...you're—Blue Roses for Laura who was quick enough to say: 'But blue is wrong for roses.' Williams has focussed on Laura's discomfiture through a dramatic device:

(*His hand slips slowly up her arm to her shoulder as the music swells tumultously. He suddenly turns her about and kisses her on the lips. When he releases her, Laura sinks on the sofa with a bright dazed look. Jim backs away and fishes in his pocket for a cigarette.*)

(*Legend on screen: 'A Souvenir.'*)

Stumble John.

(*He lights the cigarette, avoiding her look. There is a peal of girlish laughter from Amanda in the kitchenette. Laura slowly raises and opens her hand. It still contains the little broken glass animal. She looks at it with a tender, bewildered expression.*)[11]

Jim wants to resume the human link with her, saying: 'You don't smoke, do you?' Tension-filled drama is writ on Laura's face:

(*She looks up, smiling, not hearing the question. He sits beside her rather gingerly. She looks at him speechlessly—waiting. He coughs decorously and moves a little farther aside as he considers the situation and senses her feelings dimly with perturbation.*)[12]

If the breaking of a decorative glass animal was shattering for Laura, she felt the earth slipping from her feet when Jim made a disclosure of his relationship with Betty. Williams dramatises the working of double impact on Laura:

(*The holy candles on the altar of Laura's face have been suffered out. There is a look of almost infinite desolation. Jim glances at her uneasily.*)[13]

Then, in his next piece of dramatic description, Williams has shown the tormented face of Laura—trembling, biting her lip and then, opening her hand again on the broken glass figure. Finally, she places the unicorn in the palm of his hand and to close it carefully with her fingers. Seeing all this, Jim is at outs with himself:

	What are you doing that for? You want me to have him? Laura?
	(*She nods*) What for?
Laura :	A...souvenir....
	(*She rises unsteadily and crouches beside the Victrola to wind it up.*)
	(Legend on Screen: *'Things have a way of turning*

out so badly' or image 'Gentlemen caller waving goodbye—gaily')[14]

Till this stage, the hope-filled Amanda did not know about the disappointing end to her programme of getting Laura succeed with the gentleman caller, Jim. It was a catastrophe for Amanda too, for which there is a dramatic legend: '*The Sky Falls*' what follows hereafter is painful indeed. There is a heated exchange of irony-loaded remarks between Amanda and Tom. Amanda got lacerated to say to her son, Tom: '...Go to the movies, go. Don't think about us, in a mother deserted, an unmarried sister who's crippled and has no job. Don't let anything interfere with your selfish pleasure. Just go, go, go...to the movies.[15]

Amanda then comforts the forlorn, half-crippled daughter, Laura. In his own manner, Tom is also forlorn after the saddened turn to the drama. Left alone, he prepares himself to wander in the wide world with art and literary pursuit as the only defence and armour. As Tennessee Williams reflecting upon the sad story of a mother (estranged from her husband) a sensitive daughter and an art-loving ambitious son, one gets a sense of delicate pleasure, almost lyrical and sublime in its experimental content.

A Streetcar Named Desire is the second play of Tennessee Williams in which one has several occasions to experience lyrical and sublime effects woven into a painfully sad story of a tussle between a man and a woman possessing the story of a highly sophisticated Southern Belle, Blanche Dubois who visits her married sister, Stella's apartment. While Stella is settled in a family way, Blanche who is extra-sensitive has yet to commit herself to a settled life. It is at this apartment, Blanche's confrontation takes place with her brother-in-law, Stanley Kowalski. Right from the day, Blanche arrives at the sister's apartment, Kowalski develops a deep-seated dislike for his sister-in-law. It arises from the incompatibility of their temperament. Even as Blanche Dubois may be termed flighty by some—Stanley was one among them, she has a charm and elegance of her own. She is some sort of an embellished, beautiful woman, nearing 30, who has chosen a life of freedom and affirmation. She has an extraordinary flair of delicacy and movement. This trait in her character enraged Stanley

Kowalski who bore in himself the elements of a saturated male sensuousness. Blanche had her own misgivings about Stanley:

Blanche: Will Stanley like me, or will I be just a visiting in-law, Stella? I couldn't stand that.

Stella: You'll get along fine together, if you'll just try not to—well—compare him with men that we went out with at home.

Blanche: Is he so different?[16]

The two sisters were meeting after a long separation; so Blanche—the more intellectual of the two, took an initiative to know how Stella spent her married life. Both the sisters were poles apart in their outlook.

> Stella admitted: 'And when he (Stanley) comes back I cry on his lap like a baby (*She smiles to herself*)' Blanche reacting to her sister's submission observed: 'I guess that is what is meant by being in love... (*Stella looks up with a radiant smile*).

Blanche is amused to hear about her sister's happy, married life. Then she narrated how the *Belle Reve* plantation in the South was lost inch by inch, with Blanche among the living family members only to witness the sad loss: Blanche: 'I stayed and struggled. You came to New Orleans and looked out for yourself. I stayed at *Belle Reve* and tried to hold it together. I'm not meaning this in any reproachful way, but all the burden descended on my shoulders.' Blanche remained unsympathised by Stella; so she got vehement to say: 'I know, I know. But you are the one that abandoned Belle Reve, not I. I stayed and fought for it, bled for it, almost died for it.'

To Stella's unmeaningful remark, 'Stop this hysterical outburst and tell me what's happened? What do you mean fought and bled? What kind of....' Blanche got serious to say: 'The loss...the loss.' And when Stella showed surprise, she got sarcastic and lyrical to explain:

> 'I, I, I took the blows in my face and my body. All of these deaths. The long parade to the graveyard. Father, mother Margaret, that dreadful way. So big with it, it couldn't be put

> in a coffin. But had to be burned like rubbish. You just came home in time for funerals, Stella. And funerals are pretty compared to deaths. Funerals are quiet, but deaths—not always. Sometimes their breathing is hoarse, and sometimes it rattles, and sometimes they even cry out to you, 'Don't let me go.' Even the old, sometimes, say, 'Don't let me go.' As if you were able to stop them. But funerals are quiet, with pretty flowers. And oh, what gorgeous boxes they pack them away in. Unless you were there at the bed when they cried out, 'Hold me! bleeding.' You didn't dream, but I saw! saw! saw! and now you sit there telling me with your eyes that I let the place go! How in hell do you think all that sickness and dying was paid for.[17]

These extracts partake of the essential aspects of a lyrical composition. In a lyric, personal involvement is a major factor. In fact, a true lyric in its movement has also elements of sublimity; for, without the exalted view of life, no worthwhile lyrical composition is possible. When somebody says that a Belle Reve has been effaced from the social world, it can at best be a journalistic news; but when somebody makes a human assessment of the loss involved in the decay of the once-prosperous Belle Reve plantation estate, one is perforce to take a pause and think awhile somewhat deeply about the passing away of a big plantation family. This is how the rise, decay and fall of dynasties take place on the canvas of history. The above extracts become all the more poetically expressive, since Blanche Dubois stung to the very core of her being by her sister's pedestrian remarks is led to convince Stella about the loss of Belle Reve plantation and its mentors and descendants one after another through rattle of death agony as the life seraph oozed out of their bodies.... Thus one finds that Williams through the power of imagination invests the loss relating to Belle Reve plantation with human meaning. Williams' plays—*The Glass Menagerie* and *A Streetcar Named Desire*—justify the validity of Blake's observation, and in stronger and better light than his perishing mortal eye can see, does not imagine at all.'[18]

By the sheer power of imagination and poetic vision, Williams has created a highly interesting character Blanche Dubois. She is sophisticated, intelligent and sensitive. For this reason, she invited trouble on herself. If her sister was a married sister of ordinary calibre, her brother-in-law Stanley Kowalski was in complete contrast to her personality. With all her faults, maliciously exaggerated by her brother-in-law, Blanche Dubois was a refined young woman, while Stanley Kowalski (brother-in-law) was quite unsophisticated, crude and conscious of his male strength. Basically, 'refinement' and 'crudity' are deadly inimical to each other. Blanche faced her tragic end at the hands of Stanley simply for she happened to be refined. Blanche believes in illusion, while Stanley deals in hard reality. Recognising that the world is not the beautiful, ideal she would like, she tells her sister Stella: 'I can't live with him, after last night, with just those curtains between us? ...Stella: Blanche, you saw him at his worst last night. Blanche: On the contrary, I saw him at his best. What such a man has to offer is animal force and he gave a wonderful exhibition. But the only way to live with such a man is to—go to bed with him. And that's your job—not mine! ...I take it for granted that you still have sufficient memory of Belle Reve to find this place and these poker players impossible to live with.'[19]

It is true that both the sisters—Blanche and Stella had some measure of understanding between them; but Blanche could not relish, even an iota, the presence of her brother-in-law, Stanley Kowalski. So, the tenor of the conversation between the sisters on him made Blanche express herself in a pitch of fury, which acquired a lyrical intensity of its own:

> '...You can't have forgotten that much of our bringing up, Stella that you just suppose that any part of a gentleman's in his nature. Not one particle, not Oh, if he was just ordinary, just plain—but good and wholesome but—no. There's something downright—bestial—about him. You're hating me saying this, aren't you.... There's even something—sub-human—something not quite to the stage of humanity yet. Yes, something—apelike about him, and there he is—Stanley Kowalski—survivor of the stone age. Bearing the raw meat home from the kill in the jungle. And you! you have been waiting for him. May be he'll strike you or may be grunt and kiss you! ...may be we are a long way from being made in

God's image, but Stella—my sister—there has been some progress since then.'[20]

This lyrical expression ends on a note of irony. In the unquoted portion there is a reference to Kowalski's poker friends; for Blanche, all of them were apelike. In spite of her being high-strung in expression, there is nothing demeaning about it; everything is forthright; the scales of culture and civilisation are brought into focus by a woman of extraordinary sensibility.

In conclusion, it may be explained that Blanche's running into lyrical and sublime heights stemmed from her being a woman trying to defend her dignity and freedom in the midst of situation in which her innermost being was involved. Tennessee Williams also being a poet gave wings to his imagination to highlight the attendant dangers of the brute-like cussed materialism for the growth of the finer side of man and woman together. Blanche Dubois in *A Streetcar Named Desire* has expressed some of the cherished feelings of Tennessee Williams on life and culture.

NOTES

1. Richard Leavitt, ed., *The World of Tennessee Williams* (New York: G.P. Putnam's Sons, 1978) 13.
2. *Aristotle....Longinus* (Harmondsworth: Penguin, 1965) 41.
3. *IAristotle....Longinus* 108-109.
4. *Guernica* a town in Northern Spain, bombed in April, 1937 by German planes, on the side of Fascists, during the Spanish Civil War in 1930s.
5. Tennessee Williams, *The Glass Menagerie* in *Anthology of American Literature*, ed. George Michael (New York: Macmillan, 1985) 1846.
6. Sally Johns, *Tennessee Williams in Dictionary of Literary Biography,* Twentieth-Century American Dramatists Part II (Detroit: A Brucolly Clark Book, 1981) 326.
7. *The Concise Anthology of American Literature*, 1846.
8. *Ihe Concise Anthology of American Literature* 1947. The quoted line in French with an English rendering is from 'Ballads of the Ladies of the Bygone Times' by Francois Villon (1431-1463), a celebrated French poet.
9. *The Concise Anthology of American Literature* 1847.
10. *The Concise Anthology of American Literature* 1847-48.
11. *The Theatre of Tennessee Williams—The Glass Menagerie* (New York: New Directions Publishing Corporation) 228.
12. *The Theatre of Tennessee Williams* 228-29.
13. *The Theatre of Tennessee Williams* 230.

14. *The Theatre of Tennessee Williams* 231.
15. *The Theatre of Tennessee Williams* 236.
16. *A Streetcar Named Desire* 257.
17. *A Streetcar Named Desire—The Theatre of Tennessee Williams*, 261-62.
18. William *Blake, Poetry and Prose,* ed. David Erdman and Harold Bloom (New York: Garden City, 1965) 541.
19. T. Williams, *A Streetcar Named Desire* (Best American Plays—1945-51) (New York: Crown Publishers, 1970) 69.
20. Williams 70.

16

Conflict between Human Dignity and Vested Interests with Reference to Miller's Plays: *Death of a Salesman* and *The Crucible*

VINOD KUMAR MAHESHWARI

Arthur Miller (b. 1915...) trained himself in the art of dramaturgy from such illustrious men of letters as Charles Dickens and Ibsen. If Dickens gave him an insight into the framing of characterisation, Ibsen provided him with a thematic perspective as to what a drama cater to. "Every Ibsen play begins with the unwritten words 'now listen here!' and these words have shown me a path through the wall of 'entertainment,' a path that leads beyond the formulas and dried-up precepts, the pretense and fraud, of the business of the stage. Whatever else Ibsen has to teach, this is his first and great contribution.... I decided to work on *An Enemy of the People* because I had a private wish to demonstrate that Ibsen is really pertinent today, that he is not 'old fashioned,' and, implicitly, that those who condemn him are themselves misleading our theatre and our playwrights into a blind alley of senseless sensibility triviality, and the inevitable waste of our dramatic talents; for it has become the fashion for plays to reduce the 'thickness' of life to a fragile facsimile, to avoid portraying the complexities of life, the contradictions of character, the fascinating interplay of cause and effect that have long been part of the novel. And I wished also to buttress the idea that the dramatic writer has, and must again demonstrate, the right with his brain as well as his heart. It is necessary that the public understand again that the stage is the place for idea, for philosophies, for the most intense discussion of man's fate."[1]

The last line of this extract, 'that the stage is the place for ideas, for philosophies, for the most intense discussion of man's fate,' is relevant for the projected study of Miller's two plays: *The Death of a Salesman* and *The Crucible*. In these plays, he has tried to wrestle with the complexities of social life. Even as he believed in the democratic ethos, he also prized individual freedom because the cause of social freedom progressed is served better when man as an individual is susceptible to his dignified living. In modern conditions of life, to crave for human dignity is getting harder day by day. Partly, it is owing to the increasing commodification of human sensibility which gets heightened owing to the unequal distribution of wealth, fall in standard of human behaviour and unintegrated life outlook.

Psychologically, the idea of dignity goes hand in hand with one's commitment to personal integrity. In the modern world with the proliferation of ersatz culture, one may come out clever and subtle; but, it is not enough for experiencing life with personal dignity. When Cromwell wrote: "Subtlety may deceive you, integrity never will"[2], he made a very important observation. It enables us to understand modern man's dilemma: how to defend one's freedom and dignity. Since the environmental impact in its complexity on human beings partakes of both good and evil, it puts the dignity conscious individuals like Willy Loman in Miller's play, *The Death of a Salesman* into a lot of difficulties. Willy is a middle class salesman; and owing to a weird run of circumstances, his integrity comes under a reeling pressure in competitive American Society.

In bare outline, this wonderful play tells how its chief character Willy Loman who has lost his youth yet in his memory of his 'lost' youth he fights against the heavy odds of his life. He is loved by his wife, Linda, and he has two sons, Biff and Happy, whom he has tried to raise to become men of influence and power. Biff, the older son, now in his thirties, has not lived up to Willy's expectations, goals which were set when Biff was a high-school football hero. If Biff is unable to hold a job or to 'find himself,' Willy's second son has turned into an insouciant do-nothing. His two sons did not turn out to Willy's cherished expectations. From the play, one finds that Willy was past sixty-two years; and even as he found himself in economic difficulties because of the increasing cost of maintaining his family with his two sons remaining as do-nothing he hopes to turn the corner.

In the play, it is made clear that Willy Loman had started his selling career in terms of the American belief in success; but there was no such psychological boost in his two sons. There was a cultural gap of generation. While Willy Loman could dream about his future as a human being, his two sons: Biff and Happy did not have any kind of dreamy fervour in them. This difference between Willy Loman and his two sons may be attributable sociologically to the change in American capitalism and social behaviour. The Marxian dictum appears to be right that as capitalism advances from one stage to another, there is an increasing trend in the dehumanisation of social polity. Miller has taken a note of this change in social behaviour. To say the least, the process of dehumanisation is caused by an increasing reliance on monetarist methods and commodification.

Miller was conscious of this dehumanising trend when he made Willy Loman remember with gratitude the kind hearted behaviour of his earlier boss, now dead—father to the present one. The father of the present boss had human feelings for Willy; but it was not so with his son who had developed a monetarist and mechanical view of life. When the continuity from one generation to another 'is not organic but mechanical,'[3] it leads to undesirable consequences. For Willy Loman, it sealed his fate; for he committed suicide on account of his being cornered by a set of circumstances of which he had no prehension earlier. He expected human response in the American milieu; but to his great shock, the social atmosphere has taken a turn for worse. His tragic end bespeaks of his heroic defiance of the hostile circumstances which did not allow him of live his life with dignity.

A knowledgeable critic is fairly objective and justified in saying that Miller's play *Death of a Salesman*, is both a realistic study of the decline of one man, and at the same time, a symbolic presentation of the pursuit of the American dream. Miller set out to be nothing less than a modern Sophocles of everyday man in this play. "His essay 'Tragedy and Modern Man' suggests that Willy, the 'low man' on life's totem pole, is the Oedipus for this generation. 'I think the tragic feeling is evoked in us when we are in the presence of a character who is ready to lay down his life, if need be, to secure one thing—his sense of personal dignity.' Critics have denied that Miller established Willy's dignity on the grounds presented in the essay and suggest that Willy's fate is perhaps pathetic. Miller, distinguishing a lesser form from tragedy, argues that 'pathos rules where...a character fought a battle he could not possibly have won."[4]

On the basis of various dramatic situations relating to the troubles ridden life of Willy Loman in *Death of a Salesman*; and from short glimpses of the inner working of Willy's mind projected in the play by the dramatist, one comes to realise that Willy Loman was not a pathetic figure but a tragic character even in the Aristotelian sense. His being a tragic figure throws in sharp relief the dehumanising aspects of modern American life. The American dream of unending progress may be true on material plane with statistical figures on increase in commerce, trade, industry and technology; but in terms of human happiness in a deeper sense the American civilisation has failed to come up to expectations. The story of Willy Loman is the story of an American, free from the chicanery and deceptiveness of complicated social life in America as it has come to prevail there.

Death of a Salesman is cast in the setting of American life which is largely geared to the actualisation of success myth. In American novels, more specially in the novels of Theodore Dreiser, one comes across the feeling that when the cult of success is pursued beyond reasonable human limit, it has disabling effect on one's psyche. Miller has analysed beyond a reasonable doubt that Willy Loman wanted to be a good family man, a good father, a loving husband and above all a man of dignity vibrant with self-pride. But, the success myth which gets wheeled on the efficiency cult built around mechanisation and money-making vested interest shattered the masculinity and will power of Willy Loman. The main argument of this article is that Willy Loman came to a tragic end with due resplendence of a worthwhile tragic character because he could not cope with the compulsions arising out of the combined pressure of efficiency cult and the unsparing vested interest. Miller has intellectualised this interpretation in his own way: 'The deep moral uneasiness among us, the vast sense of being only tenuously joined to the rest of our fellows, is caused, in my view, by the fact that the person has value as fits into the pattern of efficiency, and for that alone. The reason *Death of a Salesman*, for instance left such a strong impression was that it set forth unremittingly the picture of a man who was not even especially 'good'—(to speak, in the conventional sense)— but whose situation made clear that at bottom we are alone, valueless, without even the elements of a human person, when once we fail to fit the patterns of efficiency.'[5]

Efficiency is a mechanical concept; and in the context of the general American outlook conditioned by the cult of efficiency, if there are individuals like Willy Loman who are sensitively alive to guard their dignity find themselves out of tune with the prevailing milieu. This is how Willy Loman came to a tragic end. Had the son of the deceased proprietor, with whom Willy was on friendly terms, not been considerate about Willy's request to provide him with a less strenuous job in his firm; and had his two sons been more receptive to the demands and expectations of their father, Willy would not have found himself shattered. Willy was undone by the hard-heartedness of the younger proprietor and that of his elder son, Biff. The filial ingratitude is a source of much consternation in Willy Loman. It all happened in the course of sequential events. His son, Biff was not good in studies. As he failed in the examination, he found himself in crisis. In this frame of mind, when he rushed to see his father, he found his father, Willy, with another woman. It created a tumultous stir in him impelling to pass highly damaging remarks against his father. It ensured a dialogue full of dramatic pathos between Willy and Biff; and let it be quoted to show how little things of life, in a moment of crisis, lead to harrowing consequences, which in the present case would mean an untimely death for Willy:

(*The Unseemly Situation*)

Biff: *his weeping breaking from him*: Dad

Willy: *infected by it*: Oh, my boy....

Biff: Dad....

Willy: She's nothing to me, Biff. I was lonely, I was terribly lonely.

Biff: You, You gave her Mama' stockings: *His tears break through and he rises to go.*

Willy: *grabbing for Biff:* I gave you an order.

Biff: Don't touch me, you liar.

Willy: Apologise for that.

Biff: You fake! You phony little fake! *Overcome, he turns quickly and weeping fully goes out with his suitcase. Willy is left on the floor on his knees.*

Willy: I gave you an order, come back here or I'll beat you! Come back here: I'll whip you.[6]

From the standpoint of actual human drama, this piece is of tense emotive equation. The text of the play makes it very clear that Willy had a highly developed sense of personal dignity. He loved his wife and children; and he wanted his two sons to grow up as well-placed enterprising individuals; but unfortunately, they belied his expectations. He was greatly disappointed over their lack of enterprising spirit; but at no stage, he had expected that his son, Biff would excitedly address him, saying 'you...liar'...'you fake! you phony little fake.' It all shows that Willy's family had run into a very pretty bad shape and chaotic syndrome. Had he been affectionately disposed towards his father, fighting his crucial battle for life, he would not have been reckless enough to insult his father with so much impertinence. Craze for money and use of machinery makes life mechanical; and as a result, human relationship loses the touch of warmth and grace. It is in this background one can understand Miller's indictment of the conventionalised American civilisation. If in the play, *King Lear*, Shakespeare made Lear say to Goneril: 'How sharper than a serpent's tooth it is to have thankless child: Away! Away!'[7] Miller made Willy to leave a sigh: 'Oh, boy, oh, boy!' which subsumes Willy's pain, frustration and suffering at the dagger-like heartless accusation of his son, Biff.[8] By composing the play, *Death of a Salesman* Miller has shown that arsenic-like element is growing at the root of American culture. Family life is in shambles if one looks at it from the standpoint of filial bond and its sanctity. The cult of efficiency geared progress is no answer. "We are unsettled at the very roots of our being," Walter Lippmann wrote in 1914, "There isn't a human relation, whether of parent and child, husband and wife, worker and employer, that doesn't move in a strange situation."[9] In the same vein, Mencken has a point when he says: "The civilised world has disposed of supernaturalism, and is engaged in a destructive criticism of the old faith's residuum—morality."[10]

Arthur Miller by creating a complicated and dignified character in Willy Loman (*Death of a Salesman*) has thrown in sharp relief the devious contradictions that have crept in American society; and that they have become more and more vicious across a period of time. In sociological term, it means that there has taken place dehumanisation in all walks of American life; and it being so, human relationship has become contrived, artificial tinged with acerbic aridity in personal attitude among family members. In saying that Willy was a dreamer—as his mental makeup was like the early American settlers who were enterprising and forward-looking. But, this was not so with his sons, Biff and Happy who lacked the enterprising spirit and the finer filial feelings.

The main shaft of Miller's criticism of modern civilisation is that pursuing the one-pointed technological and industrial progress has deleterious impact on man and his estate, which for lack of inner cohesiveness flounders on a shaky keel. In comparison to their father, Biff and Happy were do-nothing characters, with a freakish interest in womanising too. Had Biff been of enterprising nature with some maturity he would not have been so heartlessly vindictive in passing derogatory remarks, cited earlier. Even allowing some scope for their undignified behaviour on account of the generational change and gap, it has to be admitted that there is a deep malaise afflicting men and women partaking the fruits of progress in industrial societies. It is more so in America where industrialism has been sedulously nurtured right from the days of the pilgrim fathers in seventeenth and eighteenth century; and thereafter.

D.H. Lawrence felt that human life is more organic than mechanical. The machine-propelled industrialisation not only disfigures human sensibility but also deadens the finer fibers of human feelings, very much necessary for the overall well being of men, women and their families. While a large majority of people in industrial regions and pockets are prepared to down their sense of individual freedom and dignity, there still remain a select band of citizens who in spite of the debilitating atmosphere defend their personal identity and freedom. Willy Loman was one of these select band of individuals who fight for their life and destiny. Those critics who belittle Willy's tragic end should also take into account Miller's assessment of his wonderful character. He is unlike the typical salesmen who are ready to garble their feelings at the first opportunity. This man is actually a very brave spirit who cannot settle for half but must pursue his dream of himself to the end. Finally, ...this was no dumb brute heading mindlessly to his catastrophe."[11]

The significant point in this comment is that Willy Loman was fully mindful of what he was and what he was fighting for. He was mindful, but not sententious, suffering from any kind of false notion. John Beaufort, associated with the Christian Science Monitor, termed Willy Loman as 'a sad character, a vicious character....' Disagreeing with the comment, Miller explained: "The trouble with Willy Loman is that he has tremendously powerful ideals. We are not accustomed to speaking of ideals in his terms, but if Willy Loman, for instance, had not had a very profound sense that his life as lived had left him hollow, he would have died contentedly polishing his car on some Sunday afternoon at a ripe old age. The fact is that he has values. The fact that they cannot be realised is what is driving him mad, just as, unfortunately, it is driving a lot of other people mad. The truly valueless man, the man without ideals, is always perfectly at home anywhere because there cannot be conflict between nothing and something. Whatever negative qualities there are in the society or in the environment didn't bother him because they are not in conflict with any positive sense that he may have. I think Willy Loman is seeking for a kind of ecstasy in life which the machine civilisation deprives people of."[12]

It is the gravamen of machine civilisation that men and women lose a taste for enjoying life in its natural plentitude. The main reason for such an interpretation is that money-craving and the pursuit of mechanical pleasures and comforts make human life run in narrow grooves with the result man loses the inner spirit for enjoying life in a natural way. It implies not only the role of externally healthy atmosphere but also the play of uncorroded emotive responses among different members of community. Ersatz culture leads to twisted and distorted sensibility; which is the condition of most of the people under wage-earning and trade-processing social dispensation. Miller's character, Willy Loman is an exceptional one; for he had the courage to fight for his dignified existence as an experienced salesman and an honourable family man. But, the governing socio-economic atmosphere constituted of the increasing cost of living, efficiency-determined attitude of his new boss (the son of Willy's earlier employer, humane and sympathetic to him) and the self-indulgent behaviour of his two sons left Willy Loman with no other option but to commit suicide for the well being of his wife and children. In an earlier period when human society had not to contend with the modern contradictions of modern social economy, one's seeking the family welfare was more or less common; but now, as the social fabric has lost its earlier strength; but now Willy had to stake his total destiny for the well being of his family. After he had been fired by his hard-hearted employer, his already dilapidated emotive condition got to the breaking point whereby he ended his life. Miller is to the point in saying that had Willy Loman been of a pedestrian outlook he would have continued to drag on his existence with unbecoming compromises now and then. If in ancient Greek tragic play, the chief protagonist is the man who fights his fate, ordained by inscrutable Gods, Miller has drawn the very interesting character of Willy Loman, from the common stream of life, carrying in him the elements of a Greek tragic hero. In writing '*Death of a Salesman*' with a critical evaluation of the play, Miller has shown that common man is as much worthy of tragic experience and action as the high-born heroes in the Hellenic and Elizabethan plays. The only change is in the nature of superstructural forces. As against the role of fates and gods in the olden tragedies, in Miller's world-view, modern man is also subject to the inscrutable forces which are constituted of very powerful socio-political and technological influences, propertied interests and the destructive pressure-points arising out of the maladjusted male-female relationships. The overall impact is that man finds himself maladjusted with his environment. Even, the bare modicum of dignified life is becoming very difficult to maintain.

More as bodily and mental enfeeblement has taken place among the majority of men and women in the present-day governing atmosphere, there are a select number of people like Willy Loman who stand for their cherished life-values. It is an instance of moral self-affirmation. In the background of the behaviouristic legerdemain of today, the truth of Cromwell's observation: "Subtlety may deceive you, integrity never will" is very much relevant for the line of the argument. Man's sense of high tragedy coexists with the intensity with which he or she tries to defend his or her integrity. Willy Loman is a man of high integrity; and as he could not withstand the clever ways of the world, he brought his own end. It was all owing to the overwhelming burden of the money-wise, efficiency-oriented social environment.

If in his play, *Death of a Salesman*, Miller has focussed on the wider implications of social aridity and distortions, in his play *The Crucible* (1953) based on court records and historical personages involved in the Salem witch trials of 1692 he has brought to the fore, the subtle ways of the vested interests. In this play on the sinister working of the witchcraft in the seventeenth century Salem linked to the full-fledged court trial on witch-hunting Miller has tried to show the widespread ramifications of the vested interest in encouraging witchcraft; and then using the witch-hunting activities to its advantage.... In general, it is the bad social environment which is responsible for degeneration and distortion in human behaviour in any society. The clever role of a courtesan-like woman, Abigail Williams in the play determines the dramatic events which very well show how a few people at the top in the sphere of religion and politics can manipulate the public opinion in the christian community of Salem in New England. The play also makes it clear that a woman given to a distorted view of life is taken advantage of by the calculating individuals at the top of social ladder. In passing, it may be mentioned here that in India of today a politico-cultural camaraderie, like the Salem Scenario revealed at the court trial in 1692, exists between the courtesan-like females whether they may be from the ranks of the film-world or from the high-style boudoirs of upper class, wealthy people; and the powerful vested interest constitutive of bureaucrats, politicians and other class of people. It is destructive of the inner fabric of society; and harms the common human interest. The nucleus of the dramatic plot is pivoted around a beautiful, sensuous looking male, Abigail Williams, a farmer of near-perfect integrity—barring a single moral lapse, John Proctor and his wife Elizabeth Proctor. For one reason or the other, Abigail Williams who works as a maid-servant at the house of John Proctor seduces this farmer, otherwise a man of probity. Elizabeth Proctor suspecting Abigail's liaison with her husband John Proctor relieves her from household service. Abigail becomes vindictive towards Elizabeth Proctor even as she remains sensuously attached to Elizabeth's husband, John Proctor.

The temper of 'witch-hunting' in the Salem community arose out of the failure of the well-entrenched people in finding out legitimate reasons for their specific problems. For example, Rev. Parris found it convenient to explain his daughter's indecent behaviour owing to sorcery and witch-craft rather than to his own failings. In the same way, the town's richest man, Mr. Putnam taking advantages of the mass hysteria about Salem's witch-hunting found it convenient to associate his rival landowners with the practice of witchcraft. As the witch-hunting hysteria spread, a climate of fear and suspicion came to be created among people. Miller's assessment that the common men under stress of a crisis lose track of reasoning for understanding the various problems realistically is apparently justified. Abigail Williams, being a clever and ruthlessly ambitious woman also took advantage of the mass hysteria and the constitution of a trial court for settling old scores with Elizabeth Proctor. 'A shrewd opportunist, she turns her own violation of Salem Law into an occasion for naming those for whom she has little liking and, in doing so, transforms herself into a local heroine. As a participant in Tituba's forest ceremony, Abigail drank blood, believing the ritual would curse

Elizabeth Proctor, who, seven months earlier, suspecting her husband and Abigail, released the girl from their service.'[13] If Abigail Williams bore in herself strong elements of cupidity, she was equally calculative.

From this introduction to the play, *The Crucible*, it is equally interesting to find Miller arguing that there are socio-cultural factors responsible for mass hysteria and witch-hunting. Both are inter-related and are a part of a social order governed by religious and political orthodoxy. Man's sense of personal judgement is not allowed to grow by the vested interest. 'Evidently the time came in New England by the repression of order were heavier than seemed warranted by the dangers against which the order was organised. The witch-hunt was a perverse manifestation of the panic which set in among all classes when the balance began to turn toward greater individual freedom.'[14]

The very title, *The Crucible*, in its literal meaning connotes an earthen vessel in which metallic ores are melted. In an extended sense, it also means the purifying of the ores; in the same way, the periodical upthrust of mass hysteria and witch-hunting in any community is a historical process for bringing about a freshening impact on community life having gone despotic and orthodox. This is the inference one gets from the proceedings of the court trial at Salem. Witch-hunting is a terrifying experience, as the 1950s American underwent in the McCarthy era. Witch-hunting is a form of public accusation, which becomes strikingly depressive and suffocative in modern world owing to the leverage of mass media, television, radio, newspapers and other modes of printed and spoken word.

Now, coming back to the Salem scenario, it may be stated that the witch-hunting or the public accusation had a direct effect on various individuals differently. The effect differed from individual to individual depending upon the personality makeup of person so affected. Essentially, it is a psychological response; and hence, it has to be different from one person to another. Apropos this assessment, the undernoted extract by a knowledgeable critic is succinctly framed: 'As the fever (witch-hunting hysteria) grows, (one comes to realise that) its sources lie more and more in the irrationality of the human psyche as both individual and mass hysteria take over the town. Paranoia surfaces: Mrs. Putnam's unfocussed despair over the loss of her infants in childbirth turns to a more comforting hatred of Revecca Nurse. Both Mrs. Putnam and Rev. Parris see a kind of inverse election in being tormented by the devil. Miller very convincingly describes the 'positive' effects of paranoia. The 'victims' of the witches begin to value themselves more highly than those who have been left alone, since it comforts them to know that someone, even Satan, is constantly watching out for them. The culmination of the mass hysteria occurs when the girls of Salem, egged on by the calculated deceptions of Abigail, truly believe that they see the devil in the form of a gigantic bird.[15]

Thus, one finds that the cleverly good-looking, Abigail Williams playing a key role not only generates an atmosphere of witchy temper in the Salem community but also succeeds in enroping girls like Marry Warren otherwise good in intent for devilish practices during the night. Such female characters play a pivotal role in increasing the strangle-hold of unscrupulous moneyed people and their henchmen, as it has been highlighted in the play by the presence of Thomas Putnam and his aids, destructive in intent. He is imbued with materialistic craving for power and money. 'Thomas Putnam,' son of the richest man in Salem, sought restitution for the village's rejection of his candidate for minister and contested his father's will when it favoured his younger brother; Putnam's name appeared on a number of historical documents, characterizing him as an embittered, vindictive man. Francis Nurse was a frequent arbitrator in Salem, a man apparently capable of impartial judgement; he was, however, involved in a land dispute with his neighbours, including Putnam, and in the campaign for the ministerial candidate in opposition to Putnam's. It was Putnam who initiated the documents accusing the highly respected Rebecca Nurse, Francis's wife, of witchcraft, and Putnam's younger daughter who pointed hysterically and accusingly at the old woman at the hearing.[16]

Several innocent people were forced to die even as the high dignitaries of the court maintained that they were trying to endorse Salem community's heritage of 'self-denial,' 'purposefulness,' 'suspicion of all vain pursuits' and 'hard handed justice.' It is true that the evil-minded vested interest, helped by the cleverly orchestrated witchcraft activities of the unscrupulous Abigail Williams succeeded in shaping the court opinion; as a consequence of which nineteen women and men and two dogs were hanged; one man was pressed to death for refusing to plead, and 150 were imprisoned. As they were awaiting trial, a Boston court finally declared the evidence insufficient to warrant the death sentence. In the topsy-turvy world created by the witch-hunts, it was very difficult to differentiate between lies and truth. For a while, all-round confusion prevailed. Even the presiding dignitary, Deputy Governor Danforth got warped in his judgement in the surrounding confusion. Apparently, the long arm of the vested interest to influence Danforth. During the court proceedings, he was able to show consideration to an ultra-vindictive and ambitious character, Abigail Williams who wanted to create fissure between John Proctor, an upright farmer, and his wife, Elizabeth Proctor; rather, in her manipulating manner, she had tried to influence the court to consider Elizabeth Proctor as a witch so that she would be able to marry John Proctor to whom she was sensuously attached.

She would have succeeded in her design, but for the presence of mind of John Proctor who could see through the game of Abigail Williams. Along with his convulsive disenchantment with Abigail, he was equally moved by the pull and sincerity of his wife's love, that is, of Elizabeth Proctor. Ultimately, out of the courage of his conviction that one's conscience should be the arbiter, he penned his confession in regard to his sinful connection with Abigail Williams; but on the issue of naming others for witch-like act, he tore down his confession and refused to implicate others on the strength of his conviction that man's conscience is the final judge not any other authority including the Salem court. Then, John Proctor's enemies found it easy to condemn him to death. Still, in the midst of devil charged atmosphere, there were still men of sanity at Salem. One of them was Rev. Hale who was considered an expert on witch-hunting and the associated personal and institutional lapses in not adhering to the true spirit of christianity. In disagreeing with the chief judge, Deputy Governor, Danforth, Rev. Hale observed: 'Life is God's most precious gift, no principle however glorious, may justify the taking of it.' While regarding John Proctor's conduct, Rev. Hale told the Deputy Governor: "I believe him; *Pointing at Abigail.* This girl has always struck me false. She has....'[17] This difference in perception between the two high-placed man proves the old adage that an evil-minded person would be at home with the evil character, as it was so with Danforth qua Abigail Williams whom a purified thinker did not like.

In terms of *St Luke 8, (32-34)* in *The New Testament*, there is an explicit mention of devilish tendencies percolating into the mind of human beings in general. Such periodical eruptions in different societies are to be found at different periods of history. What happened at Salem was an expression of a deep-seated malaise in New England Society. All such periodical eruptions take place in different societies as and when the forces of unreason weaken the cultural values in terms of reason, equity, fair play and individual liberty associated with people who are essentially humane and good, not evil-minded. History avouches in general that the evil forces raise their head with the connivance of the propertied classes, which encourage only those people, who out of their wilful evil sustain the exploiting interests. In his plays, *Death of a Salesman* and *The Crucible*, Arthur Miller has trenchantly shown that those individuals who are conscious of their worth and dignity-like Willy Loman (*Death of a Salesman)* and John Proctor and other innocent characters in *The Crucible* suffer just because the evil forces spearheaded by the deeply entrenched vested interest do not tolerate any dissent from their established social ideology. To defeat this dreadful menace, one should know the immense worth of one's personal dignity, as it is so in *Death of a Salesman*; and Miller's mind travels from his earlier play to *The Crucible* in which John Proctor stands by his conscience. In this respect he (Proctor) affirms his destiny. After all, man's integrity at its best is realised only when he acts according to his conscience. Miller himself has acknowledged that he wrote *The Crucible* in order to find a new kind of theatre in which there is a due play of a higher degree of consciousness which was not so in the earlier plays: '*The Crucible* was written...in order to bring me, and the audience, closer to that theatre and what I imagine can be an art more ample than any of us has dared to strive for, the art of Man among men, Man amid his works.' This visualisation is equally valid for '*Death of a Salesman* because *The Crucible* is, internally, Salesman's blood brother.'[18] This is how Miller assessed these two plays which show in sharp relief the personal triumph of man in the midst of social atmosphere given to lies, deception and large-scale perversity.

NOTES

1. *The Theater Essays of Arthur Miller*, ed. R.A. Martin and Stevan R. Centola (New York: Da Capo Press, 1996) 16-17.
2. John Masefield, *William Shakespeare* (London: Thornton Butterworth, 1933) 29.
3. D.H. Lawrence, *Lady Chatterley's Lover* (New York: New American Library, 1962) 146.
4. Jeffrey Helterman, *Arthur Miller—Dictionary of Literary Biography*, vol. 7 (Detroit: Gale Research Company, 1981) 92.
5. *The Theatre Essays of Arthur Miller* 59-60.
6. Arthur Miller, *Death of a Salesman* (*Collected Plays*), (London: Cresset Press, 1985) 208.
7. William Shakespeare, *King Lear*, 4 (290-91).
8. Arthur Miller, introduction, *The Collected Plays* 34.
9. Donald Mcquade, Robert Arwan et al., eds., *The Harper American Literature*, vol. 2 (New York: Harper & Row, 1987) 1096.
10. Mcquade1096.
11. Gerald Whales, ed., *Text and Criticism on Death of a Salesman* 175.
12. Whales.
13. June Schluster and James K. Flangan, *Arthur Miller*, p. 71.
14. Arthur Miller, "An Overture to Act One," *The Crucible* in *Collected Plays* 228.
15. Jeffrey Helterman, *Twentieth Century American Dramatists*, vol. 2, 96.
16. *The Theatre Essays of Arthur Miller*, ed. Martin and Centola, 188.
17. Arthur Miller, *The Crucible* in *Collected Plays* 307.
18. *The Theatre Essays of Arthur Miller*, ed. Martin and Centola 172-74.

17

A View from the Bridge: A Modern American Tragedy

BASAVARAJ NAIKAR

Although the basic pattern of tragedy as a genre of literature remains the same, the ingredient details of this pattern have been changing from time to time and from author to author due to the changing circumstances and temperamental differences as the dramatists. Hence, the justification for a comparative and even historical study of tragedy as a literary genre incorporating a distinct philosophy or world view of its own.

The details of the pattern of Greek Tragedy or Senecan Tragedy or Shakespearean Tragedy are too well-known to be discussed here separately. Here is an attempt to examine Arthur Miller's concept of tragedy as it emerges in his relatively less known play, *A View from the Bridge*. A Study of *A View from the Bridge* helps us to see many parallels with as well as departures from the pattern of Greek Tragedy. Although Arthur Miller happens to be a great lover of the Greek culture and literature in general and of its drama in particular, he never imitates it blindly or mechanically. His originality in the contribution to drama lies in a careful and intelligent adaptation of the pattern of Greek tragedy to the modern conditions of America. He not only modernizes, but Americanizes the tragic form of drama in spite of having affinities with other forms of tragedy like the Greek and the Christian.

The similarities and the differences between Miller's concept of tragedy and the earlier ones may be examined here in some detail. The most important feature that strikes our attention is

Miller's departure from the Greek tragedy in his concept of the rank or stature of the tragic hero. Miller rejects the royal stature or the rank of the protagonist that is so important in Greek and Shakespearean tragedy and pleads for the introduction of the common man of American society as the protagonist of his plays. "I believe that the common man is as apt a subject for tragedy in its highest sense as kings were. On the face of it this ought to be obvious in the light of modern psychiatry, which bases its analysis upon classic formulations, such as the Oedipus complexes, for instances, which were enacted by royal beings, but which apply to everyone in similar emotional situations" (Miller, 1948: 17). Similarly he also rejects the notion of the Christian tragedy having a religious martyr as a protagonist dying for his faith or God. He does not believe in projecting a picture of official religion or Christianity. His protagonist is neither a king nor a martyr but a very common man of the American street who is known for his essential humanity but can be elevated to the stature of a tragic hero. The protagonist of *A View from the Bridge* is a forty year old man called Eddie Carbone working as a longshoreman at the dock from the Brooklyn bridge.

Although the setting of the play is both modern and American, its affinity with the Greek tragedy can be seen in its connection with Sicily known for its classical connotations and associations. Eddie Carbone who has now settled down in America hails originally from Sicily and has the Sicilian value-system in his blood. Miller, thus, achieves a connection between Sicily and America in terms of space as well as time thereby offering a classical resonance to American drama.

The central conflict in the play is between man and his society or environment. Miller borrows his concept of man as a social being from the Greek tragedy, although he rejects the idea of Fate as depicted by it. As he clearly states, "A Greek living in the classical period would be bewildered by the dichotomy implied in the very term 'social play.' Especially for the Greek, a drama created for public performance had to be 'social'" (Miller, 1968: 1). Instead he makes some changes in his own drama by elevating the environment itself to the level of Fate thereby giving it a socio-psychological dimension instead of a religious one. He rejects the

Greek idea of Fate as a fixed and unchangeable one and offers a post-Darwinian interpretation of man as a product of his immediate surroundings or environment which is not fixed but in eternal flux. A Steinberg points out, "an important aspect of the new drama was the post-Darwinian emphasis on environment as a shaping force in life. Man was seen as the product, and from one point of view the victim, of his surroundings" (Steinberg, 1969: 82). The protagonist of the play Eddie Carbone is thus influenced by his immediate surroundings or environment of American life, especially the Brooklyn society. He has automatically internalized the values of that society like personal 'honour' or 'respect' or 'name' and wants to be accepted by it for the achievement of happiness of life.

The external conflict between Eddie Carbone and his opponents is triggered off by the unexpected arrival of two Sicilian immigrants namely, Rodolpho and Marco who happen to be the cousins of his wife, Beatrice. Rodolpho who is like a blonde with a platinum coloured complexion is in search of a job in Brooklyn. Eddie's problem starts when he notices the growing intimacy between his niece *i.e.*, seventeen year old Catherine and Rodolpho. Eddie's external conflict with Rodolpho sparks off the internal psychological conflict between his own conscious and unconscious levels of mind. He, for example, has very filial attachment for Catherine who is not his actual daughter but who is almost like his daughter. As he feels responsible for her and is concerned about her welfare and happiness, he wants her to pursue her education and get a high job and a good husband for her. But now he notices certain subtle changes in her behaviour as she crosses the threshold girlhood into womanhood. She, for example, wears short skirts and high-heeled shoes and waves to boys in the neighbourhood. Similarly she attracts the attention of menfolk in the candy store. Eddie Carbone who has noticed these changes in Catherine's behaviour does not approve of them and, therefore, asks her to behave with dignity and responsibility. Thus, at the conscious level Eddie Carbone has a fatherly attitude towards his niece whom he wants to bring up by sacrificing his own personal pleasures and money. But he is unable to probe deep into his own unconscious mind and understand the exact nature of his attitude towards his niece. His behaviour betrays his unconscious motives, tendencies and attitudes in so many details. The growing intimacy between Catherine and Rodolpho awakens his unconscious desires which might be designated as incestuous and hence part of oedipus complex. When Rodolpho expresses his desire to marry Catherine, Eddie Carbone cannot accept it on the ground that Rodolpho is not the right kind of husband for her and that he might marry her only to become an American citizen and then to divorce her. Though he is quite right as a surrogate father to feel concerned about her welfare, his persistence in it begins to betray his unconscious incestuous attachment for her. He grows more and more possessive about her while concurrently neglecting his own wife Beatrice. His incestuous passion is evident in his kissing his niece on the mouth right in the presence of Rodolpho who intends to marry her. He also exhibits homosexual attraction for Rodolpho who looks like a girl on account of his platinum complexion and singing, by occasionally teasing and taunting him. Even when Alfieri, the lawyer advises him to recognize the natural law and allow his niece to marry the man of her choice, Eddie Carbone refuses to do so under the pretext of protecting her interests. His incestuous attachment for Catherine and possessiveness do not allow him to be separated from her. He, being an unintellectual hero like many of Miller's heroes, is unfortunately incapable of psychoanalyzing himself. Thus, unable to resolve the internal conflict between his conscious and unconscious levels of mind, he wants to solve it externally by resorting to the societal code of neighbourhood *i.e.,* by betraying the two immigrants, Rodolpho and Marco, to the Immigration Bureau. He secretly rings up the Immigration officers about the presence of two illegal immigrants in the house No. 441, Saxton Street, of Brooklyn. Consequently, the Immigration Officers rush to the spot and arrest the two illegal immigrants for taking legal action against them.

Eddie Carbone's resort to the federal law of America amounts to a heinous crime in so far as he uses it for defending his own incestuous tendency as well as for betraying the code of his own ancestral, Sicilian community. His tragic flaw may be said to lie in his violation of the moral order by choosing the federal law to betray the sub-cultural law. As the German philosopher Hegel points out, "the conflict in a tragedy need not always be between Good and Evil, but it can as well be between a higher Good and a lesser Good" (Hegel, 1975: 52). In the light of the Hegelian aesthetic philosophy, one may interpret the conflict in the present play. Though Eddie is a member of the American society now and, therefore, it is natural for him to follow the federal code of conduct, his use of it for betraying his own community or sub-culture is a great crime against the natural law of humanity.

Whenever a tragic hero tries to negate the moral order of the universe, he is bound to be negated himself by the inexorability of Law (Whitehead, 1938: 70-71). Eddie, according to this fundamental pattern of tragedy, is punished severely by Marco who spits him in the face, calls him 'criminal' and finally, kills him with his own dagger. He is hated even by his beloved wife and niece who call him a 'rat.' Eddie has, thus, lost not only his 'name' or 'honour' in the society, but also his precious life itself. Since he has negated the affirmative, natural and humanistic values of life by betraying the immigrants, he has to accept the consequences of his action by sacrificing his own life. Thus, at the end of the play there emerges a picture of the moral order of the universe. Though one is aware of the imbalance between crime and punishment *i.e.,* though we know that Eddie Carbone is punished more severely than he deserves, it also satisfies our sense of moral order and justice in the universe.

Eddie Carbone, like many tragic heroes, suffers from an obsession and remains uncompromising until the end. He has his own idea of integrity or conscience which he has internalized from the values of immediate surroundings or the society. Miller points out that "society is inside man and man is inside society" (Miller, 1978: xix). Thus, Eddie Carbone's idea of his name or personal honour etc., are all drawn from the federal society of America in which he has settled. He is so intransigent in his views that he does not wish to see beyond that or recognize the higher laws. What might be called his tragic flaw is developed from his psychic as well as sociological forces. He believes in his own idea of integrity so firmly and unswervingly that he has to sacrifice his life for that.

Although Miller replaces the Greek idea of Fate by the post-Darwinian environment, he does not believe in the total helplessness of man. He also believes in the free will of man and the possibility of right choice by man. Miller rightly believes that it was quite possible for Eddie Carbone to understand the limitations of his thinking by listening to the lawyer, Alfieri. His ignorance of himself is not something eternally fixed by his fate or gods. Arthur Miller gives a new twist to the concept of tragedy by combining the Greek and the Christian ones in a modernist way.

One thing that one misses in *A View from the Bridge* is the realization of his folly by the protagonist, which is a common feature in Greek as well as Shakespearean tragedy. Unlike an Orestes, or a Lear of a Hamlet, Eddie Carbone does not realize his folly or show signs of repentance at the end of his life, although we quite admire his uncompromising pursuit of the wrong ideals, which gives an emotional intensity to the play. Whether this lack of progress from ignorance to, at least, a belated realization is due to the protagonist's non-intellectuality or to Arther Miller's indifference to this aspect has yet to be examined.

A View from the Bridge is said to be the most classical of all the tragedies written by Arthur Miller especially in the employment of a choric character, Alfieri. Alfieri who is a family friend of Eddie Carbone acts as a one-man chorus in linking the past with the present and in commenting on or showing the dichotomy between the unconscious and the conscious motives of Eddie Carbone. Similarly he acts as the omniscient voice of the dramatist. Although as a lawyer he is concerned with legal justice, he is also aware of issues which are beyond and legal jurisdiction and belong to the moral order of the universe. In so far as he is aware of that moral order (or the natural order) and brings it to the notice of Eddie Carbone, he may be said to be a modern terrestrial substitute for Greek gods. His comment on Eddie Carbone is a fine comment upon the latter's tragic weakness:

> Most of the time now we settle for half and I like it better. But the truth is holy and even as I know how wrong he was, and his death useless, I tremble, for I confess that something

pure calls to me from his memory.... And yet, it is better to settle for half, it must be! And so I mourn him—I admit it—with a certain...alarm (Miller, 1968: 85).

Unlike in Greek or Shakespearean tragedy where verse is used for poetic elevation, in *A View from the Bridge* (*i.e.,* in the second version of it) Miller employs modern American prose, but he achieves the tragic intensity by the use of terse colloquial idiom of the Brooklyn society.

Arthur Miller's concept of tragedy may, thus, be said to be formulated from his partial adaptation and permutation of the elements of the Greek and the Christian tragedies and from the process of psycho-socializing, modernizing and Americanizing the old pattern of tragedy.

REFERENCES

Corrigan, Robert W. 1969. Ed. *Arthur Miller*. Eaglewood Cliffs, N.J.: Prentice Hall Inc.

Hegel, G.W.F. 1975. *Aesthetics* Vol. 2. Trans. T.M. Knox. Oxford: Clarendon Press.

Martin, Robert A. 1978. Ed. *The Theater Essay of Arthur Miller*. New York: The Viking Press.

Miller, Arthur. *A View from the Bridge*. 1969. Harmondsworth: Penguin Books.

Steinberg, M.V. "Arthur Miller and the Idea of Modern Tragedy," in *Arthur Miller*. Ed. Robert A. Corrian. 1949. Eaglewood Cliffs, N.J.: Prentice Hall Inc.

Whitehead, A.N. 1938. *Modes of Thought*. New York: The Macmillan Co.

18

A Week on the Concord and Merrimack Rivers: An American Travelogue

BASAVARAJ NAIKAR

Travel-literature, compared to other forms of literature, happens to be neglected by literary critics. A systematic study of the famous travelogues will, no doubt, reveal a few patterns which could be very interesting. Travelogues may be broadly classified into two categories: one, those written by natives and two, those by foreigners. Each of these categories can yield very interesting types of experience and narrative methods. Travelogues written by foreigners are generally known for their depiction of exotic life all the more exaggerated by the wide gap between two cultures. But those written by native writers are generally known for their search for details of human life belonging to the same culture which is known to the authors at least partially.

Thoreau's *A Week on the Concord and Merrimack Rivers* happens to be a travelogue written by a native American about his travel in America. The journey was undertaken by Thoreau not by way of merry-making, but with an intention of educating himself, just in line with Francis Bacon's observation that travel is part of education. He made the journey in the autumn of 1839 which actually occupied only ten days, but he compressed it into only seven days by giving it a diary structure. The journey was prompted by Thoreau's intention of escaping from the utilitarianism and materialism of the so-called civilization of America into the soothing company of Nature, thereby achieving some kind of spiritual enlightenment.

Journey which is at the heart of Thoreau's travelogue has an archetypal significance and easily brings to our mind similar motifs in John Bunyan's *The Pilgrim's Progress*, Dante's *The Divine Comedy* and Virgnia Woolf's *The Pilgrimage* and so forth. But the main difference between the fictional journey and Thoreau's journey happens to be that the former is basically allegorical or symbolic, whereas the latter is an actual one simultaneously attaining the height of symbolic one. Although the journey motif is the chief one in a travelogue, it is associated with the allied motifs like the adventurous exploration of the unfamiliar world; willingness to enrich one's experience by exposing oneself to the diversity of things, beings, customs, manners and worldviews, and yet perceive the unity behind all the bewildering diversity. Thus the spirit of adventure and philosophical quest for knowledge appear to be the motifs closely associated with that of a journey in a travelogue.

The journey undertaken by Thoreau is not a land-journey or air-journey or even a sea-journey, but a river-journey which offers him an opportunity of observing a variety of places and people within the restricted scope of the river's meandering course. Thoreau experiences have neither the unrestricted freedom of land-journey, nor the distance of air-journey, nor the exclusive acquatic surroundings of the sea-journey. On the contrary, he is privileged in his river-journey to observe both the acquatic life and the land-life along the shore.

The journey that takes place in *A Week* may be classified into two kinds: one, physical and two, mental or philosophical or spiritual which go on alternating in the whole course. Such a pattern is rightly perceived by the American critic William Drake (1962: 64). Thus Thoreau's body and mind go on indulging themselves in adventures alternately thereby giving rest to either of them at a time. Inbetween the two, the heart also is allowed a chance to drink deep into the enchanting beauty of Nature.

The first requirement for a journey happens to be sound physical health with the concomitant spirit of adventure. It also requires an extravert personality who has the patience and willingness to observe the world around him and absorb the experience sensitively. Thoreau, obviously, has all these qualities in him which enable him to undertake the physical journey. But being an extraordinary type, Thoreau had the qualities of an introvert also with poetic and philosophical tendencies. That is the reason why he could delve deep into his own heart as easily as he could go out into the external world of Nature for spiritual enlightenment. He could observe the details of phenomenal life with almost scientific precision and accuracy; he could moralise and philosophise about its essence and he could also experience the bliss of a poet on observing its bewitching beauty. *A Week* may, therefore, be called an unconventional travelogue wherein the travel-narrative is embellished with a rich embroidery of near-photographic description, philosophical observations, moralising statements, transcendental leaps, poetic outbursts, mystic raptures and so on.

He begins the journey on the Concord river on a Saturday and reaches the Merrimack river and concludes it on the next Friday. In the physical journey, Thoreau's senses, especially the eye and the ear, are busy absorbing the phenomenal colours and sounds microscopically, photographically and almost scientifically. His observation of men and Nature, the earth and the sky, the strange customs and manners of exotic tribals like Red Indians etc., is remarkable for its details and accuracy. His eyes have captured the multicoloured beauty of human and natural life with the sensitiveness of a camera lens. His ears have recorded the variety of sounds, melodies and voices of Man and Nature with superfine sensitiveness. What makes his records almost scientific is the tireless patience with which he collects and classifies the abundant data. The basic American scientific temperament is clearly evident in the record of his variegated experiences.

The names of rivers like Concord and Merrimack which mean peace and joy are not only descriptive of their local and etymological importance but also act as symbols of Thoreau's ideals of life like spiritual peace, harmony and happiness. The boat selected by Thoreau is compared by him to a fish and a bird simultaneously in order to highlight its realistic as well as symbolic significance. "If rightly made, a boat would be a sort of amphibious animal, a creature of two elements, related by one half its structure to some swift and shapely fish and by the other to some strong-winged and graceful bird" (Thoreau 1961: 25).

He proceeds with the journey after the local shore-rites are duly performed. In the course of the river journey, Thoreau, like any traveller, goes on observing a variety of objects like various aquatic creatures like fish, snakes, birds, animals, strange and colorful tribal people and enjoying their hospitality. He also hears and learns many local legends, myths and historical facts thereby enlarging the vista of his experience. The physical journey enables him to observe the minute details of the innumerable peculiarities with almost a scientist's patience, curiosity and sensitivity. But being a poet and philosopher at heart, he enlivens the otherwise arid details with his poetic response and philosophical observations. The microscopic details of the beautiful objects of Nature like sunrise, sunset, stars, sky, wind, mirror-like water, islands and falls show his communion with Nature and invite comparison with the British Nature-mystic Wordsworth. His description of the ethereal beauty of Nature is very enchanting:

> The stillness was intense and almost conscious, as it were a natural Sabbath, and we fancied that the morning was the evening of a celestial day. The air was also so elastic and crystalline that it had the same effect on the landscape that a glass has on a picture, to give it an ideal remoteness and perfection. The landscape was clothed in a mild and quiet light, in which the woods and fences checkered and partitioned it with new regularity, and rough and uneven fields stretched away with lawnlike smoothness to the horizon, and the clouds, finely distinct and picturesque, seemed a fit drapery to hang over fairyland. The world seemed decked for some holiday or prouder pageantry, with silken streamers flying... (*Ibidem*: 48).

One of the goals of a traveller is to meet or observe the strange people unexpectedly and have delightful experiences with them. One may have even bitter experiences along with the sweet ones. He should, thus, be ready to have all the unexpected experiences without any grumbling. The net result of all these strange experiences would be to realise the essential humanity of all the people and the universality of all life. The truth of Thoreau's observation that "All nations love the same jests and tales, Jews, Christians and Mohammadans, and the same translated suffice for all. All men are children, and of one family" (*Ibidem*: 60) is intensely realised by him in the course of his journey. When, for example, he meets an honest man near Merrimack he likes him for his human interest. "The best relations were at once established between us and this man, and though few words were spoken, he could not conceal a visible interest in us and our excursion. He was a lover of the higher mathematics, as we found, and in the midst of some vast sunny problem when we overtook him and whispered our conjectures" (*Ibidem*: 76). On Tuesday Thoreau enjoys the hospitality of a young woman in her house. "It's mistress," says he, "was a frank and hospitable young woman, who stood before me in a dishabille, busily and unconcernedly combing her long black hair while she talked, giving her head the necessary toss with each sweep of the comb, with lively, sparkling eyes, and full of interest in that lower world from which I had come, talking all the while as familiarly as if she had known me for years, and reminding me of a cousin of mine" (*Ibidem*: 160). Thoreau's experience with the homely and gentle lady may be contrasted with his experience with a man called Rice who is rude, ill-mannered and uncultured hunter who, in spite of all the crudities of his life extends hospitality to Thoreau in the evening. Thoreau remarks that Rice was "indeed as rude as a fable satyr" (*Ibidem*: 179). His experience with such a rude man is an education for him and a sort of training in the art of patience, tolerance and acceptance of the harsh realities of life. Thoreau is very much aware of this aspect of experience and therefore says, "But I suffered him to pass for what he was—for why should I quarrel with nature?—and was even pleased at the discovery of such a singular natural phenomenon. I dealt with him as if to me all manners were indifferent, and he had a sweet, wild way with him. I would not question nature, and I would rather have him as he was than as I would have him. For I had come up here not for sympathy, or kindness, or society, but for novelty and adventure, and to see what nature had produced here" (*Ibidem*: 179).

Thoreau had another interesting experience while he was treading the land like a pilgrim. "Farmers have asked me to assist them in haying when I was passing their fields. A man once applied to me to mend his umbrella, taking me for an umbrella mender, because, being on a journey, I carried an umbrella in my hand while the sun shone. Another wished to buy a tin cup of me, observing that I had one strapped to my belt, and a sauce pan on my back" (*Ibidem*: 263). Such unexpected experiences, no doubt, provide a good deal of humour not only to the traveller *i.e.* Thoreau but to the reader of the travelogue as well thereby easing the monotony of travelling as well as reading respectively. On Thursday, Thoreau happens to see a soldier and comments on his conceited nature:

> Far up in the country—for we would be faithful to our experience—in Thornton, perhaps, we met a soldier lad in the woods, going to muster in full regimentals, and holding the middle of the road; deep in the forest, with shouldered musket and military step, and thoughts of glory all to himself. It was a sore trial to the youth, tougher than many a battle, to get by us creditably and with soldierlike bearing. Poor man. He actually shivered like a reed in his thin military pants, and by the time we got up with him, all the sternness that became the soldier had forsaken his face, and he skulked past as if he were driving his father's sheep under a sword-proof helmet" (*Ibidem*: 269).

Such experiences hold a mirror to Thoreau's sensitive and photographic observation and subtle understanding of human nature. His coming in contact with a variety of people has, obviously, widened the range of his experience and deepened the nature of his thinking. It has also helped him to go beyond the apparent contradictions of human life by synthesizing them into a unified vision in a very broad sense. The physical journey has offered sufficient exercise for his body and given him a new vigour.

The physical journey, in turn, awakens his intelligence and imagination. Consequently his mind soars high in the sky of imagination and travels faster than his physical being both vertically and horizontally, both in time and in space. The physical journey is, no doubt, interesting in its own right, but it also serves to trigger off the mental journey inspiring Thoreau to penetrate into the world of art, literature, philosophy and religion of the whole world including both the Occidental and the Oriental. The physical journey stimulates his mind and imagination to such an extent that he seems to forget the immediate surroundings of his place and indulge in a sort of contemplation about life, literature, art, poetry, philosophy and religion mainly through the exercise of his memory and the principle of association of ideas. Nikita Pokrovsky rightly remarks that "*A Week on the Concord and Merrimack Rivers* was infused with Transcendentalist ideas, considerable space was given to the exposition of Transcendentalist conception of man" (1983: 50). Whereas his body, in the physical journey, is confined to a limited place on the surface of the river, his mind, in the psychic journey, can traverse vast stretches of time and place; jump from country to country, from continent to continent and synthesize all of them into a unified eclectic vision of life. Whereas the physical journey acquaints him with a variety of phenomenal existence, the mental journey enables him to distil the essence of his experience into poetic and philosophical observations.

Thoreau's realisation of the transcendental unity of life has enabled him to view the entire humanity with equal importance and respect. For him there is no qualitative difference between ordinary men and great writers:

> You shall see rude and sturdy, experienced and wise men, keeping their castles, or teaming up their summer's wood, or chopping alone in the woods; men fuller of talk and rare adventure in the sun and wind and rain than a chestnut is of meat, who were out not only in '75 and 1812, but have been out every day of their lives; greater men than Homer, or Chaucer, or Shakespeare, only they never got time to say so; they never took to the way of writing" (*Ibidem*: 19).

Thoreau's recognition of the great potentiality of all men and the basic dignity of human life easily makes him a champion of the ordinary man. His view is comparable to Mahatma Gandhi's respect for villagers, the downtrodden and the Harijans whom he considered to be the children of God. Though there is a difference between the cultural contexts of the two writers, their philosophies have a striking resemblance.

Thoreau has great respect for all the great and classical works of literature of the whole world. In spite of being a Westerner, especially an American, he has the open-heartedness to appreciate and enjoy the great literature produced all over the world. The Hindu works like *Hitopadesa, Laws of Manu, Visnu Purana,* the *Bhagvadgita,* the plays of Kalidasa, the Greek classics like the *Iliad* and the *Odessey,* the Persian work like Sadi's *Gulistan,* the Chinese philosophical works like the *Analects* of Confucius and the Christian works like the *Bible,* the poetry of Chaucer and the plays of Shakespeare happen to be the milestones of his literary and mental journey. His appreciative and sensitive mind travels back and forth in time from ancient days to the modern times and in space from the European continent to the Asian continent without any prejudice, but with a yogic impartiality and enthusiasm. Whatever he is unable to achieve in his physical journey is achieved by him in his mental journey. He has a special respect for mythical and legendary literature, as he rightly believes that "To some extent mythology is only the most ancient history and biography. So far from being false or fabulous in the common sense, it contains only enduring and essential truth, the I and you, the here and there, the now and then, being omitted" (*Ibidem*: 60). As the myths of the world are conveyors of superhuman intelligence, dreams and unconscious thoughts of mankind, Thoreau takes them very seriously and consequently acquaints himself with the Greek, Christian and Hindu mythology and appreciates the symbolic truths embedded in them.

A deep interest in all the major religions of the world known to him at that time happens to be part of his psychic journey that assumes an international width. A man with a serious temperament, Thoreau had no respect for cheap literature that either excites or titillates us. On the contrary, he believes in serious and morally educative literature, especially all the scriptures of the world. He, therefore, pleads for the publication of all the scriptures of the world in the same volume. "It would be worthy of the age to print together the collected scriptures or sacred writings of the several nations—the Chinese, the Hindus, the

Persians, the Hebrews and others as the Scripture of mankind" (*Ibidem*: 127). This suggestion holds a mirror to the height of Thoreau's ideal, nobility of thought and wholeness of vision. Psychologically he would travel through the exotic realms of many religions and perceive the transcendental unity behind their apparent diversity and contradictions. He could, therefore, appreciate not only Christianity but also other religions of the world including Hinduism. He could read the *Bible* and the *Bhagvadgita* with equal love and appreciation, as he saw the religious universals in them. His liberal attitude to life enables him to have a comparative picture of the world religions and even appreciate the positive features of religions not belonging to his culture. His appreciation of the Oriental, especially Hindu religion and philosophy, in spite of an element of a little exaggeration in it, is symptomatic of his magnanimity of heart. "In everyone's youthful dreams, philosophy is still vaguely but inseparably, and with singular truth, associated with the East, nor do after years discover its local habitation in the Western world. In comparison with the philosophies of the East, we may say that modern Europe has yet given birth to none. Beside the vast and cosmogonal philosophy of the Bhagavad-Gita, even our Shakespeare seems youthfully green and practical merely" (*Ibidem*: 127). Such views held by Thoreau are evidence of his yogic impartiality and appreciation of Truth, Beauty and Goodness irrespective of local habitations and names.

The journey—both physical and mental—not only embraces the present but includes the past also. In other words, all the experiences described by Thoreau are not the ones happening to him during the physical journey itself, but some of them are recalled from the past through the exercise of memory according to the principle of association of ideas. Thus the present and the past are linked together meaningfully. Most of his mental journey might be said to depend upon his recollection of knowledge earned and assimilated in the past. His physical journey is confined to the Concord and Merrimack rivers of America whereas his mental journey covers the vast space of the entire globe and the long stretch of time from the known past to the present. His mind jumps from topic to topic in a random but a reflective manner.

"...the leisurely and discursive suggests the very spirit of Concord River which for Thoreau and Emerson alike served as a symbol of the invisible stream that bears life on" (Spiller 1972: 403).

The result of Thoreau's journey—both physical and psychic; both empirical and symbolic—is the enrichment of his experience and simultaneous extension and intensification of his vision of human life. The journey has enabled him to observe the phenomenal variety, abundance and contradictions of human and natural life. Inbetween the observations it has also given him an opportunity to meditate deeply upon life. In the midst of the American countryside, he has drunk deep into the mysterious beauty of Nature and derived a good deal of spiritual consolation. "It is important that self-exploration for Thoreau is metaphorically identified with exploration of the natural world; it is not a dualism which he expresses, but an integration" (Drake 1962: 63). Like the forest philosophers of India, he is armed with a new vision of life enabling him to perceive the unity of life and experience a sort of God-realisation. Thoreau seems to have realised what he says about a saintly man. "To the virtuous man, the universe is the only *sanctum sanctorum,* and the penetralia of the temple are the broad noon of his existence" (1961: 267). He seems to have realised the essential holiness of human and natural life which is borne out by his ecstatic expression in language. It is the holiness of his vision which raises the journey from the secular level to the religious one. The journey, therefore, assumes the significance of a pilgrimage. *A Week on the Concord and Merrimack Rivers* may rightly be described as an American pilgrim's progress which shows the pilgrim's final attainment of spiritual salvation. However, one difference should be noted. Thoreau, unlike the Christian pilgrim does not go to Heaven physically, but like a Hindu yogi, returns to the business of life after achieving spiritual liberation. His pilgrimage has helped him to realise the ideals of joy, peace and harmony of life symbolised by the rivers of Concord and Merrimack. Thoreau's return to the shore from which he had started off the journey seven days ago easily brings to our mind the principle of circularity of life connoting not only the rhythmic principle of music in Nature and human life but also the attainment of wholeness of being suggested by the circle.

REFERENCES

Drake, William. 1962. "A Week on the Concord and Merrimack Rivers." *Thoreau.* Eaglewood Cliffs, N.J.: Prentice Hall Inc.

Pokrovsky, Nikita. 1983. *Henry Thoreau.* Moscow: Progress Publishers.

Spiller, Robert E. 1972. *Literary History of the United States.* New Delhi: Amerind Publishing Co.

Thoreau, Henry David. 1967. *A Week on the Concord and Merrimack Rivers.* New Delhi: Eurasia Publishing House.

CONTRIBUTORS

Arjun Kumar: Lecturer in English, Rejendra College, J.P. University, Chapra, Bihar.

Mallikarjun Patil: Lecturer, Department of English, Gulbarga University, Gulbarga, Karnataka.

Janet Wilson: Reader, Department of English, Sarah Tucker College, Tirunelveli, Tamil Nadu.

Rama Kundu: Reader in English, Burdwan University, Burdwan, West Bengal.

Prem Prakash: Reader in English, Mahatma Gandhi Kashi Vidyapith, Varanasi, Uttar Pradesh.

S.P. Swain: Department of English, Rourkela Municipal College, Rourkela, Orissa.

Sarbajit Das: Department of English, CAST, Rourkela, Orissa.

Monika Gupta: Senior Lecturer, Department of English, H.N.B. Garhwal University, Srinagar, Garhwal, Uttaranchal.

Rajeshwar Mittapalli: Assistant Professor of English, Kakatiya University, Warangal, Andhra Pradesh.

Basavaraj Naikar: Professor of English, Karnatak University, Dharwad, Karnataka.

R. Saraswathi: Chairperson, Board of Studies, Department of English, Nagarjuna University, Nagarjunanagar, Guntur Distt., Andhra Pradesh.

Abha Sharma: Department of English, Agra College, Agra, Uttar Pradesh.

Vinod Kumar Maheshwari: Reader, Department of English, Agra College, Agra, Uttar Pradesh.